THE COUNT

THE COUNT

THE LIFE AND FILMS OF

BELA "Dracula" LUGOSI

Arthur Lennig

G. P. Putnam's Sons, New York

Sections of this book have been considerably revised from the following articles and have been reprinted by permission:

"Nosferatu," *Film Notes*, edited by Arthur Lennig (University of Wisconsin Film Society, 1960).

"White Zombie," *Classics of the Film*, edited by Arthur Lennig (Wisconsin Film Society Press, 1965).

"The Titans of Terror: Karloff and Lugosi," *Persistence of Vision*, edited by Joseph McBride (Wisconsin Film Society Press, 1968).

"The Horror Film," *The Sound Film: An Introduction*, edited by Arthur Lennig (Walter Snyder, 1969).

"Bela" and "The Raven," *Film Journal*, Vol. 2, No. 2, 1973.

SBN:399-11340-1

Library of Congress Catalog
Card Number: 73-93735

Contents

Preface

ADULTS OFTEN PURSUE projects for reasons found in their childhood, and I am no exception. At the age of five an unwise sister took me to see *Dracula* and *Frankenstein*. That double bill left an indelible impression. Then at the age of eleven I saw *Dracula* again, and the early memories coalesced. Although I was no longer so terribly frightened, I was fascinated by Lugosi's unique face, bearing, and accent. In some strange way I became a victim of the Count, and my admiration grew to adoration after seeing *White Zombie* and *The Raven*.

Lugosi was by no means my only interest. Music and literature were my main concerns, but I still persisted in my adoration, despite the derision of others. In 1947 I wrote Bela a long, effusive letter. There was a reply and some photos. Then a few months later this almost mythical being came East and I had the rare pleasure of realizing a dream: I saw the Great Man on the stage in *Dracula* and met him afterward. A year later he came to my home—without doubt the happiest day of my young life. From then on, my entrancement with him was complete.

Horror films have never been highly regarded, but in my youth they were totally ignored. It was a genre that drew audiences but no writers. In terms of the film magazines, Lugosi was almost a nonperson. As far as I knew, I was the only Lugosi fan in the world. And judging from the way he treated me, perhaps I was. Certainly he proved a kind gentleman who was as pleasant off the screen as he was commanding on it.

Thanks to television, being a Lugosi devotee is no longer a full-time occupation. When I was a child, except for *Dracula* and *Frankenstein*, there were almost no revivals. The only hope was at Halloween, when theaters unearthed old horror films. I can still recall waiting impatiently for the day and then cursing my luck that I could go to only one or two theaters, when perhaps three or four were showing an old Bela film. A feast for one day, a famine for the rest of the year.

When I became Lugosi's devout fan in the late forties, his none-too-glorious career was about over. What remained were only the worst low-grade films. As I saw each of his later pictures and watched his face and body disintegrate, the experience grew painful. The photos taken shortly before his death touch chords that still disturb me.

After I had first met Lugosi, I vowed that someday I would "do right by him" and give him the tribute he deserved. Although my interests changed as I grew up, and I went on to take my doctorate in English and American literature and to become entranced with the silent film, still he remained my none-too-secret vice. Whenever I'd see a Lugosi film, it was like driving past the house of a girl you once loved. The thrill remained. In 1965 I wrote an article on Lugosi and an extensive study of *White Zombie* in an obscure book called *Classics of the Film*. Later that year, I decided to write a full-length study of him. Surely it wouldn't take too long. And of course it didn't, just nine years. A long labor pain for such an insignificant child, one could well say. Why so long? I had to see all of his films, and that was not an easy task. I also became interested in the behind-the-scenes events of his most impor- tant films. Research on these matters took an infinitely long time, for all the facts had to be unearthed. Books were of no help, for I found, much to my disappointment, that most of what had been written in histories, encyclopedias, and fan magazines on both sides of the Atlantic was substantially incorrect. After being confronted with all kinds of discrepancies, such as four different years for Lugosi's birth, I decided to go to Rumania and Hungary in the summer of 1970. There I interviewed his former friends, checked on his theatrical career, visited the church where he was baptized, and finally even found his elusive birth record.

So here, at long last, is the book. This effort was not created single-handedly like one of scientist Lugosi's evil inventions. Instead, it depended on a number of people. Above all are three: John Hand, Paul Jensen, and William K. Everson. When I was young, I was an amateur Lugosi fan, but when I met John Hand, who was still in high school, he was already a professional. He lived and breathed Lugosi and urged me on in this project. He began bombarding Hungary with questions, and it was his inconsistent information that prompted me to make the trip there myself. I am indebted to him in so many ways: for the loan of his photographs, for his facts and clippings, and for his friendship. Equal thanks must go to Paul Jensen, my literary conscience. We had once planned a book called "Titans of Terror" to cover the lives and films of Lugosi and Karloff. Although we eventually went our separate ways, we certainly had an effect on each other. He was of inestimable help in reading the manuscript and making innumerable and invaluable suggestions. I shall always be grateful for his patience and solicitude. The third person of great help was William K. Everson, who generously allowed me to screen some of Lugosi's rarer films. Someone ought to erect a monument to this man for his selfless devotion to the history and art of the film.

In addition I should like to thank Ann Dolber, Audrey Kupferberg, and Michael Mascelli for their aid, and of course, Hannelore, who did the translating in Europe. I am also deeply appreciative of the help given to me by the Rumanian Film Archive, the Hungarian Film Archive, Dr. Karolyne Berzeli of the National Theater Library in Budapest, Dr. Géza Staud of the National Theater Institute in Budapest, the Cinémathèque Française, the Theater Collection at Lincoln Center, the American Film Institute, the Library of Congress, George Eastman House, the film collection at the University of Wisconsin, and many individuals in both Europe and the United States. I am also indebted (literally and financially) to Modern Sound Pictures, Audio-Brandon, United Films, Ideal Pictures, and Willoughby-Peerless for their kindness.

January, 1974   ARTHUR LENNIG

THE COUNT

❧ 1 ❧

Bela

B AY'-LA LUH'-GAUCH-SCHEE! What these often-mispro-
nounced syllables evoke! For some people he was the embodiment of dark, mysterious forces, a harbinger of evil from the world of
shadow. For others he was merely a ham actor appearing in a type of
film unsuitable for children and often unfit for adults. Having won
immediate fame in *Dracula* (1931), he went on to become a rather
famous motion-picture star. But he was not entirely happy with being
typecast as a horror man. After all, he had been a matinee idol during
certain portions of his Hungarian career and later had starred on
Broadway. Unlike Karloff, who was grateful to be in horror films,
Lugosi kept trying to get out of them during the 1930's. By the next
decade he was inured to the fact that he would always be the villain.
Condemned to a lifetime of dying on the screen, he confessed that he
didn't mind much any more. "It's a living," he once said, shrugging his
shoulders.[1]

Suddenly the career he was always lamenting ended. Increasing age
and a supposed change in audience taste had their effect, for soon after
the end of the Second World War his type of film disappeared. The
last ten years of his life brought him only oblivion and sorrow, and his
death from a heart attack in August, 1956, proved a mercy.

If Lugosi had been neglected by Hollywood producers in the last
years of his life, he had always been neglected by film aestheticians, for
he had never appeared in a "great" film. Nor did critics, nostalgic
columnists, and various purveyors of information on the glittering stars
deign to mention Lugosi in their nonarticles and nonbooks. He was
never a popular star with the housewife set or with intellectually

[1] *Morning Telegraph*, December 30, 1941.

respectable and proper audiences. In his last years even young horror addicts, inured to the outer-space creatures of the early fifties, found his films dated and his style corny. And so Bela Lugosi, the once-famed star of the Hungarian theater, Broadway, and the cinema, had come to be a lone, forgotten, rather pathetic person whose skills had been misunderstood and whose artistic contribution lay unwanted and, for the most part, unappreciated.

The face is mirror to the soul, the romantics say. Lugosi was no exception. His final films reveal a haggard and almost unrecognizable face, the result of a transformation as profoundly shocking and disastrous as any fictional one he ever portrayed. The tall, lean frame had shrunk and become emaciated. Toward the end only the strange intonation and measured cadence of That Voice persisted, and ironically his last two film roles did not even allow him to speak.

Lugosi could not have known when he died in August, 1956, that vindication would eventually come, that his face again would adorn theaters, that his image would be used for greeting cards, that toy makers would sell plastic Count Draculas, that horror-film magazines would appear and prosper, and that the Lugosi accent would achieve a kind of folk permanence.

In many ways Bela Lugosi is a difficult figure to assess. From a purely aesthetic point of view, his films are mostly beneath contempt. A few of them are of some thematic interest, and others offer a skillfully manipulated mood, but what saves the majority of them is inevitably Lugosi himself. And yet one could never say that he was a David Garrick, Edmund Kean, and John Barrymore rolled into one; he has to be taken *con amore* or not at all. Admittedly he is an uneven performer—who would not be when faced with such frequently imbecilic plots—but it is a tribute to his talent that he made his roles as palatable as they are. If Lugosi chews the scenery at times, he chews with grandiose vigor, and often that chewing provides our only nourishment. This much can be said: he is never dull. When he is on the screen, the film moves, and when he is not, the film is generally a species of the "undead."

Lugosi did not live to relish his renewed fame, but it is gratifying to know that the passion and sincerity and emotion he placed in his performances have been recognized, that young horror-film buffs have grown tired of the bland American heroes and villains, and that now

Lugosi resides permanently in an occult shrine reserved for those who fulfill the strange mythic urges for mystery that we all have. Lugosi was not an average Joe or a humble and unflamboyant scientist; he was not a diluted human, but the distilled essence of the romantic, gothic passion. In a prosaic world his poetic self would hardly receive complete acceptance. Though he may not have gained a place in the heart of the world cinema audience, he was content to remain on the periphery—in the veins. Today he lives on, more viable than ever.

Lugosi's reputation as number-one horror man lasted from February to December, 1931, from the release of *Dracula* to that of *Frankenstein*. This short reign resulted from his unwillingness to play the Frankenstein monster—he felt it would ruin his sexy image—and so Karloff took the role and won immediate fame. As a result, Lugosi had to live the rest of his life in Karloff's shadow.

Although the two men became professional "spooks," their skills were hardly similar. Lugosi was a personality first, an actor second. He would not have been pleased with this judgment and would counter, "Well, they never gave me a chance." In a sense they never did. Except for his portrayal of Ygor, in *Son of Frankenstein* and *Ghost of Frankenstein*, and for a few minor comic roles, he was never able to escape from playing some aspect of himself. Although he found this task increasingly onerous as the years passed, it was this consistency that gave him star status and, more important, cult status. Not every Hollywood performer becomes the object of a cult. Errol Flynn, Marilyn Monroe, and Humphrey Bogart are not always regarded so much for their acting abilities as for the personality types they radiated. Bogart had a considerable range, but his most admired films are not necessarily the ones in which he acted best, but the ones in which he was most quintessentially "Bogey." Audiences like their favorite actors in "typical" roles. There were no such typical parts for Karloff. Technically a better actor than Lugosi, Karloff was able to submerge himself in various characterizations. Bela had a less low profile. Perhaps the difference was temperamental or maybe national. After all, an Englishman is quite different from a Hungarian, but whatever the reasons, these two performers differ in more ways than they are similar. Except for Karloff's unusual and indeed rather ugly face, and his odd lisp, he had no particular individuality. He is excellent at assuming a character, but does not have much of his own to exploit.

This is one reason he so often appears in heavy makeup. What he portrays he handles with skill, and seldom does he give a poor performance. He tends to underact, Lugosi, to overact.

Neither Lugosi nor Karloff would have had much of a screen career if each had not won fame in *Dracula* and *Frankenstein*. After all, what kind of future could there have been for these middle-aged men? Yet they both became stars. The horror film was kind to them, or perhaps they were kind to the horror film. Certainly they created the genre just as much as the genre created them.

Dracula and *Frankenstein* (1931) were the first sound horror films and undoubtedly two of the most successful ever made. They spawned a number of sequels and countless imitations, both direct and indirect. These two horror classics also solidified (but hardly invented) basic plots and characterizations that still persist.

Count Dracula is a creature of night; he is a spectral being casting no reflection, stemming from the occult and the supernatural—an anomaly of our century, against all logic and reason. Yet he *is*. He has not only the ability to transform himself into a bat, to live a life eternal, but even has hypnotic powers over most mortals. In contrast, the Frankenstein monster is a creature of light. He is not a product of the supernatural, but of the cerebral, the end result of logic and its application. The doctor who creates him is a real man, caught up in the Promethean quest for knowledge, who seemingly sacrifices everything to fulfill his ideas. In *Frankenstein* we are not confronted with the devious workings of Satan, the undead, the rich past of fear and superstition, but with man's own invention. Dr. Frankenstein became the harbinger of the future, whereas Count Dracula is literally a creature of the past. New myths could be invented like the mummy or old ones reworked like the wolf man, but they all work contrary to reason. Like religious faith, these myths depend on premises unprovable by logic. Such films spend much of their time creating a tone and atmosphere that would make the embodiment of the myths if not believable, at least acceptable. The scientific films, on the other hand, had a logical basis, even though the extensions of that logic were a bit farfetched. After all, there is a possibility of creating life or of reactivating dead tissue. Other plot devices such as transplanting hearts have now been accomplished, and switching brains is in the realm of possibility.

Dracula and the mummy and the wolf man (when under the full moon) are interested in their own desires. They care nothing about the world except as it serves them. Dr. Frankenstein, on the other hand, is trying to push man's knowledge perhaps beyond where it should go. He was one of the first to venture into "God's domain" and to perish for it. (Or at least in *Frankenstein* and *Bride* he was intended to die, before Universal decided to spoil the scripts and add the happy endings.)

Dracula and *Frankenstein* created an appetite for horror that Hollywood's energies would attempt to assuage during the following decades. Yet the market could bear only so many sequels. There were, however, other possibilities. Perhaps the most interesting one was the "mad doctor" series. In non-Lugosi films the doctor was a scientist who often pursued his experiments with such monomaniacal devotion that he violated the law. What were a few mortals to his earth-shaking plans? The original Dr. Frankenstein robs graves for his experiments; in later films more live sources would sometimes be sought.

Lugosi was the maddest scientist of them all. Sometimes he was cruel only to carry out his ideas. At other times he gloried in his villainy. The typical Bela role (the cult image) made him an isolated creature. His domains seem to be either castles or mansions, and only in low-budget films does he live in a mere house. Even so, no dwelling of his was without a cavernous cellar where he could carry out his experiments.

In his frequently Faustian quest for creating life, developing a superray, bringing people back to life, or just plain killing them off, the role of Gretchen is not a large one. Women appear in horror films, but they are seldom of much importance. Often they function as a means of creating terror—the girl confronted with the monster or the mad scientist—and sometimes she appears as a plot device (the nosy reporter), but for the most part the horror-film villains are a manly lot more interested in philosophical or metaphysical problems than in sheer romance.

The mad scientist always has a scheme. In *Murders in the Rue Morgue* he sacrifices women in order to mix their blood with an ape and so prove evolution. In *White Zombie* the Lugosi character, though not really a scientist, but a master of the occult, uses his magic potion to make others into zombies. In *The Raven* he is a surgeon who enjoys pain and torture—of others, that is. In *The Devil Bat* he breeds giant bats and has them tear out the throats of his enemies. In *The Ape Man* he needs spinal fluid and does not mind killing someone to get it. In *The Return of the Ape Man* he removes the brain of his assistant and transplants it. In *Voodoo Man* he captures women to use their souls to bring back his wife's consciousness. In *Bride of the Monster* he devotes himself to creating superbeings. Certainly the Lugosi scientist is no sluggard. Quite rightly, Bela has been termed the meanest man in the movies, but what would be sheer villainy and nastiness with some actors is redeemed by his own poetic intensity. His cause is just, he feels, and audiences often sympathize with his evil quests.

Lugosi was not the only mad scientist. Karloff, Lionel Atwill, George Zucco, and others were employed in the same nefarious profession. Karloff brings compassion to his portrayals, Lugosi passion to his. One does not pity Lugosi; one respects him, even in his madness and evildoing. Karloff always performs with intelligence, but his scientists are not interesting interpretations. (Perhaps one should say that he represented them for what they usually are—hardworking laboratory workers—and not for what we, as a public, would sometimes like to think of them—as half-crazed geniuses). Karloff's scientist is essentially a rationalist, a mathematician; Lugosi's is essentially a diabolist, a half-mad poet. He has the insane energy of a man concerned only with his own demented experiments, one completely indifferent to the welfare or even the lives of others. The law to Lugosi is beneath contempt. At best it stands for mere meddling, the stupid prejudice and interference of the groundlings with his Promethean experiments.

Raskolnikov's argument in *Crime and Punishment* provides the basic philosophy for many of Lugosi's films:

> People are divided into two classes, the "ordinary" and the "extraordinary." The ordinary ones must live in submission and have no right to transgress the laws, because . . . they are ordinary. And the extraordinary have the right to commit any crime and break every kind of law just because they are extraordinary. . . .
>
> The "extraordinary" man has the right . . . in himself . . . to permit his conscience to overstep certain obstacles, but only in the event that his ideas (which may sometimes be salutary for all mankind) require it for their fulfillment.

. . . If it is necessary for one [of these extraordinary people], for the fulfillment of his ideas, to march over corpses, or wade through blood, then in my opinion he may in all conscience authorize himself to wade through blood—in proportion, however, to his idea and the degree of its importance—mark that.[2]

An extraordinary man, the screen Lugosi does not worry about the welfare of his victims, nor does he ever have qualms of conscience. "Freedom and power, but above all, power! Power over all trembling creatures, over the whole ant-heap!"[3] said Raskolnikov. The screen Lugosi lived life on a cosmic stage, not in the middle-class closet. He does not care what his neighbors think. In fact, if he had his way, he'd kill them all off because they annoy him. What Lugosi appealed to, then, is the unsocial side of ourselves, a *reductio ad absurdum* of our supposed "territorial imperative." He was also, in a peculiar sense, a revolutionary. Like the Marx brothers, the screen Lugosi disliked the establishment. The Marx brothers, however, tore down the establishment, after making a mockery of it, and substituted sheer anarchy. The Lugosi character also tore it down, but was eager to replace it with his own rule. He was not, then, opposed to authority but only to someone else's employment—and enjoyment—of it. He did not want power for some utopia, but basically for the sheer joy of running the whole show his own way. Such an aim obviously had an appeal to certain segments of the film audiences. Whereas in real life we must all suffer various kinds of indignities and frustrations, Lugosi is able to triumph, at least for a while, over so-called law and order. How delightful to have an irritating colleague turned into a zombie to do your bidding. If a person remains recalcitrant, Lugosi has only to stare into his eyes to force him to his will. His authoritative command in *Dracula*, "Come here," will echo through his motion pictures. If in some films he does not have hypnotic powers, he has a strong assistant or some physical device such as a ray, a potion, a devil bat, or, more prosaically, a gun to carry out his desires.

One could well ask how such an unpleasant person could be popular in the films. The 1930's and 1940's reeked of the little man and the joys

[2] *Crime and Punishment*, edited by George Gibian (New York, W. W. Norton, 1964), pp. 248–49.
[3] *Ibid.*, p. 317.

of democracy and the American flag, and yet countless thousands went to the movies to see—at least for a major portion of the film's length—a Lugosi character revel in the free exercise of his frequently evil will. Why, the sage moralists might ask, did the people go? Why did these films, roundly insulted by the critics, pack them in? Why would people pay to see the same ritual performances?

The answer is reasonably clear. Lugosi's films dealt with the night role of human ambitions, an area that the bland Hollywood fare would not recognize. The Golden Quest for Life Eternal was one aim of the Lugosi scientist; the other was Revenge. The screen Lugosi had the skill, intelligence, money, and time to carry out his dastardly schemes. If a girl attracts him in *White Zombie*, he reduces her and her admirers to zombies and plans to have her himself. In *The Raven* he is in love with a girl, and since she is unwilling to reciprocate, thus causing him torture, he decides logically to torture her and everyone else who stands in his way. Even as Ygor in *Son of Frankenstein*, Bela remains consistent. He does not like some villagers; therefore he has his friend, the monster, kill them. In *Ghost of Frankenstein* he wants to use the monster to help gain control of the state and, in fact, has his own brain put in the monster's body so that he can have both the intellect and the physical strength to carry out his evil plans.

True, the mad scientist is a bad guy, but who are his adversaries? Usually fools, without a shred of the intelligence and culture of the master villain. Oddly enough during the thirties in America there was almost never an intelligent and cultured person on the screen. Those who did appear were included only for satirical purposes: the absentminded, fuddy-duddy professor, for example. Everyone was supposed to be average (except in looks, if one was a young man or woman). Simple solutions satisfied simple needs. An ice-cream cone at the corner drugstore, a nice game of baseball, Andy Hardy and his awful town, were more or less it. Mass values for mass consumption. The villains who appeared in these Edenic milieus were interested in money or women or both. Usually they were rather gross, crude fellows; if they were gentlemen, they often had pencil-thin mustaches and were rather oily. The mad scientists were not concerned with money or women, but power. So were gangsters, but their needs were finite: to control the South Side. Lugosi's scientists, in particular, had cosmic schemes: to pursue their experiments for the glory of science and occasionally to rule the world as well. Bitter paranoids, they puttered away in their labs, disdained most of mankind, and dedicated themselves to proving how right their theories were. As soon as their plans began to succeed, the scientists would again become interested in mankind, but only in how to control and punish it for a previous lack of respect. Sick, maybe, but fun.

That the "extraordinary" Lugosi suffers defeat at the hands of the "ordinary" folk not only returns the world to its usual pedestrian and hypocritical morality, but the defeat of his superintellect reflects and indeed reinforces the anti-intellectualism that has always been so much with us. The justice meted out to him is often deserved from a strictly moral view, but is a miscarriage in any Nietzschean sense. His audiences come back each time to see the mad scientist win, and of course, each time he loses. The only redeeming factor was that secretly we knew that in the next film he would be back with a new idea—or even the same idea—and try again.

Lugosi's horror films in the 1930's placed him in many different kinds of parts, but his starring roles in the 1940's made him almost always a mad scientist. The fact that so many of his pictures repeat the same ideas shows that these scripts were created for him. Writers knew the Lugosi character and would wring perhaps a few changes on the precise nature of his villainy, but often leave him with the same motivations and characterization. Here, then, came the cult image, but with it came numbing repetition, repetition not helped by the fact that the films were getting lower budgeted each time, with a consequent loss in good plots, dialogue, lighting, and camerawork. Often Lugosi was just let loose before some cheap sets and allowed to stumble through another performance. Lugosi complained more and more about the roles he obtained, but they were what the public wanted to see. The image had become so strong that he could not possibly have been just a nice foreign man living down Andy Hardy's street and working at the soda fountain. Imagine what audiences would think if Lugosi made Andy and his girlfriend a soda. The audience would wait, and certainly some would hope that it would be Andy's last.

Lugosi played weird roles for so long that he almost began to believe that he was a cross between vampire, superscientist, and a creature of occult powers. In fact, Lugosi the screen composite affected Lugosi the man. The pattern resembles that of John Barrymore, who also in his last years began to play a parody of his real self. Just as Barrymore was depicted as a drinker, a rake, and a has-been Shakespearean actor, and frequently even appeared under his own name, so did Lugosi begin to play himself. In 1952 he starred in a sorrowful quickie called *Bela Lugosi Meets a Brooklyn Gorilla*. Lugosi himself had now become the screen character.

Lugosi's cult image was thoroughly identifiable in appearance. With Karloff one remembers what the makeup did to modify his face, but with Lugosi his own face was remembered; he seldom used extravagant makeup. Besides his deep and penetrating eyes and, of course, his firm eyebrows, what is most clearly memorable is Lugosi's accent—one that no impersonator has quite imitated correctly. Yes, it is Hungarian, but it is also Lugosian as well. In the inflections, the certain turn of the word, the odd way his lips and jaw muscles function, he seems to speak with great effort, as if he were forcing a mouth long dead to move again. His consonants are stressed, and the vowels are heavier and more drawn out. The above phrase, "forcing a mouth long dead," becomes "forse-sink a mau-ith longk deadt." The overall effect is guttural, strong, masculine, somehow the very personification of evil, although someone once said that Lugosi's trouble was that his tongue was too big for his mouth!

Not only was Lugosi's accent unique, so was his method of delivery. Probably no actor has used more pauses per line—and to greater effect. As Dracula he says, "I bid you—welcome." The pause before as well as the inflection of the word "welcome" provide a certain ambivalency, a combination of greeting and foreboding, cordiality and superiority, sincerity and irony. Lugosi may appear as an unmitigated ham, but no one, I submit, has ever succeeded in delivering absurd lines with such dramatic power and, indeed, dignity.

Despite his many awful films, Lugosi achieved what Dracula reveled in and what many of his mad scientists strove for: life eternal. His screen character lives on. Unfortunately, like the very roles he played, he would not be vindicated until after his death. Still, as Dracula standing before his coffin or as a scientist with smoking test tube in his hand, he had the glory and the pain of venturing beyond God's domain.

Indicative of his temperament, his passion, his flair, and also in recognition of what had given him his big break on Broadway and subsequently in the movies, Lugosi merged with his screen self for all eternity by being buried in his Dracula cape—a poetic decision that redeemed much of the debasement of his final years. He remains as he had lived—the Count.

❧ 2 ❧

The Early Years

T HE LEGENDARY BELA LUGOSI entered this world more
alliteratively as Béla Blaskó on October 20, 1882, and not 1883
or 1888, as has often been claimed, in the small Hungarian town of
Lugos (now in Rumania). It was only when Bela was about twenty
that he changed his name by adapting the syllables of his native town
and becoming Lugossy (meaning "from Lugos"). The *y* ending
connoted nobility and obviously appealed to this young dreamer. In
1911, perhaps feeling that the aristocratic name was too pretentious, he
modified it and so became Lugosi.

Although American publicity releases said that Bela was the son of a
baron, his heritage was not quite so noble. His parents, in fact, were
the children of farmers. Bela's father had been born in Nyitai, a town
in the north of Hungary, near the Czechoslovakian border, and his
mother in a nearby village. When the couple wed on September 29,
1858, the husband, István (Stephan), was thirty and his wife, Paula
Vojnits, twenty. They moved south to Lugos, where their first son,
Ludovicus (Lajos), was born on May 19, 1859; on the birth record the
father was listed as *pistor magr* (master baker). These early church
records were kept in Latin, so that the father's name was spelled
Stephanus, not the Hungarian István. Four years later daughter Joanna
was born, and after a long interval another daughter, Vilma, in 1878.
This time the father's profession was listed as *pék*, Hungarian for baker.

The father had worked hard and successfully in Lugos, a town laid
in a flat but fertile plain on the banks of the Temesvár River. This
prosperous little city, of 12,500 inhabitants around the year 1900, was
divided by the river into Rumanian-Lugos and Deutsch (German)-
Lugos. The German side denoted not only the language used but also
the more financially successful people. And young Bela's father had
been quite successful. As a baker he had made good profits and decided,

along with other businessmen of the town, to form a savings bank in January, 1883. The Lugos Volksbank was a small bank, the only one in Lugos, but it made the Blaskós—at least in their own image—a little higher on the social scale. When young Bela was born, the father's profession was baker. But by the time Bela's sister Vilma married in 1896 she listed her father as *Direktor einer Sparbank* (director of a savings bank). The imagination and drive the family possessed carried on to their children as well. The first son became an engineer, Vilma married a lawyer, and of course something was to be heard of Bela.

The father no doubt counted his blessings on the morning of October 29, 1882, when he walked down Templom Street from his residence, past the cement-stuccoed houses, to the Lugos Roman Catholic parish church, where the new baby was to be christened Béla Ferenc Dezsö Blaskó. The German-speaking clerk heard the family name and, as is common with Germans, spelled it phonetically as Blaschko. The father corrected the man, and the extra letters were crossed out. Sometime later, in a more modern handwriting, a rather mysterious penciled addition—the only change in the whole volume of birth records—modified the father's profession from baker to banker.

Lugos and the land surrounding it by no means presented the forbidding geographical features so familiar to viewers of *Dracula*. The main streets have a typically middle-European look, with their multistoried houses of stone and stucco. As a youth Lugosi might easily have taken the railroad twenty-four miles to the small town of Karánsebes, where a carriage would ascend the valley of the Bisztra River for 26 miles and bring him to a 2,152-foot pass: the gateway to Transylvania.

As pronounced and intoned by Lugosi, and as depicted in many a horror film, Transylvania glows with legend and myth, an area of stark landscape sparsely inhabited by fearful peasants who cross themselves at the slightest provocation. To the natives, however, it was known more prosaically and accurately as the "forest land," for its hills and peaks are well wooded. Although Lugosi did not live far from the western border of Transylvania, the fictional castle of Bram Stoker's immortal Count Dracula lies at the other end of this supposedly vampire-infested domain. Transylvania, according to an old *Britannica*, was a place where "bears, wolves, and foxes were abundant." Probably folktales were also abundant, but whether Lugosi as a child of a middle-class family ever heard vampire superstitions is another matter. He would speak of them later in interviews in America, but he may

The peaceful town of Lugos looks the same as it did in Lugosi's day.

The parish church in which Bela was baptized.

Lugos (Lugoj in Rumanian) is still farming country.

only have been providing good copy. After all, it was not wise for the world's leading vampire to deny that he had heard about them or believed in them.

Lugosi's homeland seemed (and perhaps still seems) to be a far-off and myth-ridden place to the West European or American, but it was not really such a wild and mysterious country. Would it were so! How wonderful to think that somewhere in Europe there was a place where people were afraid to appear after dark, where bats hung over the land like a flickering pall, and where in decaying coffins lay the possibility of an eternity of "undeadness." But Hungary was part of the Austro-Hungarian Empire, and a large and sprawling civil service provided mail and certificates of birth, marriage, and death; railroads crisscrossed the rolling and mountainous land; theaters beckoned in all but the smallest towns; and banking and investment and commerce provided at least the foundations of a modern nation. Old Gypsies, superstitious peasants, broken and deserted castles there certainly were, but they were not set off by themselves in the craggy and thrusting peaks of a land isolated by time and circumstance. Hungary is not Hollywood's version, nor was it even in Lugosi's day.

But Transylvania and the surrounding area did have a long and complicated history. Controlled by the Romans until A.D. 271, the land subsequently became the battleground for Ostrogoths, Huns, Bulgarians, Magyars, and other Eastern races. The result of this influence can easily be seen in Lugosi's face, which, especially around the eyes, suggests a somewhat Oriental look, a look that Broadway and later Hollywood would exploit when they cast him as an Eastern prince, a crystal-ball mystic, or a vampire. Lugosi, occasionally to his own embarrassment but also to his financial success, suggested a land far more romantic and mysterious than it really was; it would be his salvation and his destruction. To the public, Lugosi would always be Dracula, for in a world plagued by the petty annoyances of daily living he represented something exotic: a harbinger of the unknown, a symbol of the uneasiness we all feel in the dark of night when bathrobes hanging on pegs look like ghosts and minute noises suggest unseen presences.

Lugosi's own youth was far different from what his later movie roles might suggest. He lived with his family within the town, went to a grammar school, and struggled with language, reading, and mathematics. Then he was enrolled in the Superior Hungarian State Gymnasium in 1893 and passed his first year with acceptable but by no means extraordinary grades.[1] An imaginative boy—as his choice of acting would indicate—he did not apply himself with the diligence necessary for a scholar and was often absent from class.

What his future might have been was drastically changed by the death of his father on September 11, 1894. The family prosperity waned, and a professional career became no longer possible. Instead Bela went to an industrial school at a nearby town and there began apprentice work as a *Schlosser,* a locksmith. What urged him to abandon this job is not clear, but impulsively he changed course again and decided to become an actor, a choice that did not sit well with his less prosperous but still proper family. Acting was an unsure profession, a far cry from what a banker's son should do, but at the least it had much more excitement and challenge than fixing locks. Certainly it was wise that he did not go into banking, for if there ever was a person not cautious with money, it was banker István's spendthrift son.

Years later in America, Lugosi spoke of the acting profession:

> In Hungary acting is a career for which one fits himself as earnestly and studiously as one studies for a degree in medicine, law or philosophy. In Hungary acting is a profession. In America it is a decision. A youth "decides" he will go on the stage or appear in

---

[1] Religion: sufficient, Hungarian language: sufficient, Latin: sufficient, Mathematics: sufficient, Arithmetic: good, Dancing: sufficient, Gymnastics: sufficient, Music: very good, Reading: not very satisfactory, Behavior: correct.

pictures. If the public accepts him, the "decision" automatically becomes final.[2]

An American news release once stated that Lugosi decided to become an actor when he was seventeen:

> A theatrical troupe in *Romeo and Juliet* was billed to play in the small province which Lugosi lived in. Of the population none was more interested in the forthcoming event than the young Lugosi.
>
> During the afternoon previous to the scheduled performance of the play, an unexpected bit of news exploded in the rumor channels. Romeo had been taken ill suddenly and it might be necessary to change the program for the evening.[3]

Lugosi "searched out the manager and offered his services. The manager, having a sense of humor, treated his offer most courteously and assured the young man that he would give it his serious consideration." *Romeo and Juliet*, however, had been advertised. When the manager was faced with refunding the tickets already sold, he discovered that the Lugosi family was of some prominence in the community and decided to use the young fellow. So Bela appeared, and the play was a "great success."

Press agentry being what it is, and Lugosi's imagination and memory being what they were—combined with the fact that screen reporters seldom get a story straight anyhow—have resulted in a story that is dramatic but not true. There is no record of *Romeo and Juliet* being performed in Lugos or the surrounding area in those years.

The fact is that by 1901 Lugosi had decided that he would be an actor. In those days, long before the movies, small theatrical troupes would arrive in towns of no more than a few hundred people and put on shows with primitive scenery. The productions may not have been particularly good, but at least they provided the experience that actors need. Performances were given in Lugos as early as 1829, but there was no regular theater there for many years. In 1892 a theater society was founded and a building devoted to the dramatic arts built in 1900. From then on, traveling groups of actors would regularly appear during the season.

---

[2] Press sheets for *The Return of Chandu*, 1934.
[3] Philadelphia *Public Ledger*, August 13, 1933.

Although the Hungarian theatrical encyclopedia lists aspects of Lugosi's early career, the information is not correct, as this writer discovered when he arrived in Budapest. Fortunately the National Széchényi Library Theater History Collection has more than 320,000 playbills and posters from all the towns in the old Austro-Hungarian Empire. In these wrinkled and decaying posters Lugosi's theatrical career lies hidden. The only way of checking his early years is to go through all the boxes. A thorough check would take months, for in the beginning of his career he appeared with various touring companies that performed for a day or a week in one town and then went on to another. This writer, however, devoted some days to sifting through the posters.

The earliest record that was found is for the season of 1903–1904, when "Bela Lugossy" was lucky and skillful enough to become connected with the Franz Joseph Theater of Temesvár. There he played under the direction of Ignácz Krecsányi, who, considered by many the greatest Hungarian director, centered his activities in Temesvár rather than Budapest. Bela received small roles in plays and—because he had a good singing voice—also appeared in operettas. For example, on October 11, 1903, he sang in *Bob Herczeg*, an operetta, and on October 14 acted in *Annuska*, a play; he appeared in another operetta on October 17, and on October 22 had the leading role of Pinkerton in a nonmusical version of *Madama Butterfly*. He also sang small baritone roles in operas.

At the end of the season Lugosi moved on to other troupes and in the next few years played in many towns and cities, slowly learning the craft of acting. At one time he appeared as Christ in a passion play. In 1907–1908 he traveled with the company of Béla Polgár and had leading parts, such as Danilo in *The Merry Widow*. In the fall of 1908 he moved on to Debrecen, another good theatrical town. There he played Byron's doomed hero-villain in *Manfred* on December 15, 1908. His skills were apparently appreciated, for in the next season (1909–1910) Lugosi got more leading roles. He played Pinkerton again, as well as Adam in the great Hungarian national play, *The Tragedy of Man*; Antonio in *Merchant of Venice*; and Armand in *The Lady of the Camellias*.

Most of the roles Lugosi played in these small provincial theaters have been lost in time. But a record of the rest of his theatrical performances was kept, and this writer is grateful to the Hungarian

The Prince of Darkness once played the Prince of Peace.

cultural attaché, József Kerekes, and to Dr. Géza Staud of the Scientific Institute of the Hungarian Theater, who provided the play title, role, and date for all of Lugosi's appearances from September, 1910, to January, 1919.

In August, 1910, Lugosi, still using the name Lugossy, arrived in Szeged, the second largest city in Hungary (population 90,000), and appeared in the city's repertory theater (the Városi Szinház) for the full season from September through May. He made his debut on September 2 as Romeo (this is probably the source for the much-garbled anecdote quoted previously). During that month Lugosi appeared eleven times in as many roles, in October three times, in November six times, and in December six times. He continued with the same regularity until the end of the season in May. Although not all his roles were leads—a characteristic of repertory theaters—Bela had a challenging and personally rewarding season. He did not get to play some of the meatiest parts, as he had in his earlier days, but he was kept busy. Besides playing dramatic roles, he sang in some operettas and once more portrayed the dashing Danilo in *The Merry Widow*. Many of the plays were of an ephemeral nature, popular entertainment of the period, but others were translations from Russian, German, Austrian, or English works. On December 17, 1910, he played the lead, Vronsky, in an adaptation of Tolstoy's *Anna Karenina*; on December 20, 1910, Clarence in *Richard III*; on March 9, 1911, Cassio in *Othello*; on March 31, Laertes in *Hamlet*; and on April 2, Lucentio in *The Taming of the Shrew*. All in all he appeared in fifty-four roles in as many plays during the season.

In the May 14 issue of a theatrical magazine in Szeged called *Szinházi Usjság*, Lugosi's picture appeared on the cover and an article by Béla Kálmány discussed the young star. He was described as being handsome and intelligent and having a rich, melancholy voice, a velvety voice that spoke straight to the audience's hearts. At first, however, his talents had not been completely appreciated. Lugosi had to get used to the bad acoustics of the theater and apparently played Romeo passionately but a bit too rapidly. The audiences were used to actors taking their parts slowly and getting frequent help from the prompter. Lugosi knew his part perfectly.

Before Bela came to Szeged, he had been quite successful, and silken ribbons on a wreath in his room testified to his previous successes in Debrecen. One award he won was for "the best Manfred," the demonic hero in Byron's play. The Debrecen theater had depended on him for their classical programs, and he had been their featured attraction. But in Szeged his one big classical role had been Romeo. "Beautifully fiery, passionately loving and dying Romeo!" the writer of the article described him. Lugosi played his parts with supreme passion and intensity. "He is a man and in love when he plays a man and lover. Wild, violent in love, and his aching heart almost breaking when as Romeo he sees his beautiful Juliet dead. He grabs the strings of the heart and stretches them to the breaking point." Lugosi's Romeo was a superb creation by a twentieth-century actor, the writer said, and hoped only that in the future he could see him as Manfred, Faust, or Adam.

Bela's admirer in the press was certainly impressed, but he was not the only one. When Lugosi appeared in *Sárga Liliom* (not the famous *Liliom*), the author of the play, Lajos Biró, said that of all the provincial theaters in Hungary, his play had the greatest success in Szeged because of Bela's excellent performance. When in one play Lugosi had to play a coldly calculating man of forty, he was not too effective, the article went on, but in passionate roles he was outstanding. The young star, the article noted, had been contacted by a director of a Budapest theater. "It is a pity for the audiences of Szeged . . . that he had gotten so few parts here. The director will have good box-office with him, if Lugosi is given good parts. We can predict already that he will be loved the most by the women . . . who praise his manly beauty even beyond his acting talent."

Quite a few of the ladies of Szeged must have lamented the departure of their onstage and offstage Romeo, but Bela was pleased. Here at last was the big time, the capital city of Hungary. He arrived in the summer of 1911 and began rehearsals at the Magyar Szinház (the Theater of Hungary). For the first time using the name "Lugosi," he made his debut on September 3 as Count Vronsky in *Anna Karenina* and then appeared in other plays as well. In November, 1911, he left the theater and during 1912 studied at the Rákosi Szidi Acting School. Lugosi would later claim that he studied at the Academy of Theatrical Arts, but a letter from that institution declares that he never attended. The academy demanded a broad scholastic knowledge as well as foreign languages, both of which Lugosi's youthful training had avoided. He did study at a private school, run by a former actress, the mother of the director of the Hungarian Theater, who also had an operetta theater. Perhaps she tried to make Lugosi into an operetta lead because of his good voice. On April 12, 1912, he sang the role of Fairfax in *A Gésák*. While attempting to better himself professionally, Lugosi also tried to make up for his weak academic background. His fellow actors were aware of his deficiencies, and Lugosi often had to ask what a foreign expression meant. He was diligent, however, and tried to catch up on general knowledge, was prompt for rehearsals, and at least professionally led a sober life. But he was too good-looking and enjoyed pleasure too much to spend much of his free time studying.

Early in 1913 Lugosi was hired by the Nemzeti Szinház (the National Theater of Hungary), the leading theater of the country and one of the best in all Europe, where he made his debut on January 5, 1913. In this more important institution Lugosi would get only smaller roles. The older actors of course won all the best parts, and it was natural that the still-young man would have to wait many more years. Some of the reviews of his performances, it must be admitted, were not too favorable. Lugosi was never a "great" actor in Hungary, nor was he ever a "leading" one at the National Theater, although his very presence there showed that he was among the best.

One of Lugosi's acquaintances recently offered this evaluation:

> I saw him as a young, serious actor, who came to his rehearsals punctually, with books under his arm and tried to develop the possibilities of his roles with dedication. He usually played the roles of a young lover, especially of those who were dominated by extensive passion. He was favored by the audience.
>
> In my judgment, he was a very fine actor. He was misunderstood because they wanted to make an *amoroso* out of him. Neither his voice nor his manner predestined him to this kind of role, though he had a graceful, stately, elegant figure.[4]

In 1913 Lugosi appeared in thirty-four plays in small roles, such as Rosenkrantz in *Hamlet* on March 17, 1913. Up until June, 1914, he was listed sixteen times. His life, however, would now be changed drastically by an even bigger drama, the First World War. It would again be a small role, but a painful one.

In June, 1914, he became a lieutenant in the 43d Royal Hungarian

[4] Denes Ratai, letter, March 30, 1968.

In various urbane roles and as Vronsky in *Anna Karenina*.

Infantry and served in the trenches for one and one-half years, first in Serbia and then, during 1915, in Russia. Wounded—once badly, at Rohatin, and then again while in the Carpathian Mountains—he left the service in April, 1916, and returned to the National Theater, appearing that same month as Fortinbras in *Hamlet*. By the following September he had received the larger part of Laertes.

Most of the people who knew Lugosi in Hungary are dead, and those who survive are in their eighties. Fortunately, however, their memories proved not too fallible when this writer interviewed them in Budapest during the summer of 1970. Not only were interesting anecdotes recounted, but furthermore, impressions of the young Bela tended to agree with the persona he revealed in his later life. His former acquaintances all found him to be personable, polite, friendly, but a "loner" and a terrible manager of his finances. Tall and good-looking, he had a flair for passionate parts and always wanted to play romantic roles (such as Romeo), even though he was more gifted at portraying men of intrigue or power. He gave these roles an intensity that carried over the footlights.

Around the time of World War One, Lajos Bálint (who later was literary manager of the National Theater) was looking for a place to live in Budapest. Lugosi had a nice apartment with large rooms and a housekeeper, but it was really beyond his means, especially as he had debts besides. In fact, Lugosi was always in financial difficulties but did his best to ignore them. Bálint noted that even though oranges at that time were something special and expensive, Lugosi had squeezed five of them for a glass of juice. But Bálint liked the rooms and the roommate, so he moved in and shared the place until Bela's marriage.

At the outbreak of the war, Bálint mentioned to Lugosi during a noontime conversation how everything, for example, shoes, would soon become very expensive. Lugosi asked him why. Bálint said that leather would be needed for boots for the army. When Bálint returned from work that night, he went to Lugosi's room to look for him. The actor was not there, but on the windowsills stood many white shoe boxes. Lugosi had obviously run right off to the stores and bought all the shoes in his size. Of course he couldn't pay cash for them! "I often use this anecdote," Bálint said, "to illustrate a foolish and a wise way of spending money. I had gone out and bought an extra pair, whereas he took everything in his size."

Bálint recalled that Lugosi was *simpatico,* a nice man who dressed very well, though not loudly or excessively. "You could not feel the locksmith apprentice in him. He had nice table manners, and that means something. On the stage, however, you could occasionally see it; his movements were occasionally too strong and not fine enough." He was very successful with the women, though not very selective, and none of the entanglements lasted long. Bálint recalled that one night Lugosi had a date. For about half an hour he stood in front of the mirror perfecting the knot in his tie. "Why do you fuss so?" Bálint asked him. "You'll just take it off anyway."

Asked whether Lugosi was an unhappy man, Bálint replied in the negative. "Lugosi did not have close friends—he was a bit standoffish—but he enjoyed himself and liked the good life." When this writer mentioned Lugosi's peculiar accent in English, Bálint remembered that Lugosi had a different way of speaking, not really a dialect, but somehow different.

Bálint told Lugosi one day that the only way he could cure his money difficulties was to find a rich wife. And this Bela did. Ilona "Baby" Szmik was an attractive girl whose father happened to be the executive secretary of a medium-sized bank in Budapest. She was young and very much in love with Bela. The family was, of course, cautious. The father asked Bálint about Lugosi, and the roommate replied that "he was a nice guy but needed some management and help with money."

When this writer asked whether Lugosi was very much in love with her, Bálint replied, "She was much in love with him." For Lugosi, Bálint thought, it was a marriage of convenience. But Bela didn't think so, at least not in retrospect. His fourth wife told this writer that Bela had indeed been very much in love with his first wife.

It was a big wedding on June 25, 1917, at Saint Ann's Church in Budapest, and Lugosi and his young wife settled down in an apartment near it, an apartment probably subsidized by the girl's father.

Lugosi's marriage did not improve his career. He continued to get small parts, but there was one exception. On April 7, 1918, he played the lead, Armand Duval, in Dumas' *Lady of the Camellias*. In June, 1918, he again appeared in *Romeo and Juliet*, but he played Tybalt. All in all, Lugosi's name was listed thirty-four times between April, 1916, and his last appearance, on January 10, 1919. Because his roles were minor, newspaper reviews of the plays seldom mentioned him. When he was discussed, it was not always favorably. In Hebbel's play *Maria*

Magdalena, one newspaper said, "Lugosi's Leonhard was somewhat colorless. His interpretation showed little focus." [5]

It was in 1917 that Lugosi became involved in motion pictures. Hungarian film production itself had not started until 1912. Unlike the industry in other countries, the Hungarian cinema was not begun by sheer profiteers. From its very beginning, artists and writers took the new medium seriously and tried consciously to create art, not just make money. Many of the scripts were borrowed from literature and had a kind of respectability because of their source. The budding industry made use of actors from the Hungarian theater, rather than nonactors, as did the American cinema. Although payments were small, there was a good deal of competition among the performers. Lugosi had a natural advantage: Not only was he a good actor, but he was also young and handsome and gifted with personality and a good screen presence.

In Hungary in 1913 only ten films were made, but soon a number of new companies sprang up and production rose. By 1917, when Lugosi first went in front of the cameras, more than 90 percent of the films came from works of well-known authors. This kind of seriousness affected Lugosi, and even after he had become a success in the United States he still spoke bitterly about the debased values of Hollywood and its childish scripts. This disappointment, plus his own personal problems, did not make him the happiest of men in his roles as horror star. He always lamented what might have been.

Hungarian directors were not interested in Griffith-like cutting. Instead, they were closer to the German cinema, which stressed pantomime, facial expressions, and setting. Lugosi's training at this time influenced his subsequent career. Although later criticized for his "old acting school" methods in his American films, he continued in the theatrical tradition. Whenever possible, he tried to stylize his movements. He moved cleanly across the movie sets, with few naturalistic gestures to distract from the essence of his portrayal, and often his face radiated the emotions he felt.

Unfortunately most of the early Hungarian films have been lost through neglect, deterioration, fire, or the bombings of the Second World War. In fact, of about five hundred films, only a dozen or so remain, and unfortunately Lugosi does not appear in any of them. The records for these films are lost in time, and only certain synopses

[5] *Pester Lloyd,* May 20, 1917.

indicate what these films contained and when they were produced. The following information differs from most sources for the reason that most sources are incorrect. What actual dates are supplied come from the actual release dates in Budapest. Records indicate, however, that Lugosi appeared in his first film, *A Leopárd* (The Leopard), for the Star Film Company in Budapest in 1917.[6] This company wanted to appeal to moviegoers outside of Hungary and so had their stars change their names to more pronounceable ones for European audiences. For this reason Lugosi was given the aristocratic-sounding name of Arisztid Olt.[7] Certainly to English ears this was not much of an improvement. However, in the films he made for another Budapest company, Phoenix, he used his real name. His first production for Phoenix was *Az Ezredes* (The Colonel) and was directed in 1917 by Mihály Kertész, who later came to America, where he modified his name to Michael Curtiz.

The Colonel tells the story of a vagabond (the Colonel) who breaks into the house of a millionaire and is caught in the act. In reparation for this crime, the millionaire makes the vagabond steal back a fortune that the millionaire's brother had taken. Kathe, the daughter of the millionaire, wants to prevent this, for she is in love with the Colonel. After many complications it comes to light that all the objects of the burglary are imitation: only the love between Kathe and the Colonel is true. Lugosi's role combined the excitement of being a crook with romantic appeal and no doubt pleased him.

In the following year Lugosi appeared for Kertész in *99*, a gangster story, and played in *Küzdelem A Létért* (A Struggle for Life) an architect who, as the synopsis goes,

> ruins everybody for the sake of his career. This is because his principle is the survival of the stronger. He even ruins his loves (a countess and a poor girl as well). When he believes [himself] to be at the goal, he meets his fate; the father of the poor girl shoots him.

Lugosi appeared in *Álarcosbál* (The Masked Ball); "the role of the secretary [Arisztid Olt] was played with assurance and caught the enthusiasm of the audience," according to a review of March, 1918.[8]

---

[6] The author is indebted to Dr. Karolyne Berzeli of the National Theater Library in Budapest for helping him find all these synopses.

[7] Interview with István Radó, editor of *Mozi-Világ*, in Budapest, July, 1970.

[8] *Szinházielet*, March 10, 1918.

Lugosi then had a starring role as Bertram in *Nászdal* (Song of Marriage),[9] released in April, 1918. Bertram is a famous violinist who honeymoons with his young wife in the mountains. One night while out walking they are attacked by the pianist Izau, who is in love with Bertram's wife. In the bloody duel that follows, Bertram kills Izau and escapes to the forest, where he earns a living giving violin instruction. His wife mourns because she thinks he has died. When by accident she sees the bearded Bertram, she thinks he is her husband's murderer and has him arrested. Put in prison, he takes out his violin and repeats the plaintive song he had played on his honeymoon. The wife hears it and recognizes her husband, and all is well. The plot was described as exciting and the photography beautiful. The two leads, Lugosi and Peterdi Klára, "played their very best," according to a review of the time.[10]

Lugosi played the lead in a version of Oscar Wilde's *The Picture of*

[9] Plot summary in *Szinházielet*, April 7, 1918.
[10] *Ibid.*

Jelenet a „KÜZDELEM A LÉTÉRT"-ből

Dorian Gray, called *Az Élet Királya* (The King of Life), released in September, 1918. At the end of the film, as in the book, he confronts his own portrait on the wall and in destroying it destroys himself. This role of a charming villain would often come to him in his American career. Lugosi's frequent costar was the lovely Ila Lóth. In an interview at her villa on the outskirts of Budapest, she told this author that Bela was a good player with whom to work. He always arrived promptly at the studio and showed little or no temperament despite the discomforts of early risings and frequent location trips over bumpy roads.[11]

Lugosi made other films during this period, among them *Lili*, and *Tavaszi Vihar* (The Wild Wind of Spring). By this time Lugosi had become "a favorite leading man." [12]

By 1918 forty-five directors were working in Hungary, of whom fifteen were native Hungarians, eighteen were part-time directors, and twelve were from foreign countries. Of the native directors, two would become world-famous: Alexander Korda (later in Britain) and Michael Curtiz (in Hollywood). Although Lugosi was directed by Curtiz in a few films, many of his films were directed by the prolific Alfred Deésy, who set a production record by shooting fifteen or sixteen films a year in 1917 and 1918. Years later Deésy left Hungary and worked in Germany, but returned to Budapest, where he recently died.

In the latter part of 1918 Alexander Korda summed up this period in an interview with the Hungarian magazine *Cine-Weekly*, which he had started three years before:

> In the last three years of the war Hungarian studios have achieved more than in the previous fifteen. We began to approach the standards of the great European filmmakers and our results are without parallel in the history of the cinema. I believe that in the future we'll keep above the level of Austrian and German production though unavoidably lag behind America and Britain.[13]

Korda proved wrong. Ten days before Armistice Day, revolution broke out in Budapest, and King Charles abdicated on November 13. Count Michael Károlyi, a popular though weak leader, took control as

---

[11] Interview with Ila Lóth, Budapest, July, 1970.

[12] István Nemeskürty, *Word and Image: History of the Hungarian Cinema* (Hungary, Corvina Press, 1968), p. 43.

[13] Quoted by Paul Tabori, *Alexander Korda* (New York, Living Books, Inc., 1966), p. 55.

President, but he was unable to quell even some of the social unrest.

One day, before a rehearsal began, Lugosi called over Dénes Ratai (later art director of the National Theater) and said he wanted to show him something of a private nature. Lugosi proudly pulled from his pocket a membership card from a labor union that showed he had been a locksmith. This fact of having been a worker (a union member especially) was not a wise thing to mention because of the Hungarian theater world's sense of rank and class, but he apparently had a deep faith in the cause.[14]

The theater people—especially the more successful ones—were not for the revolution, although the leading intellectuals, always an idealistic group, were overjoyed. Ratai felt that if not for the revolution, Lugosi would have had a great future.

As his film roles in America suggest, Lugosi was intense—almost a fanatic. He tended to be 100 percent for or against something. Thus, when the revolution broke out, his long resentment against the poverty he had had to endure as an actor came to the fore. With his usual passionate enthusiasm, he fell into the new liberal cause, although he had not shown any political interest previously.

On December 2, 1918, the Free Organization of Theater Employees was established, with Lugosi heading the names on the committee. Later he wrote a brief history of the trade union and said that when the first revolution broke out, the "actor-slave" dared to come to his senses.[15] At the same time the Budapest Theater Society began a countermovement and wanted Lugosi's expulsion. In February, 1919, the whole staff of the Opera House joined the society of Hungarian Civil Service Workers and formed the arts section. Lugosi and others then convinced a majority of the members of the National Theater to join the members of the Opera House. Lugosi explained, "The definite aim of my organizing activity was the raising of the moral, economic, and cultural level of the actor's society." [16] In the meantime the government continued to deteriorate. On March 17, 1919, as Károlyi wavered and then fell, the actors quit the association of Civil Servants and founded independently the National Trade Union of Actors. On

[14] Interview with Denes Ratai, Budapest, July, 1970.
[15] Bela Lugosi, "History of the Formation of Our Trade Union," *Szinészek Lapja,* May 1, 1919.
[16] *Ibid.*

March 20, 1919, Béla Kun took over the government and instituted a Communist regime. As one writer, admittedly a prejudiced one, put it, Kun "moved directly from prison into public office. . . ." [17]

Most of the middle and upper classes, including Lugosi's in-laws, were appalled. But Lugosi, along with many other intellectuals and theatrical and film people, seemed to welcome the change. Whether he saw the struggle in larger terms or not, he certainly did see that the theater, with all its bureaucracy and entrenched older actors and influential people behind the scenes, could well benefit from a revolution. Lugosi enthusiastically supported the take-over, especially when he heard the new slogan: "There is no more stagecraft of Budapest and stagecraft of the provinces—there is only stagecraft in the country." The managing directors, who had been in control, were seen as "exploiters" and cursed. In the minutes of the first statutory congress of the National Trade Union of Hungarian Actors, held on April 17, 1919, Lugosi is described as entering the room to "great cheering and applause," and saying:

> Half a year ago I launched the struggle with the decision that the national trade union of socialist actors should be established [applause]. Because I don't know Budapest actors and province actors, I know only actors and nonactors [applause]. If two actors are equally gifted . . . the actor working in the provinces should not perceive it as luck if he gets to Budapest, and the actor who goes to Budapest should not feel it a degradation if he has to work in the provinces [applause].

Lugosi went on to urge the actors of Budapest and the provinces to join other unions of technical workers and musicians. This new trade union was intended to form a superior arts council, which would, in Lugosi's words, "settle the art problems of the actors in the country, including the reform of professional training." He advocated too a protest against their low wages and wanted to be treated separately from civil servants.

Lugosi wrote enthusiastically of his belief in the actor's role in society in an article printed in May, 1919:

[17] Alfred D. Low, *The Soviet Hungarian Republic and the Paris Peace Conference*, American Philosophical Society (Philadelphia), December, 1963, Vol. 53, Part 10.

Love the actor, for he gives you his heart! It has been said more than once by our comrades—some of them, moreover, in the highest ranks of our leadership—that actors are not proletarians. Let us look at that statement. Since we assume no malice was intended, we must impute this erroneous opinion to total ignorance. What is the truth? It is that 95 percent of the actors' community has been more proletarian than the most exploited laborer. After putting aside the glamorous trappings of his trade at the end of each performance, an actor had, with few exceptions, to face worry and poverty. He was obliged either to bend himself to stultifying odd jobs to keep body and soul together (while of course being unavailable for work in his true profession) or he had to sponge off his friends, get into debt, or prostitute his art. And he endured it, endured the poverty, the humiliation, the exploitation, just so that he could continue to be an actor, to get parts, for without them he could not live. Actors were exploited no less by the private capitalist managers than they were by the state. The former ruling class kept the community of actors in ignorance by means of various lies, corrupted it morally and materially, and finally scorned and despised it—for what resulted from its own vices. The actor, subsisting on starvation wages and demoralized, was often driven, albeit reluctantly, to place himself at the disposal of the former ruling classes. Martyrdom was the price of enthusiasm for acting.[18]

Partially because of the Béla Kun regime, the Paris Peace Conference dealt quite harshly with Hungary, which lost much of its territory, including the area of Lugos, to Rumania. The Kun government, however, did not last very long, and with the assistance of the Rumanian army of occupation it collapsed by August. The counterrevolution, controlled by Miklós Horthy, succeeded, and soon the "white" officers were paying close attention to all the people who had risen to power during the Kun regime. In particular the arts were examined and the officers of the workers' councils arrested. One film director was tortured to death and others imprisoned. Some political people were hanged. Alexander Korda, Paul Lukas, Lugosi, and many others fled.[19] In 1930 Lugosi recalled these events: "I decided to go away from that place. I had no desire to attend . . . a necking party."[20]

[18] Bela Lugosi, "Love the Actor," *Szinészek Lapja*, May 15, 1919.
[19] This information contained in *Word and Image: History of the Hungarian Cinema* and provided by a letter to the writer by Dr. Géza Staud of Hungary, dated April 21, 1966.
[20] Press sheet from *Dracula*.

Lugosi fled to Vienna with his wife in the summer of 1919. The few weeks there were unpleasant. Lugosi had no money, and his wife was unused to hardship and frightened at a future that seemed far from rosy. And her father no doubt did not wish to continue financial support with his daughter out of the country. She returned to Budapest.

With no opportunity for acting in Vienna, Lugosi moved on to Berlin. Germany, itself affected by the aftermath of a lost war, was in deep psychological, economic, and political trouble, and was not much better than Lugosi's strife-torn homeland. In Berlin he found some work in theater and desperately pleaded his case at various film studios in the area. His previous reputation as Arisztid Olt and his good looks, manners, and enthusiasm proved decisive, for he soon began to appear in a number of German pictures. Some of these films were of normal length, but most of them were two-part features running altogether about two to three hours.

Lugosi's German screen career is difficult to reconstruct with absolute accuracy. Original records are not easy to come by, and even the best German filmographies are incomplete and sometimes contradictory. Furthermore, most of these early films no longer exist, and in a few instances the only evidence that Lugosi appeared in a film at all has been his face in a photograph. Some of the films also were shown under varying titles in Germany, and when they were imported to English-speaking countries, still more title changes occurred.

In July, 1920, Lugosi made his debut on the German screen (at least in terms of release dates) in *Der Fluch der Menschheit* (The Curse of Mankind). He was seventh out of the eight listed in the cast. Then in August he appeared in F. W. Murnau's production of *Der Januskopf* (literally "Janus-head," but called "Janus-Faced," a variation on the Jekyll and Hyde story). Although Lotte Eisner's definitive study of Murnau does not list Lugosi in the cast, another source (Gerhard Lamprecht's *Deutsche Stummfilme*) includes him. Supposedly he played Conrad Veidt's butler in this now-lost film. Most of the production, incidentally, was photographed by Karl Freund, who later, of course, did *Dracula*.

One month later, in September, Lugosi was seen in *Die Frau im Delphin oder 30 Tage auf dem Meeresgrund* (The Woman in the Dolphin, or Thirty Days on the Bottom of the Sea). Then in

December he played in *Die Teufelsanbeter* (The Devil Worshippers).
As can be seen, Lugosi was already playing in the kind of fare that
became his specialty in the United States, although he may not have
had the role of the heavy in these films.

Also in December came one of Lugosi's more important pictures,
Lederstrumpf (Leatherstocking), based on *The Deerslayer*, by James
Fenimore Cooper. In this production Bela played Chingachgook, an
Indian. The Germans had always been interested in tales of Indian life
in America and flocked to see this popular subject. The film was shot in
the summer of 1920 and had an absolutely authentic upper New York
state look, even though German lakes, mountains, and forests were
used. In 1923 the picture later imported to the United States, where
the twelve-reel film was unmercifully trimmed to five reels. Some of its
scenes were rearranged and long explanatory titles inserted, and it was
released as *The Deerslayer*. The surviving print, a beautifully tinted
one, at Eastman House in Rochester, is hopelessly muddled. It is loaded
with so many titles and contains so many names and people and
peculiar plot devices that its beautiful scenery and seemingly accurate
Indian costumes are buried. Also buried is Lugosi as Chingachgook.
Although he reveals an imposing physique, and with his noble nose and
body paint and stiff gestures makes a credible Indian, the plot does not
allow him to do much other than stand around and look statuesque.

Lugosi's next role was a starring one, in a rather expensive ten-reel
production directed by Richard Eichberg. *Der Tanz auf dem Vulkan*
(The Dance on the Volcano) dealt with the aftermath of the Russian
Revolution. Russia is likened to a volcano (in fact, one is shown
erupting behind the titles) and its people to the lava. The film says that
the contemporary condition of Russia was hardly satisfactory, but just
as lava will solidify and purify, so will the country develop along
democratic lines.

Bela, looking strikingly handsome, plays Andre Fleurot, a rich
Parisian who is in love with a Russian. Flashbacks show her as a street
singer and later as a barroom entertainer befriended by Ivan, a man
who is neither a revolutionary nor a royalist, but one, the film says,
who sacrifices all for the Russian people. The English titles may have
been tampered with, for Ivan looks like a classic revolutionary and not
just an idealist. In any case, he is plotting against a royalist grand duke.
So is the girl. Even though she loves Andre and he certainly loves her,

Lugosi as Chingachgook.

she sacrifices herself to the cause by becoming the duke's mistress in order to get vital information. At the end of the film she is shot by the peasants, who think she is an enemy, and as Andre runs to her corpse, he too is killed. They have a dramatic death, with Bela draped across the steps of a large staircase.

The film is not very inventive cinematically, being played mostly in long and medium shots, nor is it convincingly acted. But Bela is quite good, although he rolls his eyes almost as often as the rest of the cast. He has the main role and is certainly attractive and dashing. To see him eventually joining the antirightist group in their clandestine meetings certainly was an ironic kind of typecasting, since only a year before he had been doing the same thing, although not quite so melodramatically. In this film he appears as a handsome leading man with none of the peculiarities of facial expression or bodily movement that one associates with his villainous roles. In short, no Dracula mannerisms can be seen, proof that Bela could be entirely benign when he wanted to.

During these years in Germany Lugosi appeared in two films about which there is almost no information: *Johann Hopkins der Dritte* and *Nat Pinkerton*. Another film listed as *Ihre Hoheit die Tänzerin* and released in November, 1922, is most likely *Der Tanz auf den Vulkan* with another title. *Sklaven Fremder Willins* is yet another variant title for the same film. One other work, *Nachenschnur des Tod* (The Necklace of the Dead), is probably another title for *Der Fluch der Menschheit*.

Lugosi's life in Berlin was hardly happy. With almost no money coming in during the first year, he watched the growing disorder in the streets and lamented the results of his own politicking in Budapest. According to an interview Lugosi gave to John Sinclair in 1931, he wrote to his wife and told her that he was trying to get enough money together to send for her. "Every second day I posted letters to her. I never got an answer." Later he found out that her family had confiscated all his letters and urged her to get a divorce. Her father told her that Lugosi would be executed as a political enemy, and only if she got a divorce would he use his influence. Although this aspect of the story does not sound quite true, certainly it is a fact that Lugosi had been so involved in the Kun regime that it would be impossible for him ever to return to the government-sponsored theater. Because of his profession, he would have to remain a permanent exile. Considering the father's prestige and Lugosi's disgrace, it was not difficult to dissolve the marriage. Lugosi's roommate, Lajos Bálint, first heard of the divorce when the girl's family asked Bálint to keep a large trunk that Lugosi had left with them when he fled.

"What happened," said John Sinclair in an interview, "brought lines of unhappiness to Lugosi's face which two subsequent marriages could not obliterate." [21] Lugosi explained his feelings:

> In all his life a man finds only one mate. Other women may bring happiness close to him, but there is just one mate. The girl was mine. Possibly she was too young and fragile and lacked the necessary stalwartness of character to fight her way through.

Lugosi was no doubt embroidering the facts to make the relationship seem more romantic than it was. Perhaps, however, he genuinely

[21] Interview with Lugosi by John Sinclair (1931), reprinted in a lavish pamphlet for a revival of the stage play of *Dracula* in 1943.

looked back on those days as blissful. Certainly in Lugosi's later years he would start reminiscing about the good old days in Budapest.

Although Lugosi had found some jobs in films and theater, there was already an overabundance of German actors seeking work. The safe and somewhat satisfying career in the Hungarian theater had been taken from him by world conditions and by his own unfortunate association with the Béla Kun regime. He could not go back, he could not stay where he was in Germany, and so he looked to the United States as a haven for his talents. Therefore, at the age of thirty-eight, he left for the land across the seas.

Without money, he obtained a job as third assistant engineer on an Italian cargo vessel during the summer of 1921; he landed in New Orleans and worked his way to New York City. Since he could not speak English, his only hope as an actor was to appear in plays in his native language. Finding other émigrés, he formed a small stock company—much like the ones he had appeared in earlier in his life—and as producer, director, and star tried to put on some plays. He toured Eastern cities where there were Hungarian-speaking groups and appeared in Imre Földes' comedy *Halló*. The potential audience was small and attendance even smaller, so that scheme fell through. There were rarely more than twenty to twenty-five spectators, who were often as poor as the actors. After each performance a well-to-do Hungarian usually took members of the company out to dinner. Lugosi did not have a decent civilian suit, so he traveled in his first-lieutenant costume; he took off his sword and put it in his bag, which otherwise

Lugosi as a cowboy—in trouble again.

contained only greasepaint and a piece of dry sausage. It was around this time that he married his second wife, Ilona Montagh de Nagybányhegyes, a Viennese blond beauty, who learned short roles in Hungarian.[22]

What was he to do? As Lugosi recalled in a later interview, he was visited in 1922 by a New York theatrical manager, Henry Baron, who asked him to play the role of Fernando in a production called *The Red Poppy*. Speaking in German, Lugosi confessed that he didn't know English. "But give me a chance," Lugosi suggested. "Give me a tutor, take his salary out of my future earnings, and by the time you are ready to start rehearsal I will know my part." Whether this story is entirely true or not, Lugosi did get the role. He said he studied English at Columbia and with only a cursory knowledge of the language won the part.[23] For many years Lugosi would not really master English, and he found most of his friends in Hungarian circles even after he had gone to Hollywood. As Karloff later said, Lugosi never did learn enough English—at least by the early thirties—to understand some of the subtleties of the language. However, his heavy accent, which would be the despair of any language teacher, became one of his greatest assets.

The Red Poppy premiered in New York on December 20, 1922. The plot was simple. Claire, the Princess Saratoff, had once been an Apache, but had risen by means of a number of husbands to her present rich and noble estate. She secretly visits her old haunts and meets Fernando, an Apache of the same handsome and heroic mold as her first man. Although at first interested in her jewels, Fernando falls in love, and at the end of the play they become a Prince and Princess—of the Apaches.

The New York *Times* review, by John Corbin (December 21, 1922), said:

> Bela Lugosi is a newcomer of quite splendid mien, romantically handsome and young. Hungarian though he is said to be, he looks every inch the Spanish pirate of romance. He is a stranger to the crew of the *Red Poppy*, awaiting the blond Moll, who has at first

[22] Information from Zoltán Székely, who sent this writer a copy of his newspaper article "Debrecentól-Hollywoodig" printed in an American Hungarian paper, *Amerikai Magyar Világ*.
[23] A letter from the Records Division of Columbia University (June 24, 1970) said there was no record of his having taken a course. Perhaps Columbia became a prestige item to Lugosi just as the National Academy of Budapest had been.

Lugosi in *The Red Poppy* (1922)   The original program.

sight enchanted him, and the habitués try every means to pick a quarrel. With a forward thrust of the shoulder, with a mere glance, he quells them. And one believes it. Equally convincing is his passion of kicks and clenches. In the final scene he is not without a touch of the ` truly noble spirit. Here is an actor of fine achievement and possibly greater promise.

Although the play was not a complete success—it lasted only fourteen performances—Lugosi must have had considerable personality and skill to have become a star in a Broadway play only a year after his arrival in the country. The passionate intensity he gave to his later mad-scientist roles obviously was a vital part of the man himself.

In 1923 Lugosi appeared in his first American film, *The Silent Command.* This rather turgid drama concerned a group of spies who want to blow up the Panama Canal. A United States Navy captain (Edmund Lowe) risks his reputation and his marriage by getting himself court-martialed and thus winning the confidence of the villains.

Needless to say, the chief of the bad guys is Lugosi. The peculiar qualities that later led to his stardom were already apparent. He played the leading spy with considerable grace and style, and the almost superhuman aspects of his screen self were already exploited. Extreme close-ups of his eyes, emphasizing his strange, dark, overpowering will, prefigure some shots from *White Zombie* (1932) and show that Lugosi as master villain and as a man of powerful will were apparent from the very beginning. He had already found his screen métier, but Hollywood would take eight more years before it finally developed this aspect. One other characteristic could be noted about *The Silent Command*: his looks and manner are the only things worthwhile in an otherwise inept film. Years later Bela explained how he got the part:

> In spite . . . . of the predominance of romantic roles in my repertoire when I came to America, I found that, because of my language and the pantomime [gestures] with which most Europeans

The elegant villain in his first American film, *The Silent Command* (1923).

accompany their speech, that I was catalogued as what you call "a heavy." And at once I became identified with that class of performances. Particularly was this true in pictures, where, strangely enough no accent could then be registered, since pictures in those days were silent. If my accent betrayed my foreign birth it also stamped me, in the imagination of the producers, as "an enemy." Therefore, I must be a "heavy." [24]

Lugosi noted with some humor that the film was a propaganda picture to convince Americans that they needed a large navy. "I used to smile at the thought that for this preachment a Hungarian star had been chosen as the chief propagandist, since Hungary has no navy nor needs any!"

When *The Silent Command* opened in New York in September, 1923, the ads called it "A Mighty Drama of Love and Intrigue on the High Seas. It will make you cheer and shout." It did not, however, seem to have this effect on the reviewer of the New York *Times*, who thought it "an old-fashioned melodrama with the old school of acting . . . the villain [Lugosi], of course, turns his eyes into mere slits . . . and [then] opens his big, dark eyes, surmounted by bushy brows." [25] A bushy-browed villain he might be, but Lugosi did have something; here was a villain with class.

This film was followed by *The Rejected Woman*, released in early May, 1924. Made by a small New York company, the film starred Alma Rubens and Conrad Nagel, and Lugosi played a Continental type, receiving fifth billing out of the ten listed performers. Lugosi was not mentioned in the reviews, which, incidentally, were not especially favorable.

Lugosi was then hired by another independent outfit, Chadwick Pictures Corporation, to appear in *The Midnight Girl.* The actor's attachment to poverty-row producers would be a long one. Filmed in New York City in the winter of 1925, it was released shortly after by States Rights. The original story was by Garrett Fort, a name connected with many of the horror films of the early 1930's, including *Dracula*. Lugosi, sporting a small beard and mustache, plays a rather dashing but corrupt millionaire; he is a sponsor of opera and has a soprano mistress whose voice is not what it used to be. A title deftly

[24] Press book for *The Return of Chandu*, summer, 1934.
[25] New York *Times*, September 5, 1923.

In *The Midnight Girl* (1925).

introduces Lugosi: "Nicholas Harmon, the immensely wealthy patron of music, loved his weaknesses—and his favorite weakness was Nina." Listening to the sour notes of his mistress, Lugosi hears his foreign assistant tell him: "Always I have told you to rid of her, get. Her voice now only a noise is." Harmon decides to find another singer and perhaps another mistress. Meantime, Harmon is afflicted with an "idealistic" stepson who is supposed to be a paragon of virtue in the film but strikes one as rather vapid, moral, and dull. He has been resisting the blandishments of a society girl, one of the Schuylers, who wants him for his money and whom Lugosi wants his son to marry for prestige. The stepson and the rakish father argue, Lugosi calling him a "shiftless idler," and the two fight. The boy throws down the money his father has given him and decides to live independently. He goes to a rooming house and telephones the Schuyler girl about his situation. She is decidedly chilly. A title reads: "Would nobody ever really care for him—just for himself." Considering his personality, one would find this rather unlikely, but wondrous indeed are the machinations of movie plots.

The scene then shifts to a ship on which a young singer, Lila Lee—"a refugee from Russia's red ruin"—and her old violin-playing music teacher are coming to America. She gets a job in New York as a nightclub singer (the "Midnight Girl"). Dressed in white bat wings and appearing as a pendulum on a clock swinging back and forth, she and the boy (now a conductor) are a success in a Greenwich Village nightclub.

Meantime, Harmon tries to mend the break in the marriage plans for his stepson and concludes: "Haven't you a weenie little kiss for your possible poppa-in-law?" Harmon is also on the lookout! As a title reads, "Selecting a new sweetheart is almost as difficult as picking out a new hat." When he hears about the downtown success of the "Midnight Girl," he visits the club and is entranced with the singer. He is surprised and not too pleased to see his stepson there; neither is the boy overjoyed to see his stepfather. The proprietor of the nightclub, when he sees Harmon's interest, tells the girl, "Don't lose your opportunity with Harmon. He can make you." Pompously, the boy informs her: "Do not mar your career as a woman to further your progress as a singer." As they talk, a dope addict shoots the boy, but only wounds him. Harmon bends down to help his bleeding stepson, but carefully, so as not to bag his trousers at the knee. Solicitous, he goes often to see his convalescing offspring, but is really interested in the girl. When the stepson is upset, Harmon tells him, "Suppose we leave it to her. She might have the good sense to prefer me."

Finally Harmon asks the girl to visit him at his apartment for an intimate supper. Knowing what the main course usually is at such repasts, the girl brings along her old music teacher to referee the bout. But he promptly drinks some wine and just as promptly falls asleep. Harmon—suave, quite handsome, and very, very elegant, with his hand-kissing and affectionate arms and rather sophisticated air—is infinitely more appealing, charming, and just plain sexy than the rather Casper Milquetoast son. At times, however, Lugosi offers demonic expressions and body movements that anticipate rather uncannily some of Dracula's characteristics.

When the son finds out that the girl is visiting his father, he rushes in where sons should fear to tread and fires a gun, but misses. He does, however, hit Lugosi's rejected mistress hiding behind the curtain. Contrite, Harmon suddenly realizes how much he likes her and cradles her in his arms. The scene fades. At the end of the film the son has married the Russian singer, and the father has married his soprano mistress.

The son was ostensibly the hero of the film, but in every way the father is the really interesting figure and takes the lead, not only in acting and appearance but in the plot as well. Lugosi literally towers above everyone else in the film and is at least a foot taller than the son. Occasionally he moves in a very stage-conscious way, careful always to have his up-camera foot forward, to move his arm cleanly, to turn his head just right for the correct profile. Part of this staginess comes from his characterization as the villain, but it also shows that he had not become completely natural as a screen actor and that he still carried on some of the Hungarian acting traditions. Although his later perform-ances would be more naturalistic, he never forgot his theatrical background, which gave an air of stylization to his acting, which often set it apart from the humdrum and foot-shuffling actions of his colleagues.

Bela did not confine his sexiness to the screen. Offcamera and offstage he was quite a ladies' man in New York. His continental bearing, elegant manners, and charming accent stood him well. He was rumored to have had affairs with Clara Bow and Lenore Ulric and a number of other girls as well. If nothing else, this was certainly a pleasant way to learn English.

Lugosi's halting speech and heavy accent attracted another inde-pendent firm, Banner Productions, and he was hired to play Serge Oumansky, a communist agent, in *Daughters Who Pay*. When the film was released in May, 1925, Lugosi was not too pleased with his small role as a "heavy," but his major concern was still the stage. It was there, with the electric excitement of audiences, that he wanted to be.

On October 20, 1925 (on his forty-third birthday), Lugosi returned to the New York theater in *Arabesque*. Designed and directed by Norman Bel-Geddes, it was more of a visual extravaganza than a comprehensible or viable drama.

The play, written by Eunice Tietjens and her husband, was intended to be a light comedy of manners. Tietjens, who in 1938 recalled her adventures in a book, *The World at My Shoulder*, said that the story had been "submerged" by the director.

> Before the end of the rehearsals nobody except ourselves seemed
> even to remember that there was a story hidden somewhere. No, that

is not quite exact. Bela Lugosi realized it and tried to help. . . . Our struggles with Norman, and those of Michi Ito (dance director) and of Bela Lugosi, had at last persuaded him that the show was incoherent.[26]

Bel-Geddes then tried to shape up the play, but just threw it off more by emphasizing a secondary plot—the love story of the Sheik of Hammam and a Bedouin desert girl, "which Norman thought would please by being made extremely hot (p. 256)." The girl was given prominence, and the Sheik, Lugosi, "whose natural authority had shown through consistently despite the lack of direction, was reduced to a mere foil for her, a nothing. Only when she was off stage was he permitted to act as his talent dictated" (p. 256). The play lasted only three weeks (twenty-three performances).

The reviews for *Arabesque* encouraged Lugosi to keep an eye out for another play, and he found a part in *Open House*, which opened on December 14, 1925. The play told of a selfish businessman who asks his wife to use her charms, platonically of course, to help him sell steel and rails to foreigners. When she develops a real friendship with one of these "clients"—a Russian named Sergius Chernoff (Lugosi)—her husband becomes bitterly jealous and forces her to confess to wrongdoing that never occurred. The play ends as the husband learns his lesson.

The New York *Times* felt the work to be

> a naive and awkward melodrama. The plot is developed with little ingenuity and much artificiality. . . . The long-suffering wife . . . does as much . . . by her assignment as is possible. . . . In her support Guy Hitner and Bela Lugosi manage to make two clichéd roles—the one the family doctor and friend, the other the Russian admirer—recognizable and even bearable.

The play lasted seventy-three performances.

Lugosi was without work for a long time but returned to Broadway in *The Devil in the Cheese*, which premiered on December 19, 1926. The play's settings were again by Norman Bel-Geddes.

Act 1 takes place in the twelfth-century Monastery of Meteora, which the Quigleys, an American family, visit via derrick and hoisting

---

[26] Eunice Tietjens, *The World at My Shoulder*, pp. 248, 255–56.

The lead in *Arabesque* (1925).

1925 portrait.

basket. Mr. Quigley has arrived at the invitation of Father Petros (Lugosi) to indulge in archaeological excavations. Actually, however, Petros is really Kardos, a Greek bandit who intends to hold Quigley and his family for ransom. A separate plot involves Quigley's rejection of his daughter's boyfriend, Jimmie Chard (Fredric March), who follows her to the monastery by plane. The father, to find out what makes his daughter tick, eats a bit of mummified Egyptian cheese and so frees the little god Min, who subsequently takes Quigley into his daughter Goldina's head.

The second act takes place inside her head, where of course Bel-Geddes' settings shone. She dreams of adventure with her young hero on the South Seas, on a desert island, and finally in New York; she also envisions cooking, having babies, nursing, and some politicking from which her husband becomes President. In the third act Jimmie fools the bandit into thinking him an accomplice, turns on him, rescues the Quigleys, and is accepted by his appreciative father-in-law.

Lugosi's appearance in the first and third acts showed his ability as a character actor, according to the New York *Times*: "As the chief bandit Mr. Lugosi acts with an authority and a cadence worthy of better things." Lugosi must have made quite an impression as "an elderly Monk of fifty-two," according to the author's description, with his long black robes and heavy dark beard. In his first semivillainous role on the American stage Lugosi must have relished the lines in which he discussed the hateful, ancient Persians: "I would cut the throats of every one of them—from ear to ear. They were the enemies of Greece. Years are nothing! All time is now." [27]

In the third act of the play the author describes the bandit:

> Petros is no longer dressed as a monk. He wears, instead, the white kilt and tights, with short jacket and fez, of the Greek mountaineer. On his feet are tufted slippers. Altogether, he is a striking figure compared to his former sombre get-up.[28]

Mrs. Quigley calls Petros' demands ransom. He replies:

> Oh, Madame! Such a word. Shall we not say tax? You see—very old monastery! I am a poor man! To buy the antiques—and to hire the men—oh, very expensive for me!

[27] Tom Cushing, *The Devil in the Cheese* (New York, Samuel French, 1927), pp. 26–27.
[28] *Ibid.*, p. 154.

And, in the lines that would echo through Lugosi's future roles, he says:

Here I am the big man! I do what I want! These hills never speak afterwards! . . . I am the law here! [29]

Although *The Devil in the Cheese* received mediocre reviews, it played seventy-three performances. During the run, Lugosi was to make the acquaintance of one of the actors, a man by the name of Dwight Frye, who years later would reappear as Renfield in the film *Dracula.*

The strikingly handsome and romantic parts that Lugosi had in *The Red Poppy, Arabesque,* and *Open House* were subjugated in his new role as stage villain. It was a type that he would seldom leave again. "I do what I want . . . ! I am the law here!" would echo forever onward.

[29] *Ibid.,* pp. 55–56.

❦ 3 ❦

The Dracula Years (1927–1930)

WHEN LUGOSI WAS chosen to play Dracula, he had little knowledge of the long and gruesome tradition of vampires. To him the role was just a good one, a leading one, and not much more. He did not realize that it would prove to be both his salvation and his damnation. Despite his age and thick accent, this man would find himself a star, a star who for all his subsequent troubles would have a longer career than many of Hollywood's major figures, such as John Gilbert and Clara Bow. Although Lugosi also disappeared into relative obscurity, even at the end he was still in pictures, humbled and bowed but—in his own intonation—still "performink."

The stage play *Dracula* was, of course, based on Bram Stoker's 1897 novel, which in itself had drawn upon a few obscure facts of an actual Transylvania prince, many folktales about vampires, and horror novels of the nineteenth century. The vampire had already appeared as a literary personage in the early 1800's and had devoured the blood of victims on the Continent and in England. What Stoker did was to place the vampire first in his ancestral home in Europe and then bring him into the contemporary world of England. However, Stoker did more than the previous novelists. He made the vampire an aristocrat and gave him immense physical and mental powers. In fact, Count Dracula is more than a man who drinks blood; he is a kind of dark god, one who can command storms, transform himself into bats, wolves, and mists, and one who has hypnotic powers. Despite his abilities, his plan to leave the by-now-anemic precincts of his homeland in order to prey upon the teeming millions of England is thwarted by some intrepid Englishmen. The vampire returns in defeat to Transylvania, where he is killed just before reaching his ancestral castle.

Thus the novel. The play is another matter. Stoker realized the theatrical potential of Dracula when he attempted to protect its dramatic copyright by presenting a reading of his novel at the Royal Lyceum Theatre in London on May 18, 1897. *Dracula; or, The Undead* was announced only one half hour before playtime and was offered in a prologue and five acts, totaling a wearisome forty-seven scenes. The prologue, containing nine scenes, was laid in Transylvania.[1] Although Stoker's novel contained enough dramatic scenes to warrant an effective stage production, no one took the chance. Playwrights probably felt that audiences were too sophisticated to accept such supernatural fare. Sir Arthur Conan Doyle, in a story called "The Adventure of the Sussex Vampire," reflected contemporary attitudes when Sherlock Holmes, investigating a case that looks like vampirism, states authoritatively, "Rubbish, Watson, rubbish! What have we to do with walking corpses who can only be held in their grave by stakes driven through their hearts? It's pure lunacy. . . ." Holmes' view probably sums up what most London audiences thought.

Virtually nothing was done with the vampire idea until 1921, when F. W. Murnau, the great German director, made a film loosely based on *Dracula*. Because it infringed on Stoker's copyright, it was released on March 5, 1922, as *Nosferatu* (the "Undead," the word that Stoker himself employs in the book at one point, the same term that Van Helsing uses in the Hollywood film).

Murnau's film ignored almost all of Stoker's plotting and drew only upon the opening chapters, in which occur (1) the visit to Transylvania by the solicitor, (2) the trip in the coach and a stop at the inn, (3) the midnight greeting in the castle, (4) the vampire's sea voyage, (5) the solicitor's escape, and (6) the vampire's interest in the solicitor's wife. Except for these incidents, the script was a most free adaptation. The picture told of a solicitor who visits Dracula's castle and returns to his wife in Bremen. Meantime, the vampire has also traveled to Bremen and has moved his coffin to an abandoned building across the way from the girl. A plague, brought about by the vampire and the rats that accompany him, strikes the city. The solicitor's wife senses the evil presence, confirms her feelings by reading *The Book of the Vampires*, and sacrifices her life by allowing the vampire to come to her and sip until dawn, at which point both of them die (he from the sunlight and she from loss of blood).

[1] Harry Ludlam, *A Biography of Dracula: The Life Story of Bram Stoker* (London, W. Foulsham & Co. Ltd., 1962), p. 109.

Instead of using a present-day setting, Murnau and his colleagues placed the story back in time to 1838, under the correct assumption that an earlier period is more conducive to the supernatural. Furthermore, they tried to transform the Dracula story into a kind of primal myth, not only by infusing a sense of the past but also by providing a metaphysical plane.

Although the film has stylization, what really makes it one of the cinema's most interesting works is its treatment of the main character. The vampire is a dark and irrational phenomenon that is beyond the explanation of science. Even in the later Hollywood film, Van Helsing, the scientist, has to forsake logic and reason and rely instead on the legendary devices of wolfbane, religious symbols, and wooden stakes. But Nosferatu is more than a supernatural creature to be quelled; he is seen as a mystical principle of evil. The film recalls the ancient myths of a city (like Thebes) preyed upon by a malignant force (be it plague or vampire) until the curse has been expiated, in this case by a woman "pure in heart."

Murnau does not draw upon Stoker's rather full characterization of the vampire, but depersonalizes him so that he is less of an individual and more of a type. Nosferatu is more of an *it* than a *he*. A kind of abstract thing of evil, he has no nobility, nor does he inhabit the dark world of majestic satanic villains. Instead, he is a lower kind of evil, an obscene and loathsome creature that dwells amid decay and slime and crawling rats (the very antithesis of light). With his hairy, pointed ears, his hideous fingernails, and his lecherous and lustful masklike face, he is an image of damned flesh and not of damned soul. There is no Byronic romanticizing of him as we have in the Hollywood film, in which Lugosi's Dracula is a suave count, handsome in a fiendish way and existing in a world that is shadowy but not revolting. Although *Nosferatu* is frightening and draws upon the earlier and more ghoulish conception of the vampire, it also has a thematic richness and sense of poetry far beyond the Hollywood film.

Not long after *Nosferatu*'s release, Hamilton Deane, a British actor and producer, modified the novel and finally offered *Dracula* on stage in June, 1924. It was presented in Derby, England, with Edmund Blake as Dracula and Deane as Van Helsing, and was a tremendous success. Deane, however, was afraid to present it in London because he thought that sophisticated audiences would laugh it off the boards. Instead, he took it on the road. Three years of excellent business in the provinces prompted the formation of a second company to satisfy the demand. Finally, on February 14, 1927, Deane mustered enough courage to open in London at the Little Theatre, where Raymond Huntley starred as Dracula and Deane repeated his role of Van Helsing. Although critics, as Deane suspected, panned the play, audiences, as Deane also expected, loved it. In March, 1927, whether of necessity or merely for publicity, a trained nurse was advertised as being on hand to aid those who fainted. Later, in America, her fellow sisters of mercy would also be in attendance for the weak of heart.

In March, 1927, an audacious publisher and producer, Horace Liveright, saw the London production, sensed its possibilities, and bought the United States rights. He engaged John L. Balderston, London correspondent of the New York *World*, to make an American version (modernizing dialogue, eliminating a few characters, and tightening the plot).[2] Balderston would later go to Hollywood, where he helped write many horror films, among them *Frankenstein*, *The Mummy*, *Bride of Frankenstein*, and *Mad Love*. Bernard Jukes was imported to re-create his performance as Renfield, but the rest of the American cast was new. Who would play the role of the vampire? Probably someone had seen Lugosi in *The Devil in the Cheese*, wearing his dark robes and speaking in his Hungarian accent. Lugosi explained in an interview:

> There was no male vampire type in existence. Someone suggested an actor of the Continental School who could play any type, and mentioned me. It was a complete change from the usual romantic characters I was playing, but it was a success.[3]

Lugosi read for the part in late July, 1927, and both Liveright and his director were pleased. On August 3 Liveright noted in a letter that casting "was coming along nicely and we go into rehearsal on the 29th."[4] After a five-performance preview, beginning on September 19, the play finally opened at the Fulton Theater in New York, and history was made. The New York *Times* review by Brooks Atkinson said:

[2] In particular, Lord Gadalming and Quincy Morris (friends of the family) and one of the maids were removed from the play. Mina Harker, the wife of Jonathan, became unmarried, and her first name was changed to Lucy.

[3] "When Dracula Invaded England," *Famous Monsters*, No. 35.

[4] Letter to Alfred Wallerstein, August 3, 1927, in *Horace Liveright: Publisher of the Twenties*, Walker Gilmer (New York, David Lewis, 1970), p. 151.

The various entrepreneurs have done extraordinarily well with their initial act, and rather less well with the two remaining. . . . When they are treating this weird force as a mystery they send the customary shivers of apprehension streaming down the back, and *Dracula* holds its audience nervously expectant. When in the next two acts the atmosphere becomes more realistic than occult, the effect is not so horribly fascinating. One begins to protect one's self against the machinations of the "undead" by watching the stage machinery whirl. . . . Played more swiftly, fiercely and mysteriously, *Dracula* could doubtless scare the skeptics out of several years' growth into complete submission.

Mr. Van Sloan is excellently mysterious and apprehensive as the doctor. Mr. Jukes is weird as a lunatic. Miss Peterson makes a credible victim. Sometimes Mr. Lugosi, as Dracula, is, like the performance, a little too deliberate and confident. *Dracula* needs a frantic, tormentous rush.[5]

John Anderson of the New York *Post* also observed: "Mr. Lugosi performs Dracula with funereal decorations suggesting a little more an operatically inclined but cheerless motivation than a blood-sucking fiend." [6] The critics here already revealed the superior attitudes from which later horror films would suffer. The more culturally respectable newspapers pooh-poohed the play ("The acting is fairly awful, maybe suitably so" [7]) and took exception to Lugosi's portentous pace, but less pretentious sources, such as *Variety* or the New York *Mirror* ("Bela Lugosi is first rate as the vampire"),[8] liked the play for what it was: good, escapist entertainment.

Some of the reviewers mentioned a point in the play when the audience was on the verge of laughter. At one moment Dracula in the form of a werewolf appeared behind the heroine's couch and leaned over her. The appearance of a stuffed wolf's head spoiled the effect of the scene. Frank Vreeland in the New York *Telegram* alliteratively noted:

The minute you introduced the avowedly occult the play teeters and the audience titters. That was why the somewhat petrified audience took to grins last night when the wolf shape appeared and

[5] October 6, 1927.
[6] October 6, 1927.
[7] Gilbert Gabriel, New York *Sun*, October 6, 1927.
[8] Robert Coleman, New York *Mirror*, October 7, 1927.

why, as the Count ingeniously melted out of the hands of his captors, you might say, "I wouldn't believe it, not even if it was Houdini." [9]

The original stage production of *Dracula*.

Alexander Woollcott described the wolf's appearance: ". . . It looked so much like the good old she bear of the Christmas pantomimes that *Dracula* threatened to turn jelly then and there." [10]

Horace Liveright also noticed this blemish and, as the play's producer, did something about it. A newspaper of October 31 noted that he was going over the play and removing some of "the rash moments when the spook melodrama became so inept that the audience changed its fits from fright to laughter." [11] The werewolf was relegated to the prop-room pound, and the play went on to great success. Another reviewer incorrectly guessed that New York "would be looking for other sports" within a short period but went on to say that

[9] October 6, 1927.
[10] New York *World*, October 6, 1927.
[11] Unidentified clipping, October 31, 1927.

the play "should make an excellent movie with talking films to reproduce the unearthly voices of the crazy Renfield." [12]

If the critics had reservations, so did audiences—if they wanted a seat. *Dracula* played to packed houses and ran for 261 performances. During its run, however, more changes were made in the play. In the week of April 16, 1928, an additional character, another maid, was added.

When the Broadway version of *Dracula* closed on May 19, 1928, Lugosi went on tour with the play. In June he opened at the Biltmore Theater in Los Angeles and played there with most of the original cast, among them Van Sloan and Jukes. It was there that Lugosi was no doubt seen by various studio heads. In September the play returned to the East Coast, with Raymond Huntley (the British Dracula in Deane's production) replacing Lugosi. In 1929 the play returned to

[12] E. W. Osborn, New York *Evening World*, October 6, 1927.

Bela in 1929, with his third wife.

California, and Lugosi again performed the role. It was during the summer of that year that Lugosi married Beatrice Woodruff, the widow of one of San Francisco's most distinguished architects. The marriage lasted only a brief time, although the couple remained friends and even dated occasionally.

Later, in 1939, the play regained the boards in England when Hamilton Deane, who had always wanted to portray the title role but who had played Van Helsing because no one else in his company fitted the doctor, finally appeared as Dracula. This was the first production of the American version to be done in England. Lugosi, who was in Britain making *The Human Monster*, walked onstage after a performance and greeted Deane to tumultuous applause.

The play, though creaking more and more every year, became the bane to keep the wolf of poverty from Lugosi's door. He reappeared in the role occasionally during the thirties and had some effective revivals in 1942, 1943, 1947, and in England in 1951.

In 1930 Lugosi explained how he felt about the role:

> After I had been in the play for a month, I began to take stock of myself, and I realized that for my own well being I should make some attempt to conserve my mental and physical strength—to throw myself with less fervor into the depiction of the role. By that time I knew every inflection, every movement, every expression required of the character, and I decided that if I could go through the play somewhat mechanically—somewhat more placidly within myself—there would be no lessening of the effect of my performance on the audience, but a decided lessening of the effect on my own nervous system.
>
> But I could not do it. The role seemed to demand that I keep myself worked up to fever pitch, and so I sat in my dressing room and took on, as nearly as possible, the actual attributes of the horrible vampire, Dracula. And during all these two years I did not speak a word to any person behind the scenes during the progress of the play. And since everyone knew the strain I was laboring under, no one spoke to me. When I came off the stage after a scene, I went silently to my dressing room and did not emerge until it was again time for me to go on the stage. I was under a veritable spell which I dared not break. If I stepped out of my character for even a moment, the seething menace of the terrible Count Dracula was gone from the characterization, and my hold on the audience lost its force.[13]

---

[13] Universal's press book of *Dracula*, 1931.

In these comments, which are probably somewhat exaggerated (actors are seldom known for their accuracy and are naturally given to a certain dramatic flair), the source of Lugosi's later troubles can be deduced. He did take his roles seriously and certainly gave his performances a kind of flamboyant passion that few actors ever approached. This passion cost him in nervous tension, a tension perhaps that his later reliance on drugs attempted to alleviate.

In another interview Lugosi said that more than 97 percent of his fan mail came from women. He spoke about the females in his Broadway audiences:

> . . . It is *women* who love horror. Gloat over it. Feed on it. Are nourished by it. Shudder and cling and cry out—*and come back for more.*
>
> *Women have a predestination to suffering.*
>
> It is women who bear the race in bloody agony. Suffering is a kind of horror. Blood is a kind of horror. Therefore women are born with a predestination to horror in their very blood stream. It is a biological thing.

Despite Lugosi's dubious metaphysics and even more dubious logic, he was conscious of the deeply romantic, even sexual, and almost perverse overtones of his role as a vampire. He went on to say:

> Women wrote me letters. Ah, what letters women wrote me! Young girls. Women from seventeen to thirty. Letters of a horrible hunger. Asking me if I cared only for maiden's blood. Asking me if I had done the play because I was in reality that sort of Thing. And through these letters, couched in terms of shuddering, transparent fear, there ran the hideous note of—*hope.*
>
> They hoped that I was DRACULA. They hoped that my love was the love of DRACULA. They gloated over the Thing they dared not understand. . . .
>
> It was the embrace of Death their subconscious was yearning for. Death, the final triumphant lover.
>
> It made me know that the women of America are unsatisfied, famished, craving sensation, even though it be the sensation of death draining the red blood of life.[14]

[14] Gladys Hall, "The Feminine Love of Horror," *Motion Picture Classic*, January, 1931.

One wonders, of course, how many of the foregoing effusions were produced by the female interviewer's imagination; they certainly, however, indicate that Lugosi was keenly aware of his image.

Later, in 1932, an article describing a so-called fright-duel between Lugosi and Karloff amplified these points. Lugosi entered the room,

> smiling in his curiously knowing way. It is the smile of a tall, weary, haunted aristocrat, a person of perhaps fallen greatness, a secretive Lucifer who sees too clearly and knows too much, and perhaps wishes it were not so, and would like to be a gracious chap.

The "duel" began with Lugosi's remarks to Karloff:

> Ah, Boris, to win a woman, take her with you to see *Dracula*, the movie. As she sees me, the bat-like vampire, swoop through an open casement into some girl's boudoir, there to sink teeth into neck and drink blood, she will thrill through every nerve and fiber. That is your cue to draw close to her, Boris. When she is limp as a rag, take her where you will, do with her what you will. Ah, especially, Boris, bite her on the neck!
>
> The love-bite, it is the beginning. In the end, you, too, Boris, will become a VAMPIRE. You will live five hundred years. You will sleep in moldy graves at night, and make fiendish love to beauties by day. You will see generations live and die. You will see a girl baby born to some woman, and wait a mere sixteen to eighteen years for her to grow up, so that you can sink fangs into a soft white neck and drink a scarlet stream. You will be irresistible, for you will have in your powerful body the very heat of hell, the virility of Satan.[15]

This 1932 "fright-duel" seemed far less likely back in 1928. Although Lugosi's name eventually grew to be synonymous with the horror film, Hollywood did not quite see him at first in such a Mephistophelean light. Still, Lugosi was not ignored but appeared in small roles in a number of films. He appeared in *How to Handle Women*, a Universal "Jewel" released in June, 1928. This farce concerns an inventive cartoonist who gets the bankrupt Hendryx of Vulgaria to let him exploit the country's peanut crop to provide financial aid to the government. The villain tries to dispose of the hero by having a Turk (Bull Montana) massage him to death! Lugosi was only a bit player.

---

[15] Ted LeBerthon, "Demons of the Film Colony," *Weird Tales* (October, 1932).

Lugosi had a larger role, that of another heavy, in *The Veiled Woman*, made by Fox on the West Coast and released at the end of December, 1928. This was the first film for which Lugosi was listed in the "Work of Players" section of the *Film Daily Yearbook*. Lugosi then appeared in *Prisoners*, a First National film released in June, 1929. Made during the transition to sound, it appeared in two versions, one silent and one part talking. Lugosi had a small role.

He was then engaged by MGM to play Inspector Delzante in *The Thirteenth Chair*, released in October, 1929. It, too, had both silent and part-talking versions. Produced and directed by Tod Browning, one of the foremost directors of the macabre, who would later direct *Dracula*, this mystery was the first association of Browning with Lugosi (who here got seventh billing). The story concerned a medium who solves a mysterious crime. The New York *Times* said: "Bela Lugosi, famous Hungarian actor and creator of the stage role of Dracula, is seen as the mysterious Inspector Delzante, a Calcutta detective chief who goes to the spirit world for the solution of the uncanny murder plot." [16] Another review said: "Bela Lugosi and Margaret Wycherly cop the acting honors of this film. The former has a strong screen presence which he uses effectively every minute he is on the screen. An excellent bet where strong masculine personality is wanted." [17] The Los Angeles *Times* also praised his performance: "The casting of Bela Lugosi, as the criminal investigator, was a stroke of luck. He at times paints his acting with a phosphorescent glow and the touch of horror he thus adds to the proceedings helps in the widespread coagulation of veins." [18]

On December 4, 1929, shooting began at Fox Studios on *Such Men Are Dangerous*, released in March, 1930. The screenplay and dialogue by Ernest Vajda were drawn from a novel by Elinor Glyn, who based her fiction on the actual disappearance of European banker Alfred Loewenstein while in a plane over the English Channel. A girl, egged on by her greedy sister, is inveigled into marrying a multimillionaire, Ludwig Kranz. This bearded, stooped, and hook-nosed creature repulses her physically; neither does she like his personality, for he thinks only of material things. Every time he approaches her she feels a chill. Appalled at the consummation shortly to occur, she escapes from

---

[16] February 1, 1930.
[17] *Allen's Press Bureau*, November 9, 1929.
[18] November 1, 1929.

The Veiled Woman (1928).

The Thirteenth Chair (1929).

his immense house on their wedding night. The girl hurries back to her amazed sister, who says that "no one can afford to cross a man like Ludwig Kranz. Men like that are dangerous. There's no telling what he might do."

Meanwhile, Kranz decides on a daring plan. He hires a plane, dons a parachute, and in the middle of the Channel jumps out, leading the world to believe he committed suicide. Shortly after, he arrives in Berlin, goes to the clinic of Dr. Goodman (Lugosi), and asks to have his face changed, offering 10,000 francs. In this situation, for a change, Lugosi is a good man (as his name indicates) and takes on the case only so that he can get enough money to continue his lifetime devotion to fixing the faces of those who were maimed in the war. Lugosi is not sinister here, but quite Continental and debonair, although he has all the mannerisms of his later career—including the deliberate delivery of his lines. Perhaps no other actor could make as many pregnant pauses in what reads like rather innocuous dialogue. When Kranz, pleased with the results of the operations, offers the doctor a check, Lugosi replies in a warm but rather portentous tone, interspersed with slow gestures and precise body movement:

"I want to tell you a story, my friend—I was a surgeon in the World War—and, afterwards—I studied a [sic] small hospital—to aid the real unfortunates—those who are maimed—hopelessly scarred—and—lived. There was no money to carry on, and I was helpless. Suddenly—from somewhere—money came in—millions—to permit this work to be done—Nobody knew—who gave the money—and then—one day—I learned the name—of my benefactor.—It was Ludwig Kranz."

Lugosi, as all the pause marks indicate, delivers his lines in a studied, mannered, but nonetheless effective way. The New York *Times* said that he gave "a sincere performance," [19] and a Chicago newspaper opined that he was "very good." [20] In fact, this role of Lugosi as plastic surgeon would be reactivated in *The Raven*, although in the later film he made use of his skill for less humanitarian purposes.

Two scenes in the doctor's office were Lugosi's only appearances in the film. The rest of the picture shows how Kranz meets his wife and succeeds in having her fall in love with him so that he can humiliate

[19] March 8, 1930.
[20] Chicago *Sun-Tribune*, April 12, 1930.

her. But they fall in love with each other again, and so a happy ending occurs.

That Lugosi was enjoying at least some of the fame he had won in the stage play *Dracula* can be seen in the contract for this picture. It stipulated that he receive 25 percent of the size of the billing in the credits. During the filming of the picture the "worst catastrophe in the history of cinema" occurred.[21] Ten people, including director Kenneth Hawks, were killed when two planes crashed off the Santa Monica shore while photographing Kranz's parachute jump.

Lugosi next won a small part (he was last in the list of players) in *Wild Company*, a Fox production begun on April 15, 1930, and released in July. Leo McCarey directed this film with a "moral" about how to bring up children. H. B. Warner and his screen wife let their son run around and spend money for cars and liquor. The son also gets involved with some crooks and gamblers. Lugosi plays a rather slick but not unsympathetic nightclub owner with the unbelievably square name of Felix Brown. He is held up, and although he pleads for his life, he is shot and killed and the son accused and convicted. The son is, of course, eventually released, but the stern admonition not to let "youth" go unchecked is hammered home. Lugosi's small part doesn't give him much to do, though he does provide an elegant, Dracula-like bow at one point.

Lugosi then played another small part, in *Viennese Nights*, a Warner Brothers Technicolor operetta. The first musical to be written expressly for the screen by Oscar Hammerstein II and Sigmund Romberg, the story moves from Vienna to New York during the period from 1877 to 1930 and traces the love lives of three generations. A frustrated romance is finally consummated vicariously through the individuals' grandchildren. Lugosi played his few moments mostly with his back to the camera.

Lugosi had a larger role in his next film, *Renegades* (begun by Fox on July 14, 1930, and released in November), although he was listed last out of eight in the *Variety* credits. Victor Fleming rather indifferently directed this scenario by Jules Furthman. Four Foreign Legion privates become renegades and go over to the side of their heathen enemies. They get that far, however, and then, in the words of *Variety*, "quit renegading." [22] The last few minutes of the film show

[21] *Variety*, February 23, 1938.
[22] November 12, 1930.

them defending their old comrades besieged in a fort. They die heroes. In fact, almost everyone in the picture dies in its last few minutes.

The reasons for all this were, of course, complicated. The hero (Warner Baxter) had fallen in love with Eleanor (Myrna Loy) during the First World War and had given her information that she conveyed to the enemy. As a result, he suffered disgrace and joined the Legion to forget. They meet again on the desert, and when he scorns her, in revenge she joins up with an Arab chieftain (Lugosi). The dialogue says that he claims to be the "uncrowned king of the region" and that people "salute him as a superior." Lugosi enters one scene, swirling his cloak around imperiously. The Foreign Legion men are appalled that Myrna Loy would go to that "filthy beast." But she does. She joins his harem and tries to stir up his ambitions. "If you do this," she says, "all Africa will be yours." But Lugosi, contrary to his usual ambitious screen-self, merely yawns. That kind of conquest is too much trouble. Finally, however, she goads him on to further endeavor. Lugosi languishes on an Arabian cushion, and when Warner Baxter enters, he tells her to leave:

LUGOSI: Go, my little dove.
LOY: You're afraid of him [Baxter], aren't you? So you're going to take orders from him after all.

The villainous Arab in *Renegades* (1930).

LUGOSI: No, but first you take orders from me. If I say go, you go! If
    you don't, my little lamb, I will have you flogged. Now go, my
    little fig. Women like to make trouble [he says to Baxter when
    she leaves]. Next time when you come, I lock her up or maybe
    I just cut off her tongue. What do you think?

When Baxter has something to say to him, Lugosi shoos away the
problem: "If it is bad news, don't tell me. I feel very happy just now."
But he is told anyway, and when he finds out that one of the
legionnaires working for him has gone over to his enemy, he blows up.
"Oh, if he's alive, I—I bury him in an ant hill or maybe cut off his
hand—what do you think?" Baxter ignores Bela's rhetorical question
and says that he will take three companies to the fort. Bela replies,
"Take twenty. I'm going to crucify every dog of a Christian if he's
taken alive, or—or maybe I just burn them in slow fire. What do you
think?"

Lugosi adopts a reasonably believable Arabian accent and, in his kind
of pidgin English and inflections and almost funny expressions, gives
the role a great deal of color. One of his best lines—besides the "What
do you think?"—occurs when he and Baxter are discussing potential
prisoners. "We cook the chickens before we catch them," Bela says.

Mordaunt Hall for the *Times* reported the film as "well staged and
competently acted," but incoherent. Another review, however, was
able to figure out the plot—it was not hard—and to discern Lugosi's
skill. "Bela Lugosi, Hungarian actor of the legitimate stage, gives a fine
performance in the role of the egotistical Arab ruler on whom the girl
exerts sufficient influence to satisfy her revenge against Baxter." [23] The
perspective of time has not changed this view. Baxter's performance
now seems overdone, whereas Lugosi's remains a little gem.

Shortly after, Lugosi received sixth billing in a small part in another
Fox picture, *Oh, for a Man*, begun on September 12, 1930, and
released in January.

Meanwhile, Universal was trying to make its mind up about
Dracula, which it had first considered shortly after the play opened in
London. One studio reader of the book, in an interoffice communica-
tion, said:

> For mystery and blood-curdling horror, I have never read its
> equal. For sets, impressionistic and weird, it cannot be surpassed.

[23] *Motion Picture Herald*, November 15, 1930.

This story contains everything necessary for a weird, unnatural, mysterious picture.

It is usually the case that if a story can be played upon the stage a screen version can be written from it as well. It will be a difficult task and one will run up against the censor continually, but I think it can be done. It is daring but if done there can be no doubt as to its making money.[24]

Another reader, however, reported:

This is without doubt one of the most horrible gruesome stories that has ever been written. . . . For a picture it is out of the question . . . mostly because of the censorship. The first part of the story could be shown, but from the moment you take up the part of Lucy, you run into all sorts of difficulties.

The reader concluded that much of the story would be impossible to get across with silent titles.

For years the picture people have been trying to find a way of doing this thing on the screen and so far they have never succeeded nor have they had the nerve to try it, after they have analyzed what they can and cannot put of it on the screen or in the story adaptation. It might be a novelty—but would it pay in the end? [25]

A third reader was even more negative:

Were this story put on the screen, it would be an insult to every one of its audience. We all like to see ugly things . . . (For instance the big appeal of *The Phantom of the Opera*). But when it passes a certain point, the attraction dies and we suffer a feeling of repulsion and nausea. This story certainly passes beyond the point of what the average person can stand or cares to stand.[26]

A few months later, when *Dracula* opened in New York, another memo, dated October 6, 1927, offered the following comment:

Dracula is and always has been material for a great picture, great in opportunity for actors, writers, and directors. Great in opportunity

---

[24] Memo dated June 15, 1927, by Miss Hall.
[25] Memo from Lucille de NeVera, June 15, 1927.
[26] Memo from George Mitchell, Jr., June 15, 1927.

for photography of a wonderful sort and nature. But while it is picture material from the angle of the pictorial and the dramatic, it is *not* picture material from the standpoint of the box office nor of ethics of the Industry. It would be a thing which no child and for that matter no adult of delicate nervous temperament should see, a thing beside which *The Cabinet of Dr. Caligari* would seem like a pleasant fireside reverie.

Still, Universal did not immediately veto the possibility of filming *Dracula*. Instead, it watched the box-office success in New York and on tour. With the coming of sound, the difficulty of conveying the vampire lore to the American public was now solved. Furthermore, the censors, who had been rather strong in 1927, were again weakening against the onslaught of the producers. Such an unsavory topic became possible.

By June, 1930, Universal had had a 32-page treatment written by Fritz Stephani and then, shortly after, an adaptation by Louis Stevens. Then Louis Bromfield—whose novel, *The Strange Case of Annie Sprugg* (1929), had been described as "the combination of sinister religious influences with intense dramatic situations" [27]—submitted a 50-scene continuity on August 7. Bromfield based his version on the novel, and it is from his work that many of the best scenes of the film originated. However, his fluid, dramatic, and action-packed version was too ambitious for Universal's budget. On August 22, 1930, the studio officially obtained the rights to *Dracula* for $40,000 and set other writers to work. On September 11 a 246-scene draft (still incomplete) was made, and on September 26 a complete 372-scene version was submitted by Dudley Murphy. Unfortunately Murphy dropped many of Bromfield's scenes and substituted instead much of the action and dialogue from the Broadway play. The pursuit of Dracula back to Transylvania was replaced with the play's more tepid ending. Garrett Fort also submitted some suggestions and eventually received screen credit. The September 26 version, even though it was marked "fourth draft—final," suffered many changes during the shooting.

For unaccountable reasons the Broadway play had changed the name of Dr. Seward's daughter. In the novel she was Mina, and her friend was called Lucy. The film transferred the names back to what

[27] *New Republic*, Vol. 56 (October 24, 1928), p. 282.

they were in the book, one of the few instances in which the film adhered more to the novel than to the play.

Strange are the ways of the world and even stranger the ways of Hollywood. Some people claim that Lon Chaney wanted to star in *Dracula* and urged Universal to buy it for him, others that Tod Browning, known by 1928 as "Hollywood's Poe," was the main impetus. These theories are weakened by the fact that Chaney was known to be dying in the summer of 1930 and that Tod Browning, right up until the date of production, was not in on any of the studio's major decisions. If one is to believe the old stories that Chaney was behind the project, then the studio had bought a vehicle for a star who couldn't possibly appear in it!

Certainly the film was right up Browning's alley. Born in Louisville, Kentucky, in 1882, where he was educated, he left at the age of sixteen to play in vaudeville, became involved in a contortionist's act, and later was a blackfaced actor in burlesque. Then he became a carnival manager, joined the movies, and became a director in 1915. He worked under fellow Kentuckian, D. W. Griffith, for whom he appeared briefly in *Intolerance* and functioned as a helper. Browning directed for Fine Arts and later for Goldwyn, Majestic, Metro, Universal, Metro-Goldwyn-Mayer, and others. Lon Chaney starred in a number of his films. He died in 1962.

Browning had an odd sympathy with the carnival world and managed to capture the mystery and appeal of its vulgarity and diseased kind of milieu. His fascination with the grotesque resulted in a number of weird and sick films, among them the silent version of *The Unholy Three* (1925), *Freaks* (1932), and *Mark of the Vampire* (1935).

Browning may indeed have been behind some aspects of the *Dracula* project, but there is no written evidence. In any case, the decision to choose someone to play Dracula remained with the studio. The obvious choice, of course, was the lead of the Broadway production. But Lugosi, despite his having played parts in other Hollywood films, was comparatively unknown. Universal wanted to engage a more popular box-office draw. In July, 1930, E. M. Asher (associate producer for Universal), Louis Bromfield, and Dudley Murphy went to Oakland, California, to see Lugosi in the play.[28] But there were still reservations

---

[28] *Hollywood Filmograph*, August 2, 1930.

about Lugosi for the title role. Fortunately Lugosi must have had a loyal admirer working for *Hollywood Filmograph*, for that trade journal ran three photographs of him in the August 2, 1930, issue and said that he was "the most logical one for the screen version." On August 9 *Filmograph* put Lugosi's picture on the cover of the issue.

In the latter part of August, 1930, a stage production of *Dracula* starring Victor Jory played in the Pasadena Community Playhouse, and although Jory was praised, the review added that "one who has once seen Bela Lugosi will never be content with another *Dracula*." [29] The reviewer added:

> We can never leave a production of "Dracula" without a shudder at the tragic mutilation of Bram Stoker's magnificent novel. And our shudder was increased a thousandfold when we left the Community by the fear that Universal would produce its picture from the stage play rather than the novel. If Big U does so, it will have a screen version of an ordinary stage thriller. If Bram Stoker's tale is taken, the company will have a motion picture—and the greatest weird motion picture produced. We wait with fear and trembling.

The same issue noted that Garrett Fort was now doing the adaptation and dialogue for the film. On September 6 *Filmograph* said:

> It seems like everybody that is anybody is pulling for Bela Lugosi to play *Dracula*. . . . Those who have seen his performance in New York, on the West Coast and abroad, say that the story is made to order for him, since he has the voice along with the appearance that is necessary for the part.

But indecision still reigned supreme at Universal, and in the September 13 issue of *Filmograph* it was rumored that Ian Keith had gained the part over Lugosi and over William Courtney, whom the New York office had seen in another Broadway version of the play.

Still unsure, Universal gave Lugosi a screen test and at last saw the light, for in the September 20 issue of *Filmograph* a headline announced that he was signed for the part. The magazine was pleased at the choice:

> It was *Hollywood Filmograph* that first called to the attention of Universal that Bela Lugosi . . . was the proper man to play the role. . . .

[29] *Hollywood Filmograph*, August 23, 1930.

We kept continually picturing the artist in many moods and poses
in the very selfsame character, and Ye Editor personally went to the
bat and talked to everyone that had any power to give the final word
in favor of the noted artist to play the role.

The article noted that other parts in the film would soon be cast. If
Universal had finally decided on Lugosi, it had decided on little else.
Even up to the last moments before the film went into production, the
studio was remarkably unsure of everything. The October 4 issue of
Motion Picture Herald—the information printed probably being no
more than one or two weeks old—reflected the studio's indecision:

> After puzzling for a week as to whether *Dracula* . . . should be a
> thriller or a romance, Carl Laemmle, Jr., and Tod Browning decided
> to make it both. Accordingly, Lewis Ayres . . . and Helen Chandler
> have been cast as the two lovers. . . . Universal chiefs expect *Dracula*
> to achieve a popularity equal to *Seventh Heaven*.

Obviously Ayres was dropped and the far more British-sounding
David Manners added instead. And, needless to say, the script was by
no means a *Seventh Heaven*.

Filming finally began on September 29 and was planned to be done
in six weeks. The unit soon was behind schedule, later episodes were
done hurriedly,[30] and after seven weeks the film was completed. Lugosi
was paid $500 a week for his work, the only money he ever received
from Universal's bonanza. Slightly more than midway in the shooting,
a Spanish version using the same sets was begun by George Melford on
October 23, with an all-Spanish-speaking cast. The art of dubbing had
not yet been perfected, and many studios in the first years of sound
made several foreign-speaking versions.

Meanwhile, Universal's executives were shivering from fright—not
fright from the weird accent and strange countenance of Lugosi or
from the misty photography of Karl Freund, but from what they feared
Dracula would do at the box office. The original comments by some of
the studio's readers that the public was not ready for such an outright
horror film reasserted themselves. It seemed better to play up the
story's romantic, sexual aspects. On November 15 in the *Motion*

[30] As John L. Balderston said in a memo to Universal in January, 1934, discussing his treatment
for *Dracula's Daughter*: "The last one-third [of *Dracula*] . . . dropped badly. In the case of
Dracula this was due to being behind schedule and financial pressure, I am told."

Picture Herald an ad appeared: "*Dracula*: the story of the strangest passion the world has ever known." In the December 20 issue a large ad said: "Dracula will get you if you don't watch out. The Universal thriller with the box-office grip. The crimson kiss of Dracula will thrill them to the core!"

Universal was not known as the most lavish of studios, but it spent a considerable sum on the giant sets for Dracula's Transylvanian castle and British abbey. After the film was completed, the castle set remained standing and was still being used more than ten years later: At the end of *Sherlock Holmes and the Voice of Terror* (1942) some scenes take place among its "broken battlements."

The propmen searched around for exotic old furniture, the technicians spun an eighteen-foot spider web made out of rubber cement that was shot out from a rotary gun, and masons built a giant fireplace big enough for a man to stand in and placed a real fire in it. Unfortunately the fire created some difficulties. The crackling of the wood made so much noise that it was picked up by the rather unselective microphones then in use, and the dialogue scenes had to be postponed until the fire died down.

By the second week of *Dracula's* filming, the *Hollywood Filmograph*, still pulling for Lugosi, interviewed him.[31] The Hungarian acknowledged the aid that Browning was giving him in his portrayal:

> On the stage, the actor's success depends wholly on himself. He goes onto the stage and gives his performance in what, to him, seems the most effective manner. But in the studio the responsibility is shifted to the director, who controls the actor's every move, every inflection, every expression.

Lugosi and Browning worked well together, but there was considerable confusion on the set as Browning disregarded many of the moving camera shots indicated in the script and many suggestions by Karl Freund. The fluid effect that Freund wanted (and later achieved in *Mad Love*) is only occasionally present in the film.

After the opening titles of *Dracula*, accompanied by a rather mysterious-sounding passage from Tchaikovsky's *Swan Lake*, *Dracula* starts with a shot of a coach moving among the precipitous peaks of the wild and forbidding terrain of Transylvania. Needless to say, the actual

[31] October 18, 1930.

region is not quite so hostile and stark. But the Hollywood film, if not topographically and horticulturally correct, does create an appropriate area where peasants are fearful, where castles harbor flickering denizens of the night, and where such creatures as vampires could possibly exist.

The coach contains Renfield, an English solicitor. In Stoker's novel the visitor to Dracula's isolated castle was Jonathan Harker, but the film script merged this character with an insane inmate of Seward's sanatorium named Renfield. As a result, the Harker of the film became a bland character who was betrothed rather than married to Mina and, except for being slightly jealous, had little to do with the story.

As a consequence of trying to blend the Broadway play with some of the remaining bones of the novel, the film becomes confusing. Indeed, upon scrutiny, its script barely holds up. Aspects that are clear in the novel become hopelessly muddled when introduced into the film. Renfield is bitten by Dracula, yet he also goes crazy, obsessed by flies and spiders. Why? And why does Dracula visit Renfield at night and talk to him as a wolf ("He howls and howls"), and why does he promise him things? In the novel he is promised things because Dracula, like many supernatural creatures, must be invited into a house—he cannot enter at first without being bidden.[32] With this point omitted in the film, the relationship between the two makes little if any sense. Renfield's refusal ("Don't ask me to do that: not *her*, master!"), although in the novel meaning that he is being asked to invite Dracula in to sip the blood of the heroine, is meaningless, since Dracula is already a houseguest. Renfield seems to be only a helper, and not a very effectual one at that. (Dracula kills him at the end.)

Dwight Frye, who plays Renfield, was not in the original Broadway cast, but he was a Broadway actor of some fame. A slight suggestion of a lisp and a somewhat queenish intonation were part of Frye's vocal delivery and are evident as his Renfield minces considerably in the early part of the film when he is sane. These characteristics tend to vanish in his portrayal of the lunatic. In any case, he forms a vivid contrast to Dracula—short, high-voiced, effeminate.

The coach stops at an inn—an exterior scene of a hillside (on the Universal lot) with a cross standing out against the darkening sky. The coach driver does not want to proceed any farther, but Renfield argues

[32] See Coleridge's *Christabel*, for example.

that he must go on, for he is to meet Count Dracula's carriage at midnight. The innkeeper hears the altercation. "Dracula?" he says in surprise. "To the Castle Dracula? No, no," he says, in a routine that seems classically campy today but that must have been quite effective in 1931. Even more effective—and still valid—is the innkeeper's wife, who walks up to the young man and gives him her crucifix, saying, "Vear dis for your mutter's sake." A moment later Renfield and the coach depart.

Within these first few moments the motion picture creates a plastic, fluid continuity and a growing sense of the ominous. The film is controlled here by visuals, not dialogue, so that even if there were no sound but only titles, the action would still be gripping. It is only later, in England, that the dialogue instead of the camera becomes dominant. The exposition here is economical: this first reel establishes the locale, shows Renfield's necessity for meeting Dracula, explains (via the innkeeper) that Dracula is a vampire, and provides an air of dread. One must remember that this was virtually the first time in American films a vampire had appeared, and all the lore pertaining to that creature would have to be established. Today's vampire films, in contrast, do not have to spend time explaining what a vampire is, and so they can concentrate solely on action and conflict.

After the coach pulls away from the inn, there is a long shot of some mountains (actually the Rockies) and the coach rumbling toward them—a trick scene that is impeccable. Then the scene dissolves to a view of Dracula's castle and dissolves again to a shot that moves through the cobwebbed and musty crypt and stops before a coffin that begins to open, revealing Dracula's hand slowly and grotesquely emerging. Then Browning, in a momentary slip from his so-far good taste, shows a giant bug crawl out of a coffin. The coffin is in actuality no more than two to three inches long, and the bug is small. The result is absurd, for the creature looks exactly like what it is: a small bug in a matchbox-size coffin. Fortunately the shot does not stay on the screen for more than a fraction of a second.

This sequence differs from the way Universal's scriptwriters had fully described the vampire's introduction. The camera was to move down a flight of stairs into a "dank, moldy" crypt. The camera was then to dolly close to a coffin to show Dracula's hand emerge (as it does in the film) and then was to retreat to a full shot of Dracula, with his back to the camera, as he surveyed two wooden boxes, "lids off, piled high with earth." This precise establishment of the boxes was omitted; as a result, other references in the film to his boxes now seem obscure. After the vampire looks at his boxes, he faces "the camera for the first time and, moving into fore[ground], towards stairs" starts to ascend. "This movement brings his face into camera until the entire screen is filled with the menace of his inhuman eyes. . . ." The finished film stays in long shot and does not realize this effect.

Oddly enough, Universal's hard-working screenwriters did not have a very good ear for dialogue, but they did have a remarkable visual sense. They described many inventive camera movements to create an impressive atmosphere of the supernatural. Browning ignored some of the overly explicit dialogue, but unfortunately he ignored the camera directions as well. If he had followed these suggestions, *Dracula* would have been a far more fluid film. Browning showed that he did not seem to know a good idea even when given one, a fact that should be kept in mind by those critics who are so convinced of the director's cinematic genius.

After the introductory shots of Dracula, the camera next shows Dracula's wives—three women in long white dresses, white faces, and dark makeup around the eyes. Though Browning intended the women to look like animated corpses of an earlier period, they appear more antiquated today because whatever 1930 influence on their makeup and hairdo that intruded has also dated. As a result, they are even more convincing as the living dead. Here is an aspect of cinema—admittedly, an extraneous one in terms of "pure" art—that helps the film; the intervening decades have made the whole picture "dated," and so what happens on the screen is in some ways more acceptable now because of its archaic quality than when it was supposedly in the "present" day.

After a few more shots—one showing Dracula standing by his coffin (he is never shown completely rising from it because not even the lithe Lugosi could get out of a coffin gracefully and stand up without looking rather awkward)—the image dissolves to a night scene at Borgo Pass and to Dracula's waiting coach. The vampire wears a black hood that covers the top and sides of his head and sets off with startling effect Lugosi's hawklike face. His luminous eyes shine in the foggy night. This sequence contains some of the best atmospheric shots of the film and certainly one of its most frightening scenes. When the other coach arrives, Renfield's luggage is thrown off, and a second later the frightened driver rumbles off into the night. Slowly, Dracula's shrouded figure turns in a smooth motion, and a hand indicates that the not entirely nonplussed Renfield should enter the waiting coach. The ride is a bumpy one, and when Renfield leans out the window to remonstrate to the driver, he sees nothing but a bat fluttering over the horses. Apparently Dracula was wise enough to change his form rather than experience a Transylvanian road.[33] The coach finally pulls into the courtyard of the castle, and when Renfield dismounts to complain, he sees no one. The great door of the castle creaks open.

Now the second reel begins, one of the greatest single reels in the whole genre of horror films. Renfield enters the immense deserted and dilapidated hall of the castle, that pride and joy of Universal's design department. Dracula, with candle in hand, descends the long staircase, and Renfield turns in surprise as the stealthy figure approaches. "I am Dracula," Lugosi intones.

This scene of the Innocent Man meeting the Bogeyman is played in such a manner that the audience shares Renfield's own fright and yet can also laugh at his fear as well. Certainly the creature that Renfield meets hardly makes an attempt to appear normal. Dracula is strange from the very beginning, and one can well share Renfield's growing anxiety. The wolves howl, and Bela announces in his intense style: "Listen to them, the children of the night. What music they make!" Dracula turns, starts up the staircase, and apparently walks through the large cobweb.

It was in one of the earlier drafts of the script that the giant spider web was conceived. Renfield, with match in hand, enters the main hall of the castle. The camera then "becomes Renfield" as it approaches the main staircase and comes to a sudden stop before a giant dust-covered spider web. The camera "holds this for a moment" and then "tilts up to the head of the stairs," where Dracula appears, descending the stairs slowly, with a "huge taper" in his hand. Renfield is startled and afraid. (Note: the italicized parts were retained in the film.)

DRACULA: *I am Dracula.*
RENFIELD: *It's really good to see you—I—I don't know what happened to the driver and my luggage—and—and with all this—I thought I was in the wrong place—*

[33] Having traversed this area myself, though by Volkswagen, not coach, this writer can well understand Dracula's desire for comfort. Most of the road is still unpaved.

DRACULA: The walls of my castle are broken—the shadows are many—but, come—*I bid you welcome.*

Dracula is seen in front of the cobweb, there is a reaction shot of Renfield, and then Dracula appears on the other side of the obstacle. Needless to say, Renfield shows some astonishment and, after hesitating, takes his cane and breaks the web. Disturbing a spider, Renfield hears Dracula say: "The spider spinning his web for the unwary fly. The blood is the life, Mr. Renfield." In the original script Dracula's lines are far less terse (the capitalized portions had already been crossed out, and other parts would be dropped during shooting):

> AN INTERESTING ILLUSTRATION OF the eternal struggle for life—each living creature must have blood to live, EVEN DOWN TO THE LOWEST FORMS OF EXISTENCE—*the spider, spinning his web for the unwary fly—the blood is the life, Mr. Renfield!* [This final line, used in the film, stemmed from Van Helsing's comment to Renfield in the Broadway play, "The blood is the life, eh, Renfield?"]

Actually this statement contains an evil parody of Christ's words:

> Except ye eat the flesh of the Son of man, and drink his blood, ye have no life in you.
>
> Whoso eateth my flesh, and drinketh my blood, hath eternal life. . . .
>
> He that eateth my flesh, and drinketh my blood, dwelleth in me, and I in him.[34]

One characteristic of this scene, and indeed of the film in general, is Browning's habit of cutting into the action with stationary close-ups of Lugosi's face. These close-ups of his intense stares are all silent footage inserted within the longer sound takes; the effect is a bit choppy, but the shots help create Dracula's mystique. Indeed, the combination of Lugosi's deep voice and odd inflections and the carefully lit close-ups help form an extraordinary characterization, one that would remain unique in the annals of the American screen.

Some critics have complained about Lugosi's heavy-handed and

[34] St. John, Chapter 6, Verses 53–56.

strangely one-dimensional creation of Evil Incarnate. Lugosi himself was aware of his larger-than-life interpretation:

> In playing in the picture I found that there was a great deal that I had to unlearn. In the theatre I was playing not only to the spectators in the front rows but also to those in the last row of the gallery, and there was some exaggeration in everything I did, not only in the tonal pitch of my voice but in the changes of facial expression which accompanied various lines or situations, as was necessary.
>
> But for the screen, in which the actor's distance from every member of the audience is equal only to his distance from the lens of the camera, I have found that a great deal of repression was an absolute necessity. Tod Browning has continually had to "hold me down." In my other screen roles I did not seem to have this difficulty, but I have played *Dracula* a thousand times on the stage and in this one role I find that I have become thoroughly settled in the technique of the stage and not of the screen. But thanks to director Browning I am unlearning fast.[35]

Much of the conversation in Dracula's apartment was pared down considerably from the script. For example, except for the one line in italics, this whole sequence was out:

> DRACULA: Your supper awaits you—
> RENFIELD: That's very kind of you, Count Dracula, but I'm afraid I haven't much appetite.[36]
> DRACULA: At least then—a glass of wine to refresh you—*I trust you've kept your coming here a secret*—
> RENFIELD: Oh, quite, sir. You see, I'm the only member of my law firm—in fact—[smiles boyishly]—I AM the firm.
> DRACULA: You've destroyed all your correspondence—?
> RENFIELD: Yes.
> DRACULA: My mission in England is one of vital necessity—I've relied upon you to arrange the details of my journey there with the utmost discretion.

The part of the scene used, though considerably cut from the original script, contains some of its better lines. The "I'm taking with me only three—boxes" survived, but certain of Renfield's observations ("I'll be

[35] *Hollywood Filmograph*, October 18, 1930.
[36] At this point a penciled "Start here" was written on the script. But Dracula's line about the wine is cut so as not to detract from the more effective scene later.

glad to get to bed—it's been a tiresome trip—and an unusual one")
have been wisely dropped.

The next episode, one of the most famous in the film, was modified
slightly when shot. After Renfield pricks his finger, the script described
what happened: Renfield cries "Ouch!" and starts to "suck the
wounded finger." A flash close-up of Dracula follows, "his eyes
gleaming at sight of the blood." Renfield takes out a handkerchief to
dry his finger as Dracula approaches "with swift stealthiness." His
"long, prehensile fingers reach out convulsively," but when the cross
suddenly swings into view, Dracula wheels around in horror. During
the shooting, Tod Browning made an improvement. After the
"Ouch!" Renfield just examines his finger as Dracula starts to
approach. When the cross swings into view, the vampire turns in
horror. Only after that does Renfield suck his finger, as Dracula
watches with an evil countenance.

Although this scene does not occur in Stoker's novel—indeed, the
solicitor is never attacked—a similar incident does appear in the second
act of the play. Van Helsing is opening a parcel (containing, as it turns
out, wolfbane) in the presence of Dracula when he cuts his finger and
holds it up covered with blood:

> Dracula starts for Van Helsing with right hand raised, then keeping
> control with difficulty, turns away so as not to see blood. Van
> Helsing stares at him a moment, then walks up and sticks bleeding
> finger in front of him. . . .

> Dracula, baring teeth, makes sudden snap at finger. Van Helsing
> turns away quickly; ties handkerchief around it. Dracula again
> regains poise with effort.[37]

Somehow Dracula's stealthy approach in the film seems far superior to
his snapping at Van Helsing's finger like a nasty puppy.

After Renfield stops sucking his finger, Dracula offers him wine—a
far better time to do so than in the original script. It is here that the
immortal lines occur:

DRACULA: This is very old wine. . . .
RENFIELD: Aren't you drinking?
DRACULA: I never drink—wine.

[37] Hamilton Deane and John L. Balderston, *Dracula* (New York, Samuel French, Inc., 1933),
p. 49.

The other lines of the shooting script are more verbose, though explicit about the Count's activities:

> DRACULA: And now I shall leave you to enjoy your well-earned rest.—I may be detained elsewhere most of the day tomorrow —in which case, we will meet here—at sundown.—Good night, Mr. Renfield (*with a peculiarly diabolical inflection which is not lost upon Renfield*). [Only the "Good night, Mr. Renfield" and its diabolical inflection remain in the film.]

Then, according to the shooting script, Renfield goes to the bed, takes off the cross, puts it under a pillow, and starts to unlace his shoes. The "camera swings around to semi-close shot" to put Renfield in the foreground with a door visible in the distance. As the door starts to open, "the camera moves swiftly forward, past Renfield, to a close-shot" of the door, which opens "as yet by an unseen hand." Beyond is a large chamber "in complete ruin." The "camera continues moving forward, more slowly now, to [a] large close-up" of the door as the faces of the three women appear around the edge. As they move forward, the "camera moves quickly back to the bed." There is a close shot of Renfield removing his shoes. Then, as he sits on the edge of the bed, something intuitive warns him of his danger. He rises and goes to the window, the "camera panning to follow him." With some difficulty he flings open the window and looks down into the courtyard below.

EXT. COURTYARD, MED. SHOT

A rickety-looking dray is standing in the courtyard. . . . . This is shot from Renfield's angle—on the dray are two coffin-like boxes.

INT. CLOSE SHOT RENFIELD AT WINDOW

As he looks down, a mist comes rushing in, and with it a gigantic bat. Renfield, dizzy from the blow, recoils, and in doing so, strikes his head against the window and collapses, unconscious, upon the floor.

This whole foregoing scene was severely modified. The active use of the camera, reflecting the German techniques that Karl Freund had mastered, vanished almost completely from the film as shot. Obviously Browning's sense of the camera was far more sedate and conventional.

Not only the camera work but also the action had been changed. In the final version Renfield seems to be affected by a drug and goes to the window, where he falls. The three women, entering, approach his body, but Dracula enters through the casement and with an imperious gesture motions them away. He then approaches the drugged man's neck as the scene fades.

Photographs do exist that show Dracula standing by the boxes, near a wagon that will transport the strange cargo to the ship, but this episode has been completely cut. The release prints show the title "Aboard the Vesta—Bound for England" superimposed over a sailing ship on a storm-tossed ocean.[38]

On board the vessel, Renfield, now crazed, is shown opening Dracula's box and pleading with him for the blood of small things. Dracula ignores his slave and goes out on deck to survey the crew. At this point some of the action that Murnau had included in *Nosferatu* (which in turn had been borrowed from the novel) should have been used. Dracula should have stalked the crew one by one until the only

[38] In the play Dracula flew to England in a three-engine German plane, apparently one engine for each box. The film reverted to the sailing vessel as being more traditional and dramatic, although the film does not draw as imaginatively as it could have upon the concept of the evil menace approaching.

man left, aware of the horror, straps himself to the wheel in an attempt to steer the ship and avoid the vampire. But Browning just shows Dracula going out on deck and then cuts to shore, presumably a few days later, where the boat has drifted into the harbor. A voice (Browning's, as a matter of fact) explains that the whole crew has vanished and that the captain was found dead at the wheel. The whole drama of why the captain is at the wheel is skipped entirely. This mishandling of a potentially dramatic vignette is typical of the rest of the film, which departs further from the novel and adheres closer to the play.

Louis Bromfield, who had fashioned many of the early scenes (the wonderful castle opening, for example), made one other lasting contribution to the film, the dialogue in the theater scene. In Bromfield's early version Dr. Seward, his daughter Mina, and Jonathan Harker come out of a theater and wait for a taxi. Dracula, passing between them and the camera, is struck by the girl's appearance and looks over his shoulder at her. "She shivers and shrinks back under his gaze. . . . As if hypnotized, her eyes follow the figure of Dracula offscene." This fateful meeting was permanently removed. However, Bromfield's next scenes showing Dracula arriving at the Seward house, where he is introduced to the family, were retained. Subsequent scenario writers transferred Bromfield's excellent lines to a scene in a theater. Now Dracula in London walks down a fog-shrouded street, sees a girl flower vendor, and stops for a bite before going to the theater. Then he enters the concert hall to the imposing chords of the *Meistersinger* overture, hypnotizes the girl usher, and has her announce that Dr. Seward is wanted on the telephone. This allows Dracula to "overhear" Seward's name and to introduce himself. Here follows, although with some modifications, Bromfield's original dialogue. The reason for the switch in locale is obvious. Browning or Universal wanted some background music, and since they did not (in late 1930) feel that films should have musical accompaniment without an actual source, the scene was changed from the Seward living room to the theater.

When Dracula states that he has leased Carfax Abbey, his listeners think that it would look nice after extensive repair. In the original Bromfield version Dracula answered that he would do very little repairing and adds: "There is something about it that reminds me of the broken battlements of my own castle in Transylvania." This line replaced two of Dracula's comments in the play (which originated in the novel): "The walls of my castle are broken, and the shadows are many, and I am the last of my race," and, "When I hear the dogs howling far and near I think myself back in my castle Dracula with its broken battlements." [39] In the film the line was pared down to the terse and perfect: "It reminds me of the broken battlements of my own castle in Transylvania."

Lucy, impressed by the Count's odd manner, quotes an old toast: "Lofty timbers—the walls around are bare—echoing to our laughter— as though the dead were there." And then she adds, "Quaff a cup to the dead already, Hurrah for the next to die—" Mina interrupts, but Dracula muses: "To die, to be really dead, that must be glorious." Then he adds: "There are far worse things awaiting man than death." In the original Bromfield version the line was: "There are worse things waiting for man than death," and in the margin someone had added the comment "Excellent lines." Slightly modified and improved, they would remain so. During these lines the houselights dim, and the ominous beginning chords of Schubert's Eighth Symphony begin. The scene concludes with a close-up of Dracula staring intently.

Although the film takes place in the present time (1930), the opening reels could easily have occurred one hundred years before. Renfield rides in a coach to the castle, and the *Vesta* is a sailing ship; only when Dracula arrives in London does the contemporary world enter with the automobiles in the street scenes and the clothes of the people in the theater. The film actually has a double time sense; it is both modern and historical.

In the theater scene in particular and in subsequent scenes as well, Lugosi radiates the aura of knowing too much of life (and death, perhaps). This approach added dimension to an otherwise bogeyman role. Unfortunately neither the script nor the director developed Lugosi's odd personal appeal, an appeal that John Barrymore was able to create in *Svengali* (1931) and *The Mad Genius* (1931). After all, women find a fatal fascination in demonic villains, and both Lucy and Mina are certainly attracted to the Count. Perhaps a greater sense of his own damnation would have given Dracula an even more tragic dimension, but Browning was more interested in scaring his audience

[39] Deane and Balderston, *Dracula*, Act 1, p. 24.

than in revealing the depths of character that must have been developed in a count who has lived five hundred years.

Directly after the scene in the theater, Lucy and Mina talk about the strange man from Transylvania. Mina playfully imitates Dracula's "broken battlements" line, but Lucy is completely enthralled. Mina prefers her Jonathan, for he is much more "normal." Shortly after, a bat appears at Lucy's window, and soon Dracula—again, no camera trickery—is shown approaching her bed. As he bends down to bite her neck, the scene fades. Unlike the newer Dracula pictures, no blood is shown.

Next occurs one of the more cinematic episodes in an otherwise rather stagy film. A shot shows an operating room, and the doctors say that despite transfusions they were unable to stop the loss of blood. A doctor in a closer shot leans over the body and says, "And on the throat of each victim the same two marks." The whole point of her death, its cause, and its results are conveyed within just a few seconds. Unfortunately such economy would not be exercised in other portions of the film.

Soon after, Van Helsing is consulted and immediately concludes his diagnosis by saying, "Nosferatu. . . . Gentlemen, we are dealing with the undead." When his listeners seem incredulous, Van Helsing speaks a line that would long echo in horror-film dialogue: "I may be able to bring you proof that the superstition of yesterday can become the scientific reality of today." He travels to the Seward house, interviews Renfield, and confronts him with a sprig of wolfbane. That night Dracula appears in the garden and talks to Renfield in his room. Renfield begs the master not to ask him that, but finally bows his head. The next scene shows Dracula, at first in bat form, enter Mina's bedroom and bite her neck.

The scene shifts to the Seward living room, where Mina tells Jonathan about a dream that she had of a face coming out of the mist and moving toward her and touching her. Van Helsing overhears her comments, examines her neck, and asks how long she has had those marks. "Since the morning after the dream," she answers, implying that what happened occurred earlier than that morning. When Harker asks what could have caused the marks, the name "Count Dracula" is heard, as if in answer, although actually it is the maid announcing the visitor. Browning would not use sound cleverly again in the rest of the film.

The Count enters the room, and Van Helsing observes that Mina becomes strangely animated. Then Seward introduces Van Helsing to Dracula, and only a few moments later Van Helsing notices that Dracula does not cast a reflection in a mirror. When he confronts the vampire with the glass, the Count smashes it and leaves. There is no suspense or uncertainty here; within a very short time Van Helsing knows that he is dealing with vampirism, that Renfield is connected with it, and that Dracula is the cause.

Mina, in the obligatory white gown, now leaves the house and goes to Dracula, who, in a fog-shrouded shot, stands next to a stark and ominous-looking tree; he puts his cape around her—an effective and beautiful way of showing his possession of her—and leads her away.

Renfield then enters the living room and, when questioned by the professor, hears the squeaks of a bat and talks to it. Naturally any doubts that Van Helsing may have about Renfield's connection with Dracula are here resolved. The maid runs in and says that Mina is outside, and everyone exits but the maid and Renfield. She sees him, hears his laugh, and faints; in a gruesome scene he crawls toward her as if to bite her neck. Meanwhile, Harker carries the unconscious Mina back to the house as Dracula watches from behind a tree.

The next scene fades in at night, near what looks like cemetery gates, and Lucy is shown walking. This shot dissolves to Martin, the asylum guard, reading aloud to two nurses a news item about a mysterious lady who entices children and bites them on the neck. Instead of showing these scenes, the film talks about them. In fact, the brief scene with Lucy is the only one that remains in the print. She actually was dispatched by Van Helsing, but this episode, along with others, was not in the release prints.

By this time the action of the film has slowed down considerably. The first reel, less the credits, contains sixty shots; the second, seventy-four. By the time of the sixth reel the action has severely bogged down so that it contains only thirty-six shots. One "take" of Mina talking to the professor and then to Harker lasts 251 feet, almost three minutes.

The pace picks up momentarily when Dracula enters the house and tells Van Helsing that "my blood now flows in her veins" and that she will live through the centuries to come as he has "lived." Van Helsing replies that he will destroy her. Enraged, Dracula commands Van Helsing to come to him, but though the old professor wavers, he finally steps back, winning Dracula's comment "Your will is strong. . . ."

Note the chalk marks on the floor.

Dracula then starts to attack, but Van Helsing whips out a small cross and defeats him. At this point the original premiere audience exhibited its relief by applause, described in the New York *Times* as "handclapping such as is rarely heard during the showing of a motion picture." [40] The audience liked this scene, of course, for its content, but also, though perhaps unconsciously, because it was more cinematic. In fact, within this brief scene of about 200 feet (two and one-third minutes), twenty shots appear on the screen, a welcome contrast to the interminable dialogue scenes surrounding it.

Not long after, Mina sits on the porch outside with Harker and, under the influence of Dracula, almost bites him on the neck. But she is stopped and finally put to bed. Later that night Dracula again visits Mina and, after feasting, takes her back to the abbey. But Renfield decides to visit Dracula, and Van Helsing and Harker follow him. Dracula is shown on the immense staircase of the abbey (actually 129 steps without a railing, forming a gentle curve—a set in which Universal's art director took great pride). When Dracula discovers that he has been followed by the two men, he blames Renfield, chokes him to death, and throws him down the stairs. With dawn almost upon him, Dracula picks Mina up and runs through the gothic doors, just as Harker tries to catch him. Finally, as dawn comes, Harker and Van Helsing get through the doors and find two wooden boxes. Van Helsing opens one, sees Dracula's body, and starts to open the next box, but then tells Harker to find something to drive home the stake. When the second box is opened, they discover that Mina is not there, so as Harker hurries off to find her, Van Helsing hammers a stake through the vampire's heart. Mina cries out, and although she suffers sympathetic pains—her chest moves in rhythm to the blows of the stake—she is freed from Dracula's influence when he dies. Harker and Mina return to Van Helsing and ask him to leave with them, but he replies, "Not yet, presently." The two go out alone.

The original plan for the ending was to have Van Helsing say, "I shall remain and fulfill my promise to Renfield." As Mina and Harker exit, the script said that the camera was to pan "around following him [Van Helsing] into a medium shot as he moves back to where the coffin lies." Then he crosses himself before Dracula's box "with a shaft of morning sunlight bathing it in a golden glow—dust particles glinting

---

[40] February 22, 1931.

in the rays." This scene was filmed, but the last part of the shot was cut, so that the film dissolved from Van Helsing's comment ("Not yet, presently") straight to Mina and Harker ascending the stairs. Organ music was planned in the original script, but most prints today have a dubbed-in chord of orchestral music as the couple ascend the stairs. But in the original release print—and even in some 16mm copies that still circulate—the final shot of the couple walking up the stairs is accompanied by the sound of church bells. Then a brief flash of Universal's whirling globe with "The End" appears, followed directly by a shot of Van Helsing standing near the corner of a proscenium arch with a motion-picture screen in the background. He steps quickly forward and holds up his hand in a gesture of command:

> Please! One moment! [looks out into audience and says, with a smile] Just a word before you go. We hope the memories of Dracula won't give you bad dreams—so just a word of reassurance! When you get home tonight and lights have been turned out and you're afraid to look behind the curtains—and you dread to see a face appear at the window—why, just pull yourselves together and remember [pause] that, after all, there are such things! [Quick fade. Then "The End" appears again, with "It's a Universal Picture."]

Van Helsing's comments are usually omitted from current prints because today's audiences would find these final words campy, another example of Hollywood's cornball taste. The remarks, however, come word for word from the final curtain speech of the Broadway play, which according to the published script "is one of the best parts of the play." [41] In Van Helsing's speech to the audience "He practically kids them all through until he reaches the words, 'There are such things—' This is read melodramatically, which throws the chill back into their marrows and sends them out of the theatre quaking." [42]

There have long been rumors that in present prints of *Dracula*, scenes besides Van Helsing's curtain speech have been trimmed. However, Universal's continuity script and the dialogue submitted to the New York censor in February, 1931, show that the film was released as it now stands. Whatever cuts it suffered occurred before its release, not after.

[41] Deane and Balderston, *Dracula*, p. 105.
[42] *Ibid.*

In November, 1930, while *Dracula* was being assembled by the studio, Lugosi wrote an open letter to the actors and artists of Hollywood and urged their cooperation in the civic theater movement in Los Angeles. Although he was not officially connected with the repertory theater, his interest, said the press, stemmed from his previous experience in Europe. Lugosi said that the future of the drama in America is closely dependent on civic theater movements and offered his services to the group.[43] His allegiance to the stage was still strong. Later, in June, 1932, he appeared in *Murdered Alive* in Los Angeles and during the subsequent years would try to do more stage work.

By December at least one finished print was sent to the New York office, although there was a two-month wait before it was released. In the meantime, the Spanish version was shown in the first week of January, 1931, and was liked by the critics. Lugosi also saw it and thought it "beautiful, great, splendid." [44]

Final release prints of Lugosi's version were made in both silent and sound versions (many theaters in the world had not yet switched to sound), and the talking version was offered finally to the New York public on Valentine's Day, 1931. It would mark the beginning of a long love affair between Lugosi and his public. Actually the film was originally booked for the thirteenth, but that was a Friday. An advertisement appeared in *Variety* containing a facsimile of a telegram from Tod Browning, dated February 7:

> DEAR ROXY DON'T BLAME ME BUT I WAS BORN SUPERSTITIOUS STOP JUST HEARD YOU ARE OPENING DRACULA FRIDAY STOP THAT BAD ENOUGH BUT FRIDAY THE THIRTEENTH IS TERRIBLE STOP I HAVE PUT EVERYTHING I HAVE INTO THIS PICTURE AND AS A FAVOR TO ME CAN'T YOU OPEN YOUR PRESENTATION THURSDAY STOP BEST REGARDS
>
> TOD BROWNING

To comply, Roxy shifted the date to the fourteenth. The advertisement read, "First a best-selling book—then a sensational play—now, still greater as a talking picture."

Mordaunt Hall in his New York *Times* review said:

---

[43] *Hollywood Filmograph*, November 15, 1930.
[44] *Hollywood Filmograph*, January 10, 1931.

Mr. Browning is fortunate in having in the leading role in this eerie work, Bela Lugosi. . . . What with Mr. Browning's imaginative direction and Mr. Lugosi's make-up and weird gestures, this picture succeeds to some extent in its grand guignol intentions. This picture can at least boast of being the best of the many mystery films.[45]

The rest of the critics, although they had reservations about the film, were generally quite taken with Lugosi's performance. The New York *Herald Tribune* said that he was "even more effective than he was on the stage, which is something of a tribute," [46] and *Film Daily* felt that he gave "a convincing performance" and that he "creates one of the most unique and powerful roles of the screen," [47] while the woman reviewer of the *Daily News* perhaps summed it all up by saying, "He's simply grand." [48] Unfortunately this was about the last time critics would have a kind word for Lugosi's performances in horror films. After a year or two of grace the critics decided that they did not approve of the genre on general principles and so found it fashionable to adopt a smart and superior tone. Almost every subsequent horror film, whether good or bad, was usually considered beneath contempt by the so-called respectable newspapers. Only the trade press, with fewer intellectual pretensions, tended to judge the films on their own merits.

Few critics showed the sensitivity and intelligence of the writer for *Hollywood Filmograph* who had originally championed Lugosi. Although he was pleased with the casting of *Dracula*, he was well aware of the faults of the film:

Had the rest of the picture lived up to the first sequence in the ruined castle in Transylvania, *Dracula* would be acclaimed by public and critics. It would have been a horror and thrill classic long remembered; and a splendid example of true motion picture. However, after this grand introduction, Universal elected to desert the Bram Stoker novel and follow the stage play. . . .

The greater portion of this popularity will result from the work of Bela Lugosi, who at all times contrives to make Count Dracula a

[45] February 13, 1931.
[46] February 13, 1931.
[47] February 15, 1931.
[48] February 13, 1931.

believable and thrilling figure. Lugosi outdoes any of the performances of the undead count which we have seen him give on the stage.
There are times when the force of the evil vampire seems to sweep
from him beyond the confines of the screen and into the minds of the
audience. His cruel smile—hypnotic glance—slow, stately tread,
they make *Dracula*. But some day Bela Lugosi will appear in a film of
Count Dracula as Bram Stoker wrote him, and then the world will
see the true, full genius of this man.

The reviewer stated what many lovers of the horror film have often
felt:

> *Dracula* should have been a thing of shadows and mists. The dialog
> should have been much sparser. The characters should have moved
> slowly, dazedly, save only Van Helsing and Count Dracula, the two
> great antagonists. The action should have taken place in the period of
> which is was written—with crowded, ugly architecture. A modern
> operating room and modern telephones? God forbid! It belongs to
> the latter part of the nineteenth century. The battle between Van
> Helsing and Count Dracula should have been longer, harder. And
> the film should have closed with that mad race over the roads of
> Transylvania, when Van Helsing struggled with coming darkness,
> and Count Dracula sought to reach his ruined castle and safety.[49]

The sad fact is that Louis Bromfield, had he been allowed to work
further on the script, would have provided just this. But he unfortunately was dropped. Lugosi, himself, was well aware of these
shortcomings and hoped through the remainder of his life to do a
remake. But that was not to be.

Even though *Dracula* was a flawed film, it was still a considerable
success. Lugosi was pleased with his newly won fame, but he was
already fearful for the course of his career:

> Circumstances made me the theatrical personality I am, which
> many people believe is also a part of my personal life. My next
> picture, *Murders in the Rue Morgue,*, will continue to establish me as
> a weird, gruesome creature. As for my own feelings on the subject, I
> have always felt I would rather play—say, Percy Marmont roles than
> Lon Chaney types of things.[50]

[49] April 4, 1931.
[50] Interview with Lugosi by John Sinclair (1931).

Later, in an interview Lugosi gave in the spring of 1934,[51] he told of how his acting life had changed:

> A strange thing happened to me following [*Dracula*]. . . . I discovered that every producer in Hollywood had definitely set me down as a "type"—an actor of this particular kind of role. Considering that before *Dracula* I had never, in a long and varied career on the stage of two continents, played anything but leads and straight characters, I was both amused and disappointed.
>
> Of course, it is true, that every actor's greatest ambition is to create his own, definite and original role—a character with which he will always be identified, but on the screen I found this to be almost fatal. It took me years to live down *Dracula* and convince the film producers that I would play almost any other type of role.

Lugosi went on to speak about the cinema:

> It is the greatest medium of expression an actor knows. While the stage is near and will always be dear to me, I cannot truthfully say I would rather be back on the stage. While it is true that a screen actor has no audience before him other than his fellow workers, he is nevertheless compensated in the knowledge that millions will see his performance at one time, where only hundreds could see it on the stage.

And there was one other factor. Not only could millions see the performance, but it would be available for generations; indeed, like his fictional portrayal, Lugosi will "now live through the ages to come."

[51] Universal's press book for *The Black Cat*.

To Gertrude Soeurt sincerely Bela Lugosi

4

The Thirties

SOON AFTER *Dracula's* box-office success, Universal decided that a series of horror films might be one way of staving off the financial wolves baying at its doors. The plan proved quite profitable and the results artistic. Between 1931 and 1933 most of the horror films now considered classics were released. Universal produced not only the immortal twins, *Dracula* and *Frankenstein,* but also *Murders in the Rue Morgue, The Mummy, The Old Dark House,* and *The Invisible Man.* Other studios offered *White Zombie, Dr. Jekyll and Mr. Hyde, Svengali, The Mad Genius, The Mystery of the Wax Museum, Dr. X,* and *King Kong.* During this period almost all the basic horror myths were established and given definitive treatment. Only the Wolfman was missing, but even that personage had been considered in an unproduced script written by Robert Florey for Universal in 1932.

Although Lugosi had been featured by Universal in *Dracula* and was likely to become an instant star, he did not capitalize properly on his fame but continued to appear in minor parts. Before *Dracula* was released, he took a bit role in an Olsen and Johnson comedy, *Fifty Million Frenchmen,* released in March, 1931. Then, two days after the premiere of *Dracula,* on February 16, he took a small role in *Women of All Nations,* issued in May. It featured the eternally argumentative pair of marines, Captain Flagg and Sergeant Quirt, of *What Price Glory* fame. These two competitive lechers are attracted to a wife of Prince Hassan (Lugosi), who is blessed with a large harem. The boys make a play for one of the women, but the Prince unexpectedly arrives, and the two would-be seducers flee. Lugosi received eighth billing (Humphrey Bogart got ninth).

In his next film, *The Black Camel,* released in June, 1931, Lugosi or at least his agent had the good sense to demand a clause in his contract stating that he would not be listed less than third in the credits. The film opens in Honolulu with a movie company shooting on location. When a female star is murdered, Charlie Chan is called in. He levels his inscrutable gaze on a rather suspicious-looking group and momentarily furrows his brow at Tarneverro (Lugosi), the dead woman's personal fortune-teller. Although the beturbaned crystal-gazer looks like a prime suspect, there is also the murdered woman's ex-husband (played by Victor Varconi, one of Lugosi's fellow actors from the Hungarian theater) and many others who look capable of dispatching the woman to the life hereafter. Although much of the acting in the film is stagy and dated, Lugosi as usual survives quite well. His performance, while hardly naturalistic, seems believable, far better than Dwight Frye's overacted bit as the butler. There is one delightful scene in which Charlie Chan asks Tarneverro to ride with him in an old automobile. The car lurches down the road with an almost oblivious Charlie at the wheel. The great Tarneverro loses his mystic detachment, and his facial expressions become a sheer delight as he apprehensively glances at the inscrutable Chan and then at the countryside swirling past. Finally Tarneverro diplomatically inquires how long Charlie has been driving! Lugosi plays the scene just right and shows that he did have a flair for comedy.

Although Tarneverro is by no means as important a character as Dracula, and a red-herring part in the bargain (the first of many), *The Black Camel* was not a step down, for it was not the quickie production that Charlie Chan films eventually became. Lugosi's photograph dominated the New York *Times* ads, and his name immediately followed Warner Oland's. A trade review singled Lugosi out for praise, saying, "Warner Oland has never given a better performance than that of Charlie Chan in this production, but he shares honors with Bela Lugosi, whose portrayal of Tarneverro is masterly." [1] *Variety* added that "Bela Lugosi, the crystal peeker, and Victor Varconi, as the first husband, are boys who can always look guilty under the right conditions, and in this instance the conditions are perfect between dialects and scowls." [2] And dialects and scowls there certainly were.

Shortly after the release of *The Black Camel* Lugosi took the oath of allegiance to the United States on June 29, 1931, in Los Angeles and became a citizen. In his application he stated that he was not sure

---

[1] *Motion Picture Herald*, May 16, 1931.
[2] July 10, 1931.

which government was in control in Lugos, so he rather grandly renounced both the government of Hungary and Rumania. His birth date on the application, according to the newspapers, was 1892, although perhaps an error was made, since he usually did not depart from the truth more than to 1888.

In July, 1931, First National offered *Broad Minded*, starring Joe E. Brown and directed by Mervyn Le Roy. A rich man grows tired of the irresponsible exploits of his son and orders his offspring and a companion (Brown) to heed Horace Greeley's old advice and go West to avoid New York's temptations. The two wastrels agree and drive across the country. They stop in a diner where Pancho (Lugosi), a hot-tempered South American, is having lunch. Brown spills salt and throws some over his shoulder on Bela, who naturally grows angry and then absolutely livid when Brown explains the white array as dandruff. Then the unrepentant Brown borrows Pancho's pen and accidentally squirts ink all over the irate man's strawberry shortcake. Stifling the urge to kill, Pancho departs in his automobile only to be bumped a few miles later by the unobservant Brown. Pancho sputters, "First you spoil my food and now you ruin my rear end!" He adds indignantly, "If I had you in my country, I'd kill you." This scene is great fun, for Lugosi as a man of indignation and short temper is a perfect foil for Brown's idiocies.

Later Brown and his pal and their new girlfriends go to a nightclub. In the adjoining booth Pancho explains to his ladyfriend about his trip. "I had a little trouble with what you Americans call a fresh punk," he rages. "He not only insulted me, but he stole my fountain pen!" With great conviction he announces, "If I ever see him again, he will not forget it for a long time." Lugosi's face freezes as he hears Brown in the next booth saying that he had met "a big bozo." Pancho turns around and peers over the top of the booth. This shot of Lugosi's head coming slowly up over the edge and the expression on his face as he gazes furiously down at Brown are hilarious. The humor is compounded by Brown, who continues to talk about his encounters with the "bozo." Brown finally sees Pancho's eyes intensely glaring at him, and after a few awkward attempts at rectifying the bozo's image, he flees, the raging Pancho in close but unsuccessful pursuit.

Still later, to solve a complication in their love lives, the boys ask Pancho's lady friend (who is an actress) to impersonate one of their girlfriends. Of course Pancho arrives unexpectedly to see the lovemaking scene and declares heatedly that Brown not only ruined his shortcake and his car but now his girl also. Finally Pancho is talked out of his anger, but Brown, unaware of the change of heart, scurries about like mad to evade Pancho, who is rushing after him. Eventually all ends happily, and in a rare denouement for him even Lugosi wins his girl.

Broad Minded (1931).

The film is not terribly funny or successful when the boys are chugging through their wearisome antics, but as soon as Pancho comes on the scene, the film becomes quite amusing. Bela Lugosi talking about "strawberry shortcake" in his deep accent and raving about his bumped "rear-end" make a marvelous companion piece to his dignified role of the Hungarian Count. He proved himself capable of playing in comedy, although *Variety* accused him of "retaining his 'Dracula' mannerisms." [3] This observation was unkind and not accurate. True, Lugosi doesn't make any attempt to create a South American accent, but he plays a perfectly normal, though irritable human being, and is by no means supernatural in any way. In fact, he is quite the gentleman, elegant with his hand-kissing, and sexually attractive too. Significantly, the script was not written for Lugosi, and no changes

[3] July 7, 1931.

were made between the first story outlines and the finished film to accommodate the role to him. Unfortunately all the Continental roles that he could have received in Hollywood were lost because of his Dracula image.

Although the part was a good one, Lugosi again showed little business sense. Instead of holding out for significant billing and an impressive salary—after all, he had just starred in an expensive Universal film—he ended up second from the end in the credits and was not even mentioned in the advertisements.

With the success of *Dracula* at the box office, Universal decided to go ahead with its plans for *Frankenstein.* It wanted Lugosi to play the monster to fulfill the second performance called for in his contract. In the April 18 issue of *Hollywood Filmograph* Lugosi was listed as star, and in the first week of May, Robert Florey was mentioned as director. Florey was also working on the script. Behind these announcements, however, a good deal of resentment was brewing, and although most of the infighting is now misted over by time, certain facts are reasonably clear. Lugosi, after the initial success of *Dracula*, was excited at last to be a big Hollywood star. He saw himself as a sexy, romantic man who played the part of a vampire and not a "horror" man. Universal, on the other hand, felt that Lugosi would be their new Lon Chaney. The former Hungarian matinee idol was not entranced with the heavy makeup and love for grotesquerie that marked Chaney's career.

Lugosi had mixed feelings about his part in *Frankenstein.* At first he was enthusiastic—after all, it would be another starring role—but he was afraid his image would be ruined. How could he shine as a star when his face could barely be seen and when he wouldn't be allowed to speak? Anybody, he felt, could do this. In any case, work on the project began. In June, 1931, Florey went on to the still-standing *Dracula* set and shot some test reels, using Paul Ivano as cinematographer. Lugosi had his own ideas about the makeup and apparently did much of his own and ended up looking a bit like the Golem, with a head larger than usual and with a massive hairpiece. During the tests, Ivano made a big close-up of the monster coming to life. When Lugosi saw the result, he said, "Ivano, my close-up was magnificent!" and handed him a whole bunch of dollar-apiece cigars. Ivano, not a devotee of cigars, gave the bunch to Florey. Ivano concluded that Lugosi was a likable but "screwy" guy.[4]

[4] Interview with Paul Ivano, May 26, 1973, by Richard Koszarski.

Lugosi may have liked the close-up, but he continued to have misgivings about the film ruining his image. Meanwhile Universal did not care for the makeup or for Lugosi's complaints either. He could have played Dr. Frankenstein, but the studio was convinced that he had to be the monster. Considering the perfect performances of Colin Clive and Karloff, one can be grateful that Lugosi was not given the one role and had lost the other. But this omission proved to be a serious mistake, for Karloff scored great notoriety in *Frankenstein*. The film was better than *Dracula*, more dramatic and frightening, and made an even greater triumph at the box office. As a result, the producers gave Karloff a great deal of credit for its appeal, and overnight the obscure British actor became the biggest horror star at Universal. This situation was a source of continual pain and torment to Lugosi through the ensuing years, as his rival continued, despite his unimposing physique and rather unhandsome face, to outrank Hungary's contribution to the cinema.

Universal had paid $40,000 for the rights to *Dracula* and $20,000 plus 1 percent of the gross for *Frankenstein*. Although the first film had made a considerable profit and even larger hopes were held for *Frankenstein*, the company felt the effects of the Depression in early 1931 and was reluctant to invest additional money in horror properties. Instead, the studio's writers rummaged among works in the public domain to find an idea. Edgar Allan Poe seemed a likely prospect, and so his literary remains were exhumed, and by the first week of April, 1931, a treatment of *Murders in the Rue Morgue* was completed. There was some hesitation, but finally *Variety* on May 27, 1931, reported that "Universal is going ahead" with the project and that Lugosi would play the lead, with George Melford directing. Lugosi liked the role because it allowed him to appear more or less as himself, a monster of intent but not of appearance. However, the confident announcement in the press hid a number of facts, the most important of which was the difficulty in concocting a script. Poe's story was more of a detective than a horror tale, and its construction was not easily adapted into a workable scenario. Writers studied the story, stared at the wall, smoked cigarettes, and labored throughout the summer to come up with a better plot. Meantime, the studio started to make changes in its plans for *Frankenstein*. Although Lugosi was still listed as starring in the film, Florey was dropped as director at the end of June, and James Whale was put in charge. Florey, who had also been working on the *Murders in the Rue Morgue* project, was given that instead, and Melford, who was to direct, was diverted to another film. The July 11 issue of *Hollywood Filmograph* said that Florey "will be able to begin direction of *Murders in the Rue Morgue* in early August." On July 18 the same magazine said that Lugosi had "been released from his role in *Frankenstein*" because he did not want to play "a dumb brute" and was signed to do *Murders in the Rue Morgue* instead. The new film would "require a great deal of his unique talents in dialogue as well as pantomime. . . ."

While the script of *Frankenstein* was being revised and the settings planned, Universal's scenario department was mining its new treasure trove of horror. The July 14, 1931, *Variety* announced that the studio was seriously considering a sound remake of *The Hunchback of Notre Dame*. Since Chaney was now dead, "the next best," according to the article, was Bela Lugosi. This plan, however, fell through.

Unfortunately the summer of 1931 brought financial disaster to Universal. The telephone line between New York and California hummed about the quarter's whopping deficit. Around the beginning of September, studio executives panicked and questioned the desirability of another horror story to follow *Frankenstein*, then being shot. E. M. Asher, supervisor at Universal, decided to economize. Unwilling to spend money on costumes and period sets, he ordered that the *Murders in the Rue Morgue* story be advanced from its originally planned period of 1845 to the present day. Contemporary settings had been used, although a bit uneasily, in both *Dracula* and *Frankenstein*. Ulcers churned at Universal for a few days, and then the order was rescinded. Saner minds agreed that the story, which was based on an attempt to prove evolution, while perhaps credible a century earlier, would be dramatically absurd in 1931. "You may have your time period," Florey must have been told, "but we'll have to save money." So the budget was cut from $130,000 to $90,000. Florey, annoyed, stalked out. The announcement in the *Hollywood Filmograph* for September 12 that *Murders in the Rue Morgue* was "shooting" proved premature. Two issues later, on September 26, the project was listed as "preparing." Finally Florey was persuaded to return.

But return to what? The script, which had been violently gyrating among the various studio factions throughout the summer and had barely survived the last-minute decision to change its time period, remained a problem. The difficulty: to establish a motive for the murders and to give the story some love interest. Finally, after enduring six complete rewrites, including some later contributions from the young John Huston, the film went before the cameras in the third week of October. Except for the fact that an ape stuffs a woman up a chimney and that people overhear strange chatterings and attribute them to a foreign language, even Poe's ratiocinative skills could not have identified his own story. It was pure Hollywood.

Universal cried efficiency. Not long after Karloff's monster lumbered out of Dr. Frankenstein's laboratory, Lugosi, ape, and assistant arrived on the same gothic watchtower set for a few scenes. Florey worked quickly, and on November 18 the film was completed. Then a certain amount of time was allotted so that *Frankenstein* would have a chance to make headlines and disappear before another horror film was offered to a hopefully insatiable public. But this waiting was not good for Florey's film. During the interval, the executives examined it carefully and did not quite like what they saw; they decided that the much-revised script, which almost everyone had scrutinized, had a basic fault that had been overlooked. The order of the events was wrong, they concluded, and so the beginning reels were cut apart and juggled, and the result was finally released in February, 1932.

Such countless visions and revisions ideally should have resulted in a highly original work, but this did not happen. *Murders in the Rue Morgue*, although interesting, is a derivative film. The shooting script adhered to the dramatic strategy and many of the plot devices of *Frankenstein*, just as more successfully a year later *The Mummy* drew heavily upon *Dracula*. *Murders in the Rue Morgue* has a mad scientist crazed with the dream of proving his theory, willing to break the law to achieve his ends, living a solitary life devoted only to experiments, employing a not-too-bright assistant, and "creating" an extremely strong and unpredictable creature that eventually turns upon him. The film also drew upon the visual style of *Dracula*, with its fog-shrouded streets and low-key lighting. This is no coincidence, since Karl Freund shot both films. He and Florey also reveal the influence of *The Cabinet of Dr. Caligari* in some of the lighting and sets. The writers of *Murders in the Rue Morgue* also knew about this classic and showed their appreciation by appropriating some of its plot elements: the exhibition of the creature by the doctor at a carnival, the doctor's command to have the girl captured, the creature's violation of his master's orders after seeing the girl, and the chase over the rooftops.

This eclecticism of subject matter and visual style resulted in a film that does not hold together very well. It is also marred by poor dialogue, especially in the romantic scenes, which are so overwritten as to be ludicrous: "You're like a flower, soft and fragrant, pure and beautiful; you're like a star—a bright morning star. And your hair, it's full of star dust. You're like a song the girls of Provence sing on May Day . . ." and so forth. The acting is spotty, with the hero (Leon Waycoff, later known as Leon Ames) sounding uncomfortable even when speaking his less effusive lines, and the female lead (Sidney Fox) portraying rather dully an overly sweet little thing. Only Lugosi shines through the tarnish in all his demonic splendor.

The underlying idea of the film, which could not actually be filmed but only suggested, was to have the ape cohabit with the girl so that, through pregnancy, the ape's kinship with man would be proved. This threat of a fate even worse than the "fate worse than death"—being fondled and indeed attacked by a giant ape—would later recur in *King Kong*. The sexual element was watered down (or "blooded down") in *Murders in the Rue Morgue* by having the mad doctor try to mix the blood of a gorilla with that of a human.[5] This milder version makes the doctor's need for a young woman to prove his theory unnecessary, although certainly more fun.

The first version of the film began in Paris, 1845, on a foggy night—photographed in Freund's wonderful misty style—as two men fight at the edge of the Seine over the favors of a woman, who stands by a lamppost screaming. One man stabs the other and walks away in triumph, but the second momentarily recovers and throws a knife to dispatch his rival. Meantime, a carriage, which had pulled up a moment before in the fog, emits a strange, tall, black-garbed figure (Lugosi), who approaches the camera, his face unseen in the deep fog. When he moves into close-up, he pauses and says with a strangely sardonic intonation: "A lady—in—distress?"

Sobbing, the girl turns. "Who are you?"

"Come with me."

"Where?"

"My carriage," he whispers.

[5] Oddly enough, this concept is not as farfetched as it sounds. Apparently a team of Russian scientists, as late as 1932, according to the American Association for the Advancement of Science, was trying to create a man-ape hybrid by means of artificial insemination. Ah, those Russians! R. E. L. Masters, *Forbidden Sexual Behavior & Morality* (New York, Lancer Books, 1962), pp. 62–63.

"No . . . no. . . . Your hand is cold. It chills me."

"Come," he says, leading her to his carriage and enfolding her in his cloak, "I will help you."

The next scene was to be set in the man's laboratory. The girl is trussed to two vertical beams forming an X, and she screams as Dr. Mirakle removes a specimen of the now-intermixed blood from her arm: "Are you in pain, Mademoiselle? It will last a little longer. Ah, you are stubborn! Hush! It will last only one more minute and we shall see, we shall know if you are to be the bride of science!" Through this whole scene she is crying and sobbing. Moving to his microscope, the man examines the blood sample and then pushes the instruments aside in anger. "Rotten blood!" He goes up to her, shaking his fist. "Your blood is rotten, black as your sins. You cheated me, your beauty was a lie." Her head drops and her body relaxes. "Dead. You're dead." He looks sad now, bows his head, clasps his hands, and falls to his knees before this figure, in a composition suggesting some grotesque religious tableau. His mood changes, and he calls his servant—Janos, the Black One (Noble Johnson)—commanding, "Get rid of it. Get it away." Janos takes an ax and chops the ropes that hold her hands and feet, and she plummets through a trapdoor into the river. The camera cuts back to a long shot showing the whole laboratory, which is really just a large room with beams and a table with apparatus on it. "Will my search never end?" says the doctor as the scene fades out.

Later that night the woman's body is found along the quay, and some wharf people talk about how she is the third suicide in recent days. Not long after, a medical student named Pierre Dupin visits the morgue and examines the body. He says, in a phrase that was already starting to have a familiar ring at Universal, "the same marks." Pierre also notes "the same foreign substance in the blood of each victim" and concludes that "all three died of the same cause."

This opening, modeled after Universal's pattern in *Dracula* and *Frankenstein* of providing lots of atmosphere right in the beginning and then digging into the exposition and main plot, was changed after being shot by transposing the first scenes to a later position. The film now opens at the carnival, where the doctor meets the heroine, Camille.[6] With the scenes in the original order, Dr. Mirakle's interest

---

[6] As a result, there are some minor continuity errors because scenes which had once been separated were now spliced together; for example, in one shot the carriage contains the ape, yet in the next it does not.

Murders in the Rue Morgue (1932).

in Camille is far more sinister, because the audience knows what he wants to do with her. As the film now stands, this interest perhaps seems more lecherous than diabolical.

In any case, the release version begins with Pierre and Camille and another couple roaming through the crowds at the carnival and coming upon a tent. A barker outside says:

> Behind this curtain is the strangest creature your eyes will ever behold: Erik, the ape man, the monster who walks upright and speaks a language—even as you and I. The ruler of the jungle whose giant hands can tear a man in half. Erik, the ape man, the beast with a human soul. More cunning than a man and stronger than a lion.

The couple enter the tent, and Dr. Mirakle advises Camille to sit in front, where she can see everything. They comment on the doctor. "What a funny looking man; he's a show in himself." Someone else says, "Did you notice his accent? I wonder where he comes from? I never heard an accent like it."

Then Dr. Mirakle, in a scene reminiscent of *The Cabinet of Dr. Caligari*, steps onto the stage and in excellent Lugosi style—the accent heavy, the intonations odd, the pattern of speech containing unpredictable but dramatic pauses—begins by intoning, "Silence!" And then he offers his monologue, the high point of the picture, a high point that unfortunately comes at the start of the reedited film. The words might read flatly, but Lugosi's facial expressions and delivery make the speech menacing and somehow even poetic.

> I am Dr. Mirakle, Messieurs and Mesdames, and am not a sideshow charlatan, so if you expect to witness the usual carnival hocus-pocus [he says the word marvelously] just go to the box-office and get your money back. I am not exhibiting a freak, a monstrosity of nature [the second syllable of "monstrosity" drawn out, the last syllable of "nature" brought up with a strange inflection] but a milestone in the development of life! The shadow of Erik the ape hangs over us all. The darkness before the dawn of man. [Here he shows the ape to the audience, which is frightened.] Listen to him, Brothers and Sisters, he is speaking to you. Can you understand what he says, or have you forgotten? I have relearned his language. Listen. [Here he mutters to the ape in a strange language, and the ape replies.] I will translate what he says. "My home is in the African

jungle where I lived with my father and my mother. [And when the ape mutters, he adds:] And brothers and sisters. But I was captured by a band of hairless white apes [a phrase said with pure disdain] and carried away to a strange land. I'm in the prime of my strength! [Lugosi says this with proud passion.] And I am lonely." [Then he moves to the chart and points.] Here is the story of man. In the slime of chaos there was the seed which rose and grew into the tree of life. Life was motion. Fins changed into wings, wings into ears, crawling reptiles grew legs. Eons of ages pass. There came a time when a four-legged thing walked upright. Behold the first man! [The audience stirs, he points to the ape, and someone yells, "Heresy."] Heresy? [And then the doctor says with superiority and contempt:] Do they still burn men for heresy? Then burn me, monsieur. Light the fire. Do you think your poor candle will outshine the flame of *truth?* Do you think these walls and curtains are my whole life? They are only a trap to catch the pennies of fools. [And then he says, with great sincerity, touched with insane passion, lines that perhaps sound hammy but could not be done by any other actor in quite Lugosi's way and have them succeed:] My life is consecrated to great experiment. I tell you I will *prove* your kinship with the ape. Erik's blood shall be mixed with the blood of man!

After this declaration, most of the audience gets up and leaves, but Dr. Mirakle prevails upon Camille to "make the acquaintance of Erik." The ape snatches her bonnet. "Erik is only human, Mademoiselle. He has an eye for beauty." And then, with great enthusiasm, he says, "You have made a conquest, Mademoiselle." When the ape ruins the bonnet, the doctor offers to give her a new one, but the boyfriend refuses to tell him where she lives. Mirakle sends Janos to follow them. It is at this point in the release print that the waterfront fight, the screaming prostitute, and her disposal through the trapdoor occur.

In the meantime, Mirakle has sent a new bonnet to the girl. Later she and Pierre go to the park, and in a bit of showy film direction, the camera is placed in front of the girl on a swing and moves back and forth with her as she and Pierre talk. (Freund had used a similar scene in *Variety*, a German silent film.)

Later Pierre visits the doctor's tent and says that Camille will not be coming, a fact that disappoints the doctor. Pierre explains that he is a medical student and asks whether Dr. Mirakle has written any papers. He replies in ominous tones, "None—to be shown." Mirakle says that he is leaving Paris that night and dismisses the young man, but Pierre overhears the carnival workers say that Mirakle is staying, follows his carriage, and discovers where he lives.

Mirakle arrives at Camille's house and tries to convince her to accompany him. He says most strangely, "There is something you must know," as he tries to force his way through the door. Here he is just a plain bogeyman and so unwise and extreme in his dialogue that she asks, correctly, "Are you insane?" and locks the door. The doctor, not easily deterred, sends Erik up the side of the house. The creature kills the mother and carries away the screaming girl. Meantime, Pierre has discovered that the foreign substance in the blood of the dead prostitute is from a gorilla and hurries back to check on his girl's safety.

He is too late. It is at this point in the story, when the ape makes his attack, that the script finally coincides with Poe. A number of people offer their opinions about the strange chatterings they have heard. A German thinks it was Italian, an Italian thinks it was Danish, and a Dane thinks it was German. This comedy-relief argument rages while Mirakle returns home with the girl and starts his experiment. Finally Pierre prevails upon the police to believe him, and they arrive at the doctor's house, the exterior of which is reminiscent of an expressionistic set. Janos, looking out through the window, sees the police, and the doctor sends him down to keep them away. Janos descends the steps

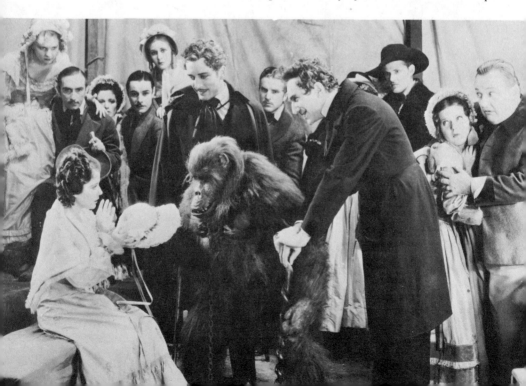

(the same ones used in the watchtower of *Frankenstein*), and is shot for his troubles by an officer. The ape, however, is attracted to the girl and does not want her hurt, so he kills the doctor and carries the girl off over the rooftops. He is finally shot, and Pierre and Camille are united on the roof, a scene that provoked "irreverent squeals" when the film was first shown in New York.[7] *Variety* opined: "At the Mayfair a cynical audience hooted the finale hokum, but away from Broadway the chase and its finish shouldn't meet such hard-boiled resistance." [8]

Murders in the Rue Morgue is not really a frightening film by present standards and was not even too frightening back in 1932. There are some melodramatic moments, but they are based more on adventure than suspense or fear. Despite the occasionally imaginative sets, the director fails to create much of a sense of mystery. Events happen too matter-of-factly. The best buildup of all in the film was the original opening, but inserted later into the film, its foggy scenes seem inconsistent, and the silhouetted form of Mirakle picking up the girl becomes pointless, since we already know what he looks like from the tent episode.

Here the mad scientist was already starting to become a stock figure, and the ape, which had often been used in comic situations, was now to be taken seriously, which apparently audiences couldn't do. (That is, until the next year with *King Kong*.) One reviewer found the film to be "both feeble and foolish." [9] Still, the New York *Post* felt that Lugosi made "an imposingly sinister figure," [10] while the review in *Photoplay* showed an awareness of Lugosi's nonrealistic acting style, saying that "although folks who like the repressed school of acting will get a little annoyed with his tactics, he is, nevertheless, the perfect type for this sort of film." [11] Certainly Dr. Mirakle is on the verge of being one of Lugosi's best performances, but the actor is so hampered by a stodgy script and by the uninspired direction of Robert Florey, as well as by an excess of bad comedy relief, that the film as a whole is only mildly interesting and by no means up to what one would expect, considering the creatively rich period during which it was made.

After completing *Murders in the Rue Morgue*, Lugosi was ap-

[7] New York *Times*, February 11, 1932.
[8] February 16, 1932.
[9] New York *Herald Tribune*, February 12, 1932.
[10] February 12, 1932.
[11] March, 1932, p. 49.

proached by the Halperin brothers, who had a scheme for a movie about zombies. They had obtained their inspiration from a Broadway play called *Zombie*, which had opened on February 10, 1932, in New York and played for twenty-one performances. Taking place in Haiti, the play told the story of a plantation owner who is not sure whether his wife loves him or his friend, a doctor. The husband drinks a potion, a prescription prepared by the doctor, seemingly dies, and goes stalking around scaring everybody.

On February 20, 1932, the *Motion Picture Herald* announced that negotiations were taking place and that the play would soon be made into a film. Shortly after, the Halperin brothers had Garnett Weston concoct a rather different script and offered Lugosi the leading role, but not much money. The actor later said that they bid $500 for his services. Afraid to create another rival, anxious to play a leading role, and unwilling to let the money pass from him, Lugosi accepted. In fact, after his *Frankenstein* error, he seemingly never said no.

When Kenneth Webb, the author of the zombie play, read that the Halperins were going to make *White Zombie*, he brought suit in March, 1932, for copyright infringement, stating that the proposed film weakened the commercial possibilities of his own work. The Halperins argued that Webb's play had not been much of a box-office success and that the film could not possibly have ruined the play's future. They stated further that Webb had no monopoly on the word "zombie." They won their case.

The subject of the argument, *White Zombie*, proved to be a lucrative investment for the brothers Halperin, but it was no help to Lugosi's professional standing and in fact was mocked and derided by most critics. The *Herald Tribune* said that it was "clumsily wrought and unhappily acted. Bela Lugosi proves that a good makeup cannot conceal a bad actor." [12] *Variety* felt that its "atmosphere of horror is well sustained and sensitive picture-goers will get a full quota of thrills," but went on to say that although Lugosi "gives an exceptionally good performance," the film is "not quite up to Broadway." [13] The New York *World Telegram* was far more critical: "As entertainment it is nil. . . . *White Zombie* is such a potpourri of zombies, frightened natives, witch doctors, leering villains, sinister shadows, painted sets

[12] Richard Watts, July 29, 1932.
[13] August 2, 1932.

and banal conversation on the black magic of the island that the actors of necessity just move along. There are, however, moments when they get a chance to act. But the less said about that the better." [14] This criticism was not unwarranted, for the hero and heroine were quite poor. Madge Bellamy, who was making a comeback, played her whole part so woodenly that the difference between her zombie state and normal one was almost indecipherable. The poor acting plus the rather low budget made the film an early step in the downward course of Lugosi's career. But time has proved quite kind to *White Zombie*. Although dismissed as a piece of inept and juvenile film-making, its plot and cinematic skill prove it to be a minor masterpiece of the genre. Indeed, what had seemed corny in 1932 has gained a kind of period flavor, and Lugosi's performance, although played to the hilt, appears now as the definitive interpretation of this type of villain.

The premises upon which the zombie tradition in the movies began are based on actual practices in Haiti, beliefs examined by reputable anthropological observers and theologians, and are not merely figments of the imagination of Hollywood scriptwriters. When Africans were introduced to Haiti in 1510, they brought with them native superstitions that came from more than thirty different areas of Africa.[15] When these superstitions were mixed with Spanish Catholicism, a curious amalgam called voodooism resulted. One of its strangest procedures is the creation of a zombie.

> On occasion an apparent death is felt not to be a real death, but rather the simulacre of death brought about by the machinations of a sorcerer. If poison has not been administered . . . or if the body was not stabbed, after the funeral the sorcerer recovers the body, which, deprived of its soul, works for him as a zombie; only returning to the grave when the time decreed by God for his natural death is reached. . . . Though the concept has been presented in recent years with unjustifiable sensationalism to the reading public, it is indisputably a living one.[16]

Among the believers in voodoo, it is thought that piercing a wax image of a victim is an excellent way of killing an enemy.[17] More sober

---

[14] William Boehnel, July 29, 1932.
[15] Harold Courlander, *Haiti Singing* (New York, Van Rees Press, 1939), p. 2.
[16] Melville J. Herskovits, *Life in a Haitian Valley* (New York, Knopf, 1937), pp. 245–46.
[17] "Cuban Authorities Battle Cult Practicing Kidnapping and Human Sacrifice," *Literary Digest,* CXXIII (January 2, 1937), p. 29.

analysis has shown, however, that the power of suggestion and hopelessness on the victim's part bring about such deaths.[18]

Despite the film's concern with zombies (a relatively new bit of folklore), its treatment, its whole conception, is that of some of the morbid creations of the gothic-romantic period. True, the film must be taken *cum grano salis,* but salt in this case enhances the flavor.

The character that Lugosi depicted in *White Zombie* was in some ways close to the man himself. The press sheets for the film described Lugosi as a far different kind of person from most Hollywood actors:

> There is something of a mysterious, hypnotic quality about the man himself, particularly about his deep-set eyes, and the reason appears to be that he has probed life too deeply.
>
> But probing life is just what he has devoted his thought to. Seldom has he dwelt upon this ambition, for he has few intimates and with the exception of his studio visits, he is seen in public infrequently. He remains in his inaccessible retreat in the Hollywood mountains, and his constant companion is a half-wild malamute dog which howls at night . . . [a little hyperbole here, to say the least].
>
> The star unintentionally put all of his philosophy into one paragraph one day recently, when an interviewer managed to corner him at his home. Lugosi had been looking off into space toward the Pacific Ocean, when he suddenly swerved around and said:
>
> "People—thousands of them—chained by monotony, afraid to think, clinging always to certainties and terrified by the unknown. They live like ants. I want to get away from people. I must get away somewhere where I can be free.
>
> "And I can do it soon, too. Not many more years and I will have enough of this world's goods to pursue my own course and to pay for whatever research I desire to make. I'm going into the mountains completely away from people, to study."

These remarks were noted by the interviewer as about "the longest speech anyone ever heard Lugosi make in Hollywood."

> "I have lived too completely, I think," he said on a subsequent occasion. "I have known every human emotion. Fear, hate, hope, love, rage, despair, ambition—all are old acquaintances, but they have left nothing to offer me. Only study and reflection remain. I must

---

[18] See, "Evidence Is Lacking for Voodoo Deaths," *Science Digest* (December, 1961), p. 19; also "Voodoo Kills by Despair," *Science News Letter* (May 7, 1955), p. 294.

know what I have learned. I must analyse all my theories and be alone to think."

The interviewer went on to speak of Lugosi's specialization in eerie roles. "And those who know as much of him as it is possible to know are convinced that there is something in his own nature which mirrors these odd roles."

The interviewer continued:

> Certainly, Bela Lugosi is an unhappy man. He is given to unaccountable moods, spells of silence during which he seems to be conversing with some unseen presence. . . . Only one thing can be certain about him, and that is that any weird ingredients in his nature are bound to be marshalled upon the side of good rather than of evil. . . . For one of Bela Lugosi's fondest hopes is to exert some force in the agitation for a more utopian existence.

Lugosi's utopian predilections hardly found an outlet in *White Zombie*. In essence, the film is a fairy tale; at least it is structured along those simple, yet firm outlines, but it is a tale that deals more with evil than with good:

There was once a handsome young man and a beautiful young maiden destined to be married. But a jealous suitor, unwilling to lose her, visits an evil sorcerer, who bewitches the girl and takes her to a faraway castle. However, when the suitor sees her masklike face and soulless expression, he repents of his evil and asks the sorcerer to remove the spell. But the evil wizard now wants the maiden for himself and so bewitches the suitor. But good will not be vanquished, and the handsome young man, aided by voices and an older friend, finds his way to the perilous castle, where the sorcerer is outwitted and killed. The spell is broken, and the young man and the maiden live happily ever after.

The fairy-tale structure, as well as the symbolic interplay of light and dark (the girl equals light and goodness, and thus is "white," whereas the sorcerer equals dark and evil), was probably not intended by the creators of the film and thus is unself-conscious. Although Jungian archetypes and universal myths and fables can be found if the critic *wishes* to find them, these aspects appear in the script not because the author was so subtle, but because he was working in the tradition of romanticism, a tradition replete with suggestive overtones.

As the sorcerer in *White Zombie* (1932).

The villain of *White Zombie* is the sorcerer "Murder" Legendre, portrayed by Lugosi—a character who stands with the dark villains of the romantic period and could well have been conceived by Byron, M. G. Lewis, and Shelley at one of their ghoulish get-togethers. Lugosi's role is not so much a new kind of villainous creation as it is the end product of a long tradition, the culmination of the tendencies of the previous century. His "bad" behavior is not psychologically or sociologically motivated. A drunken father or life on the other side of the tracks is not the cause; a caseworker would thus be stymied, for there are no *outward* reasons for evil. The sorcerer is evil because he likes to be; he does not need a reason. He is not the servant of circumstance, but the master of it. As Legendre's makeup indicates, he is satanic: his forked beard, dark eyes, pronounced widow's peak, tall, spare figure, and Continental appearance (Satan is always a foreigner) create an imposing personage, one whose manner makes his later conduct credible.

A girl, Madeline, has journeyed to Haiti to marry. Aboard ship she has met Beaumont, a wealthy but unscrupulous plantation owner, who has fallen in love with her. Although she refuses him, she consents to having her marriage ceremony performed at Beaumont's place far in the Haitian interior.

As the film opens, Madeline and her husband-to-be travel in a horse and carriage along the lonely roads of the province, but their journey is halted by a funeral. A corpse is being buried in the middle of the road so that no one will steal the body and transform it into a zombie. Shortly after, as the couple go deeper into the country, a close-up of Lugosi's eyes dominates the screen, as if his evil will pervades the land itself. The carriage halts on a deserted road next to the tall, dark-garbed, and silent Lugosi. He approaches the carriage and looks in. Frightened at his expression, and especially at his eyes, the heroine draws back, but the sorcerer clutches her shawl. The cry of "Zombies!" comes from the scared driver's mouth when he sees slow-moving figures crossing the hillside. As the carriage jerks forward, the shawl slips from around her neck. Her hands go instinctively to her bruised throat. Although she has momentarily escaped Lugosi, to the audience the touch is only a premonition of what is to come, for the shawl that once kept her throat warm will now aid in her "death." She is falling into the hands of evil.

Beaumont, at whose place they soon arrive, appears disheveled and debauched, a Byronic figure in his riding boots and white trousers. Almost insane with passion, he disregards his servant's advice to be careful of the sorcerer. He will risk everything to win Madeline. A carriage arrives in the courtyard, and Beaumont hurries down to it to be carried away by a zombie to Lugosi's mill, where undead blacks, their eyes dully staring into nothingness, push slowly but automatically the arms of a large capstan that is grinding sugarcane. One of the zombies trips and falls in, but the other men continue. The only sound is the grinding and creaking and groaning of the wheel.

Lugosi approaches Beaumont and offers his hand in greeting, but Beaumont will not shake it. He refuses to touch such an evil creature. In the dialogue that follows the reader need not be reminded that Lugosi's deep voice and accent lend a strange beauty and somberness to his lines. His words are given an extra meaning, a kind of ominous doomsday import. Lugosi begins:

"I've been on a journey—getting men—for my mills."

"Men?" Beaumont asks disgustedly.

"They work faithfully; they're not worried about long hours. You could make good use of men like mine—on your plantations."

"No," says Beaumont, "that's not what I want."

The power of Lugosi's eyes. *White Zombie.*

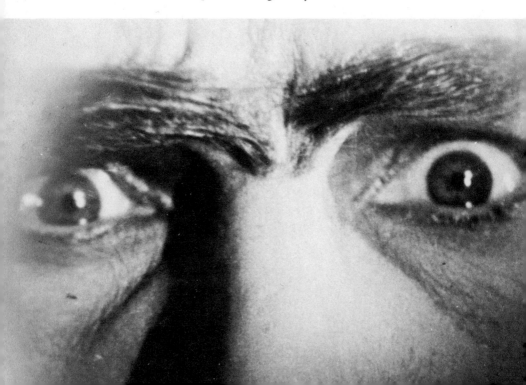

And Lugosi answers, the first instance of his strange insight: "Then perhaps you want to talk about the young lady who came to your house this evening."

Beaumont asks excitedly, "You've seen her? When?"

"The road, tonight." Then Lugosi pauses, the first word coming out slowly, as if drawn from some hellish depth. "There—was a young man with her."

Beaumont says, "They're to be married tonight. If *she* were to disappear. . . ."

"What do you hope to gain by her disappearance?"

"Just give me a month, one little month. . . ."

Lugosi replies, "Not in a month nor even a year." The line that follows indicates the kind of insight he has: "I've looked into her eyes. She is deep in love," and adds sardonically, "but not with you!"

Beaumont ignores this. "They are to be married within the hour. There *must* be a way," he says in despair.

"There *is* a way," Lugosi says in a tone of evil finality.

The camera cuts to a zombie. Beaumont recoils in horror. "No, not that." Lugosi shows him a potion, his eyes lighting up in demonic enthusiasm: "Only a pinpoint, Monsieur"—the voice emphasizing the word "pinpoint"—"in a glass of wine—or—perhaps, a flower?"

This romantic image of wine and a flower recurs throughout the film as a kind of leitmotif. The wine, of course, suggests the old world, upper-class living, elegance, the drama of a toast, the beverage of ceremony and ritual. The other image, the flower, hints of purity and beauty. It also suggests the speaker's cynical and condescending attitude in seeing the girl as a flower, as a transitory and fragile figure to be plucked and admired briefly. The coupling of these two images of wine and flower, which respectively suggest happiness and beauty, to the contrasting state of unhappiness and death, is profoundly steeped in romanticism and draws upon hundreds of years of lyric poetry. This device of a festive toast and an innocent bloom bringing about evil has long been an element in the literature of the fable and the fairy tale: from luscious lotus blossoms in *The Odyssey* and the poisonous apple in *Snow White* right down to the ingenious parody in *Alice in Wonderland*.[19]

[19] The potion appears frequently in literature. See the medieval *Tristan and Iseult* and later Wagner's *Tristan und Isolde* for a variation of the death-love potion. In *Romeo and Juliet* again the potion appears; Juliet seeks a temporary death in order to have her Romeo. In nineteenth-century

Handing the zombie potion to Beaumont, Lugosi says encouragingly, "You must do your share if I'm to help you." But Beaumont does not want the potion.

"Keep it, Monsieur," says Lugosi. "Keep it. You may change your mind."

But Beaumont does not like Lugosi's cynical inference. "I'll find another way," he says.

And Lugosi answers, "There is no other way."

Later, just before the wedding, Beaumont again pleads with Madeline, but she refuses him. In desperation, Beaumont picks up the poisoned rose lying on the table and hands it to her. This simple flower seems to glow with a kind of evil significance as she inhales its mysterious fragrance and places it within her bridal bouquet. The organ starts to play the wedding march. Meanwhile, in the courtyard of Beaumont's house, another ceremony begins: the bewitchment of her soul. Standing between two lanterns with a vulture perched upon one of the pillars, Lugosi puts the finishing touches on a wax replica of Madeline. He is invoking the primal device of sympathetic magic, in which the fate of a human being depends on the treatment afforded its likeness. Although this seems a pagan doctrine and alien to Western cultural traditions, just such a procedure had been used by the medieval Christian Church.

Lugosi takes the carved object, wraps it with the shawl that Madeline had worn, and puts it into the flame of the lantern. As the wax melts, the vulture screeches overhead at the bewitchment of a new victim. The bird, the "familiar" of this wizard, also reinforces Lugosi's unique relation to death.

Meanwhile, Madeline, at her wedding feast, is reading her future in a glass of wine. Looking at the wine's glistening surface, she says, "I see happiness, I see love, far more than I deserve."

"Is that all?" asks the new husband.

"I see—" she says, looking into the glass, a giant close-up of which appears on the screen. "I see—" she continues, beginning to reel back and forth as Lugosi's demonic eyes are superimposed over the wine. "I see—I see death." She slumps down dead as her husband cries out her name again and again.

---

romantic writing potions often appear. Hawthorne uses it in "Dr. Heidegger's Experiment," Stevenson in *Jekyll and Hyde*, Wagner in *Siegfried*. The bewitched flower does not appear as often, though Hawthorne uses it in "Rappaccini's Daughter."

This counterpoint of marriage and death, of pure love and profane, of freedom of the will and subjugation, and of good and evil occurs to the accompaniment of a demonic musical score.

The next scene opens in a bar, where Neil (the husband), drunk, seems to see the white form of Madeline hovering within every shadow and calling out to him. Later, at the cemetery, Beaumont, Lugosi, and his servants stand before her mausoleum to take away her corpse. Lugosi's comments are the clearest explanation of his powers over life and death. He indicates his servants and says: "In their lifetimes they were my enemies." The camera surveys the mindless lot. Lugosi takes obvious pleasure in his menagerie and proudly points them out one by one. "The witch doctor, once my master. The secrets I tortured out of him. . . . Von Gerde, the swine, swollen with riches; he fought against my spell even to the last. Scarpia, the brigand chief. And this, this is Chauvin, the high executioner, who almost executed me!" And then he concludes, "I took them"—pause—"just as we will take—this one." This statement defines in many ways what Lugosi's role is: he is the Dark God to whom a person is a mere body, a mere "one." This use of the impersonal "one" suggests that at this moment, at least, Madeline is only another for the collection. His use of the verb "take" implies that he can have whomever he wants, that he can literally *possess* those

Stealing the corpse. *White Zombie.*

whom he wants. Beaumont is appalled at this. "But what if they regain their souls?"

"They would tear me to pieces," Lugosi says, smiling, "but that, my friend, shall never be." He says this confidently; there is no question in his mind of his absolute power. They then go down to the mausoleum and carry away her coffin. Meanwhile, the hero is approaching the cemetery and crying out her name. Lugosi and his "men" hear his voice and hurriedly leave the vault. A moment later Neil arrives and rushes down into the empty mausoleum. After a moment's pause his mad, tormented screams reverberate weirdly in the underground chamber as the scene fades.

Shortly after, Neil goes to the missionary who had married them, and in one "take" lasting more than five minutes he is told about voodooism and zombies.

As the next scene opens, Madeline is at the sorcerer's immense gothic castle. Still garbed in her wedding/funeral white, she sits at the piano playing *Liebestraum* mechanically. Her eyes are vacant. Beaumont puts jewels around her neck, but there is no reaction. What he says does not register on her now-unconscious brain. What he has loved, that spark of personality, has now vanished. Only the shell remains. Overcome with the enormity of his deed, he says in despair, "I must take you back!"

"Back to the grave, Monsieur?" Lugosi answers, leaning over the gothic railing of the staircase.

"Anything's better than that awful emptiness," Beaumont says desperately. "You must put the light back into her eyes and bring laughter to her lips. She must be gay and happy again."

Lugosi, with the slightest suggestion of a sneer, answers, "You paint a charming picture, one that I should like to see myself."

Beaumont says again, "You must bring her back!"

Lugosi tries to reason with him: "How do you suppose those eyes will regard you when the brain is able to understand?"

Lugosi's question has a hideous logic in its impersonal view toward the girl. She is no longer a person with a soul but rather "eyes" and "brain" as if she were a mere mechanism. And to the sorcerer perhaps this is exactly what all people are.

But Beaumont's answer, if not as practical as Lugosi's question, is far more humanistic. "Better to see hatred in them than that dreadful emptiness."

White Zombie: the new zombie.

It doesn't pay to drink with Lugosi.

Lugosi, sensing trouble, pretends to agree. "Perhaps you're right."
And then with great mockery, "It would be a pity to destroy such a
lovely flower." Once again she is linked to the flower, and now in a
moment the wine image too will return.

Lugosi says, "Let's drink to the future of this flower," and secretly
puts some of the potion in the wine. Beaumont drinks it, but the taste
makes him look up questioningly. "To the future, Monsieur," Lugosi
says, his face beaming satanically.

Beaumont asks desperately, "You, what are you trying to do to me?"
And Lugosi answers in all his demonic passion, "I've taken a fancy to
you, Monsieur." This line is perhaps the most sinister in the film. The
sorcerer's power can be seen here as capricious; the word "fancy" sums
up his contempt for mankind and for Beaumont as its representative.
To trifle with a man's life and, even more, with his soul because of a
"fancy" is perhaps the height of evil. In turning Beaumont into a
zombie to remove a conscience-stricken accomplice and a potential
rival, Lugosi also, of course, amuses himself. Beaumont will now join
the ranks of his "men." His previous line from the cemetery comes to
mind: "I took them—just as we shall take—this one."

Madeline's husband and the missionary head for the castle to rescue
her. Meanwhile, the drug has been working on Beaumont. Lugosi, in
what is psychologically one of the cruelest scenes in all horror films, is
shown sitting at the table carving a wax figure of his victim. He studies
Beaumont's struggles with a mixture of curiosity and indulgence. Now

mute, Beaumont tries to touch Lugosi's hand, but the sorcerer withdraws it. "You refused to shake hands with me once—I remember." Lugosi brushes his hands together in a rather dismissive manner and says, "We understand each other better now." He is not one to forget a slight.

Although Lugosi controls Madeline's soul, he does not yet possess it entirely, nor can his malevolent will prevail against good (good here suggests not the powers of God, but rather those of love).

Madeline drifts onto the exquisite gothic balustrade of the vast castle to the accompaniment of mystic emanations, symbolized by humming voices. They seem to float out upon the air and rouse the fever-ridden Neil. Visually this point is made even clearer by use of the split screen. She is seen in the left top corner of the frame, and he leans forward in her direction and cries out her name. Soon after, Neil climbs the perilous mountain and enters the castle, but collapses from fever. Lugosi becomes aware of Neil's presence and, with a Mephisthophelean look on his face, decides the appropriate fate of the husband. Using his hypnotic powers, he summons Madeline. Garbed in a white dress with an embroidered pattern suggesting a gothic design, she slowly descends the staircase (the camera framing her with a similarly shaped cutout in the banister supports), goes to the table, and picks up the knife with which the sorcerer has been carving Beaumont's waxen image. Ascending the stairs, she stands over the unconscious Neil and is commanded to plunge the knife in his throat, but she hesitates. As she begins to bring the knife down, the missionary arrives and stops her. Stirred by this experience, she rushes down the staircase and runs to the edge of the cliff. Neil wakes and runs after her and stops her. Lugosi, his perverse pleasure thwarted, summons the zombies. When Neil asks Lugosi who these creatures are, the sorcerer replies, "To you, my friend, they are the angels of death." The zombies approach while Neil, at the edge of the precipice, shoots them to no avail. But Lugosi can barely savor this moment of triumph before the missionary sneaks up behind him and knocks him out; the zombies, continuing their last order, mindlessly walk off the edge to perish in the ocean depths below.

Madeline now begins to show signs of recognition, but when Lugosi regains consciousness, she soon returns to her trancelike condition. In the confusion, Lugosi tries to escape, but Beaumont, in the last exercise of his will, grapples with him, and they both plummet over the cliff to death. Madeline wakes, recognizes her husband, and says, "Neil, I—I dreamed."

White Zombie is not for all palates. But despite its melodrama and too-obvious attempts to frighten the viewer, the film is one of the few of the genre that has a strong touch of poetry, in both its visual and verbal imagery. The photography by Arthur Martinelli is particularly noteworthy. Careful attention is paid to light and shadow and especially to composition. There is frequent use of forefronts to create a three-dimensional effect. The camera shoots through archways, the grillwork of the sugarcane mill, festoons of flowers at the wedding, the sides of the vault as the coffin is slid, and the gothic filigree of the ornate banister. These shots were made in the studio, but others were done outside on location to save money. Although pieced together from various places, they present a convincing sense of the particular locale.

The film is fluid and fast-moving, marred only by some long expository scenes of the missionary talking. The picture also makes imaginative use of sound: the grinding of the mill, the coffin sliding into the vault, the hero's echoing cry of despair in the tomb, and of course the background music. Although the score uses some stock themes, it brilliantly reinforces the frenzied and evil content and is a major factor of its success. There are also blacks chanting, loud and piercing screams of the dying, the screech of the vulture, and of course Lugosi's sublime bass voice, intonation, and diction. The press sheets for the film stated that Edward and Victor Halperin

> have long since felt that the motion picture has been marring its possibilities since the advent of the talkies by the employment of too much dialogue.
>
> Only where a line of dialogue is absolutely essential does a character speak in *White Zombie*, and the result is a revelation. This means that for 85 per cent of the picture's length the story depends entirely upon camera action.

Whether this somewhat exaggerated percentage stemmed from economy or from a convinced theory of aesthetics, the proportion is a valid one. *White Zombie* has a good balance and is more cinematic and exciting than the much larger-budgeted *Dracula* of less than two years before.

To most people, however, *White Zombie* is a terrible film. Audiences tend to scoff at it, and even many horror buffs do not accept it graciously. The acting by the hero and heroine is poor, and the missionary (Joseph Cawthorne) is good if one disregards that divine's somewhat Yiddish accent.

Beaumont (Robert Frazer), although a bit stagy, fits the part well with his slightly dissipated good looks and splendid voice. When he and Bela have a scene to themselves, the film reaches a higher plane than most horror films. Perhaps this plane is corny to some people but not to this writer. Although blemished, the film has its moments. And some of these are tremendously imaginative. The film remains valuable for its almost pristine fablelike plot, its rather pure gothicism in story, attitude, and setting, and even at times in the poetry of its dialogue. Above all, the film provides Bela with an excellent role, and he in turn gives it an intensity that perhaps no other actor but John Barrymore could have accomplished. He is the demonic villain in the best of the gothic-romantic tradition.

Lugosi's next film stemmed from a more modern tradition, though it too had its forebear—radio. One of the more popular radio shows at this time was *Chandu the Magician*, a series of exploits broadcast five nights a week. The title character, a master of Yoga, devotes most of his time to quelling the forces of evil. Fox studios thought that a film based on this idea would share the success of the radio series. After some extravagant sets were created by William Cameron Menzies (who also codirected), the film was begun on July 14, 1932. Lugosi's reputation for diabolic nastiness had obviously spread, for he was chosen for the villain and given third billing under Edmund Lowe and Irene Ware (later to play in *The Raven*). When premiered in September at the Roxy Theater in New York City, the film proved that the cinematic hand was less deft than the radio's voice, for the reviews were, to say the least, not adulatory. The *Herald Tribune* probably summed up the picture most accurately: "If *Chandu* were bad enough to be funny, it would have its virtues, but it has the misfortune to fall dismally between the burlesque and the dramatic, with the result that it offers scant entertainment." [20] *Variety* concurred by saying that the film

> carries the fantastic, the inconsistent and the ludicrous to the greatest
> lengths yet achieved by the screen. Were it to be taken seriously,

[20] September, 1932.

The former Romeo in his home, seemingly at peace, 1932.

Bela and his "devil" dogs, 1932.

there'd be no enjoyment for anyone. If it's accepted strictly as hoke growing out of the development of the horror cycle, it's not so bad, but it's still hoke.[21]

As the film opens, a native hits a gong (evoking the later J. Arthur Rank trademark), the word "Chandu" appears, and then a hand moves across the screen wiping on and off the credits. The camera tracks through miniature mountains to a glowing castle on top of a peak and then dissolves to the interior of a Near Eastern temple, where Chandu seems to be receiving his doctorate in Yoga. As the New York *Sun* reviewer put it: "Why he has gone there I don't quite know, unless he possibly wanted a vaudeville career." The recipient of the degree is a stolid, bland, unemotional Edmund Lowe, a far cry from the bawdy Sergeant Quirt, whom he played in *What Price Glory* and its sequels. A less effective portrayal could hardly be conceived. He plays Chandu with a flat voice and expressionless face, lacks a sense of mystery, and casts a pall of dullness over the film without ever giving any inner sense of his supernatural powers. He seems incapable of besting Lugosi in a battle of wills and would not even be an odds-on favorite against one of the camels inhabiting the set.

Lowe quickly proves that his powers exceed his personality in what one assumes is his graduation exam. To prove his mastery, he performs the Indian rope trick, projects an astral self, and walks through fire. The high priest approves of his unlikely candidate's gifts and tells him that "the world needs thee" to fight for good and to oppose evil—in particular, the outrageous and dastardly evil of Roxor, (Lugosi), whose diabolically resplendent face promptly appears in a nearby crystal ball. The priest tells Chandu that fate has chosen him to vanquish Roxor, who with "the brain of a madman" is a "human monster" who lives near the third cataract of the Nile and who is not only plotting the doom of the entire world (no small task at that time) but also interfering with Chandu's sister and in-laws. Chandu's brother-in-law, with apparently nothing better to do in his spare time, had developed a death ray, and Roxor, of course, finds this instrument just what he needs for his nefarious scheme of world domination.

After this exposition the scene shifts to a laboratory, where the brother-in-law, played by Henry B. Walthall, is working on his death ray. He checks the electrical equipment—a fine array of hums, buzzes,

[21] October 3, 1932.

flashes, tubes, and dials—and turns on his ray (really a disintegrating ray), which soon proves its efficacy by dissolving a giant block of stone. Walthall enjoys his success for only a few seconds, because he is captured by Roxor's men and taken to an Egyptian temple. There Roxor tries to force the inventor to make a giant ray capable of destroying half the world. (Roxor's theory is that the other half would then capitulate.)

Chandu finds out that Roxor is at a wine cellar in an Egyptian town. The password at the door is "Open in the name of Osiris, blind eyes, sealed lips, death is." This mouthful, intoned by Chandu, has its effect, for he is allowed to enter. Meantime, Princess Nadji arrives, and Roxor tells her that with this ray he will blow up a dam and drown the people. She accuses him of wanting to be Pharaoh. But that is not enough for Roxor: "I shall be greater than any Pharaoh!" He will reduce civilization to ashes and return man to primitive savagery. "Then there will be only one supreme intelligence: Me!" Roxor tries to keep the Princess with him, but Chandu hypnotizes Roxor's henchmen, starts a fire, and walks through it, escaping with the girl. Although Chandu is in love with the Princess, he shows absolutely no enthusiasm (although he is supposed to) and tenders his affections to her as if his vital organs had already been bathed in the death ray.

Roxor, in the meantime, is still trying to convince the inventor to give over the secret of the ray. When he refuses, Roxor has his daughter sold at a slave market. A delectable item, with only a slight gauze covering her breasts, she understandably fetches a high price. But the bidder is Chandu, who has transformed himself into an old Arab and pays with coins that change into frogs when brought back to Roxor. Outraged that the girl has escaped, Roxor finally concludes that Chandu's gifts are a result of hypnotism and that if the mystic's eyes could only be covered, he would be helpless.

Soon after, Chandu is attacked by tear gas, and both the Princess and he are captured and put in a cell. "Well, Chandu, we meet at last," Roxor exults. Chandu is manacled and put in an Egyptian coffin. When warned that yogis can live for days, Roxor replies, "But not under water." He has the weighted coffin thrown into the Nile. Meantime, Roxor has imprisoned the inventor's family and threatens them with death. To save them, the inventor capitulates and helps Roxor ready the machine. "At last I am king of all," Roxor says. Grasping the death ray, he exults, "That lever is my sceptre." He

The evil Roxor, in *Chandu the Magician* (1932).

envisions the destruction of the world. In superimposition, Lugosi's face laughs as cities are annihilated in puffs of smoke. "All that live will know me as Master and tremble at my word! Paris—city of fools—England—" He draws himself up: "They shall bow before me, worship me, Roxor!"

At this supreme moment Chandu returns from having freed himself from his by now soggy coffin, and the battle of wills commences. It does not last long. The director does not allow even one close-up of Lugosi's eyes because they are far more impressive than Chandu's dull orbs. In fact, Roxor succumbs to Chandu's spell with hardly a murmur. Frozen to his machine, which the inventor had, of course, sabotaged, Roxor, instead of coming into his kingdom, is blown into kingdom come, while a happy ending is enjoyed by everyone else.

Chandu the Magician is an odd combination of some excellent sets mixed in with some rather patently cheap and obvious studio mockups. But if the art direction saves the film at times, the acting does not. The performances alternate between the acceptable and the ridiculous. Of course the main burden rests on the inadequate shoulders of Edmund Lowe as Chandu, and the film picks up only when Lugosi enters. The as-usual-snide *New Yorker* did not sense any improvement. The film "is about yogis and death rays and the Nile, but none of the atrocities described seems as fearful as the acting." [22] Often the action is filmed in economical long shots rather than in more carefully planned and time-consuming closer shots. Probably some of this method comes from Menzies, who conceived of cinema more as a scenic delight than an actor's paradise. The camera does not punctuate or enhance Lugosi's more evil sayings or capture his intense eyes and dramatic facial expressions. As a result, he plays his scenes rather broadly. One review said: "Mr. Lugosi, the original movie Dracula, still had his property room satanic look and his same old clutching hand school of acting." [23]

True, Lugosi seems more theatrical here than in his other performances of the period, but this was a consequence of the direction. Had he underplayed, the film would have been impossibly dull. In spite of his melodramatic gestures (it is difficult to underact lines like "I'll be greater than Pharaoh!"), he still comes off much better than anyone else in the cast. His megalomaniac scientist is far more evil than the

[22] October 8, 1932.
[23] New York *Sun*, October 4, 1932.

mild Dr. Mirakle of *Murders in the Rue Morgue*. Here he is unmitigated evil, obsessed with ruling not only his private domain (like Dr. Vollin in *The Raven*) but also the whole world. This role he would often play in the ensuing years.

Lugosi next appeared in one of the sickest and cruelest and yet most fascinating films of the horror genre, Paramount's *Island of Lost Souls*, directed by Erle C. Kenton and released in January, 1933. Starring Charles Laughton as the scientist (it was his fifth film, all made in 1932), the picture was based on H. G. Wells' gruesome *Isle of Dr. Moreau*. It was the tale of a scientist living on an isolated and otherwise uninhabited island who attempts to prove his theory that "all animal life is tending towards human form." By means of plastic surgery, blood transfusions, and gland extracts, he has succeeded in speeding up the process of evolution in various animals. He has already created a panther woman, an ape-man, a dog-man, and other equally weird beings who have the powers of speech and thought. Lugosi portrayed the small role of the leader of the furred creatures, called "the Sayer of the Law."

The cast was quite a menagerie. As Laughton would later recall, "I remember each horror and monster had more hair than the one before. Hair was all over the place. I was dreaming of hair. I even thought I had hair in my food." [24]

Dr. Moreau could easily have been portrayed as one of those Continental scientists who grandiloquently and passionately carry out their mad dreams. Laughton plays the role far differently. His Dr. Moreau is a logical, albeit cruel, scientist with overtones of the sexual deviant. There is something slimy and unhealthy about him. As the *Herald Tribune* phrased it, he was "an engaging combination of child, madman, and genius." [25] With his little tuft of beard, thin mustache, and soft, almost infantile face, he is an excellent example of what Hannah Arendt described as "the banality of evil." Laughton, in fact, modeled his makeup on an eye specialist he had visited several times. Moreau is not in the mode of the Promethean scientists of Lugosi's type. Lugosi was much more old-fashioned, an obsessed experimenter, part poet, part madman, part scientist, but by no means a grotesque case history out of Krafft-Ebing. Lugosi is the mad scientist we would

[24] Kurt Singer, *The Laughton Story* (Philadelphia, John C. Winston Co., 1954), p. 103.
[25] January 13, 1933.

like to envision; Laughton is more the type he might actually be. Laughton soft-pedals many of his lines and with his sardonic humor, nonchalance, and casualness gives them a kind of menace even more disturbing than Lugosi's. When Laughton says, "Mr. Parker, do you know what it means to feel like God?" his gentle manner makes the presumption even more sinister and hateful. Most reviewers favored Laughton's approach, and he received a good amount of praise, though the film itself was liked less well. It was considered tasteless and gruesome and perhaps even blasphemous in America, and in England, where vivisection was a sensitive issue, the film was banned outright.

The story begins as an American (Richard Arlen) is abandoned on Dr. Moreau's island along with a shipment of animals. The doctor escorts him around the island, where strange creatures cower in the bushes. They look upon the doctor as their Creator, the Being who made them, the One who heals them, and He who runs the House of Pain, the laboratory where the doctor has cruelly but successfully advanced the evolutionary process. Moreau is a god to his "men," and the leader of them is the Sayer of the Law (Lugosi), who leads his fellow creatures in a curious litany:

> LAUGHTON: What is the law?
> LUGOSI: Not to eat meat, that is the law; are we not men?
> CHORUS: Are we not men?
> LAUGHTON: What is the law?
> LUGOSI: Not to spill blood, that is the law; are we not men?
> CHORUS: Are we not men?

Toward the end of the film Moreau is forced to use his gun to kill, thus breaking the law that he himself created and causing at first consternation among his creatures and then complete rebellion.

> LAUGHTON: What is the law?
> LUGOSI: Law—no more.
> LAUGHTON: What is the law?
> LUGOSI: Not to spill blood.
> OTHER: He tell me spill blood!
> LAUGHTON: What is the law!!?
> LUGOSI: Law no more.

The creatures, aware now that they are "Things! Part Man! Part Beast!" attack, take Moreau off to his House of Pain, and there vivisect

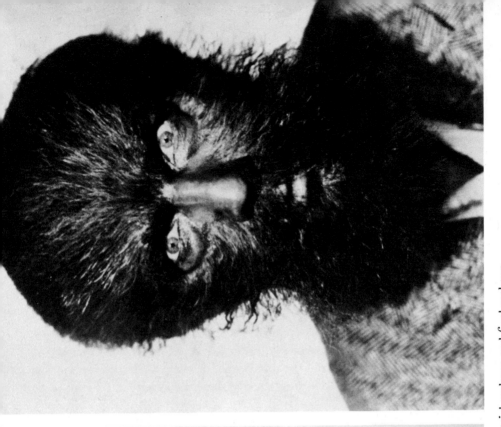

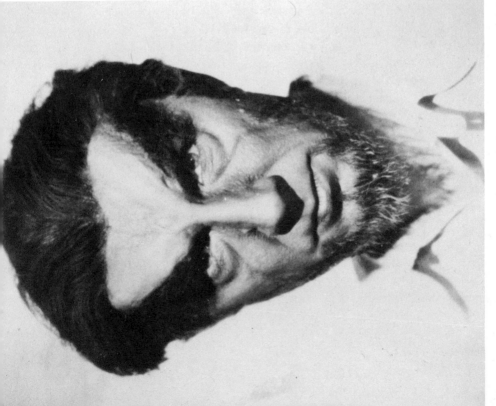

Island of Lost Souls (1932): trial makeup and final makeup.

him. This ending, as horrific as the one in *Freaks*, was indeed a shocker and too strong for the taste of 1933.

This role did not aid Lugosi's career. Although he was adequate as the ape-man, the character was too simple to reveal any new facets of his acting abilities. It does indicate, however, that the reticence he had shown in refusing to appear as the Frankenstein monster because of the heavy makeup had now left him, but it happened too late, for the fame that Karloff had won as the monster stayed with him in the ensuing years, and Lugosi, despite all his efforts, could never quite get back to being Number One again.

In the last week of January, 1933, another film with Lugosi, *The Death Kiss*, opened in New York. This murder mystery begins as a girl steps out of an auto containing two men and kisses another man just coming out of a nightclub. The surprised recipient tells the doorman that he does not know the girl, and then is shot down by guns from the car. A voice then yells, "Cut," the camera reveals that we are in a movie studio, and the director calls for a retake, complaining that the death did not look realistic—and then discovers that the actor really is dead.

Everyone, of course, is suspected. The police investigate, but as usual overlook clues that are obvious even to a young scenario writer (David Manners), who sets out to investigate on his own. He is fond of the heroine, who is under suspicion because the dead man was her former husband. Only after two more murders is the crime finally solved. Lugosi played Joseph Steiner, one of the studio executives, and, as in *The Black Camel*, he looks villainous enough to distract viewers from recognizing the real killer. The fact that Lugosi was used as a decoy was praised by the reviewer for the New York *Times* (January 28, 1933):

> Perhaps the most ingenious element in the film is that which makes Bela Lugosi a leading suspect up to the very end. Mr. Lugosi's reputation in these cinema crimes makes it almost impossible for the amateur sleuths out front to dismiss him from suspicion. As a smoke screen, Mr. Lugosi is rather more effective than he has been recently in the more showy roles of ghoulish madmen.

However, in years to come, Lugosi's effectiveness as a red herring was lessened because he took that role so often.

Although Lugosi was probably foolish to follow prestige films with a poverty-row quickie like *The Death Kiss*, the picture does not look as cheap as it was. It took place at a movie studio, and therefore many scenes could be made without having to build sets. It had a good cast; in fact, three of the principals of *Dracula* were in it, Edward van Sloan (Van Helsing), David Manners (Harker), and, of course, Lugosi. The film, however, is by no means a horror picture. Instead, it is a reasonably well-plotted and motivated detective story and has some good suspense. Reviewers preferred these saner, more normal pictures and considered the film far superior to *White Zombie*, which in a sense it was. But *White Zombie* had some imaginative moments and, despite its dreadful cast, had Lugosi in a great role. *The Death Kiss* gave him only a few minutes of screen time. Lugosi was faced with a dilemma. Some of the films in which he had done remarkable work (such as *Murders in the Rue Morgue* and *White Zombie*) were not received as well as more normal but less interesting productions. Unsure of his own judgment and afraid that his fame would not last, he diluted his reputation by accepting, seemingly, whatever parts were offered. Audiences grew leery of his name on a marquee, not knowing whether he had the lead or just a minor red-herring role. A trade ad for *The Death Kiss* is a case in point. "He made the two greatest box-office pictures for the exhibitor in *Dracula* and *White Zombie*. Here is the third."

At this time Lugosi left the horror genre temporarily to play a comic heavy in another Paramount picture, *International House*, released in May, 1933. Starring W. C. Fields, Burns and Allen, Peggy Hopkins Joyce, and a host of other personalities, the film is a hodgepodge of miscellaneous acts held together by the flimsiest of plots. Dr. Wong, an Oriental inventor, is staying at the International House in Wu Hu, China, and demonstrating an early form of television called a radioscope, which he plans to sell to the highest bidder. Among the host of adventurers and international wheeler-dealers who arrive are a bumbling Stuart Erwin (from an American electric company), a money-hungry and often-married Peggy Hopkins Joyce, and General Petronovich, her former but still-jealous husband (Lugosi). In the beginning of the film the General is interviewed by a newsman and asked whether he has had a nice trip. "I *always* have a nice trip," he answers positively, and then goes on to explain that he is "General Nicholas Branovsky Petronovich, formerly of the Russian Imperial

Guard, at present General Manager of the Moscow Utilities Company." Fixing his tie and smiling for the newsreel camera, he pompously announces that "I am here to buy the rights for my company," and then strides away and falls over the tripod holding the microphone.

Later Peggy Hopkins Joyce checks in at the hotel, where she is accosted by her ex-husband. When she says that they are divorced, he replies, "Ah, that means nothing. In my country you're still my wife."

"Nicky, darling, don't go dramatic on me. Everything is finished."

"Never! Any man who comes between us, *he* will be finished," Lugosi says in tones worthy of Count Dracula.

In an attempt to prevent the American representative from bidding on the radioscope, the General connives with the local health authorities to have him quarantined. But they make a mistake and instead quarantine the whole hotel, and the General cannot get in. A soldier recommends the Lotus Garden Hotel across the street. "That horrible place," Lugosi laments. But he checks in there anyhow and that night watches Fields—who has arrived at the hotel and cannot get a room—sneak into Miss Joyce's suite. As angry as if Van Helsing had dropped him in the midst of a crop of wolfbane, Lugosi grabs his gun and tries desperately to pry open the window, but it is stuck. A few minutes later, discovering that it is just latched, he easily lifts the window and aims at Fields, who meanwhile has crawled out onto the balcony to elude the hotel manager. The gun barrel, however, has been bent by its use as a crowbar, and the bullet misses Fields. The sight of Lugosi glaring impotently at his ineffectual gun is not easily forgotten!

The next morning the raging General calls his wife. "There's no use lying. I myself through the window saw everything." Getting more and more violent, he says, "I could take his throat in my hands and I will squeeze and break it." At this point the telephone receiver disintegrates in his hand. Determined to enter the hotel one way or another, the General gets a number of men to break down the hotel doors. In the meantime, the quarantine has been removed. The General and his men, with a monstrous battering ram, head for the hotel doors, but as they rush forward, the doors are opened, and unable to stop, they all smash into the lobby's main desk. Dressed in a snappy suit, wearing a straw hat, and brandishing a cane furiously over his head, Petronovich leads his nonplussed entourage through the entire

"In my country you're still my wife," he says in *International House* (1933).

"That horrible place?"

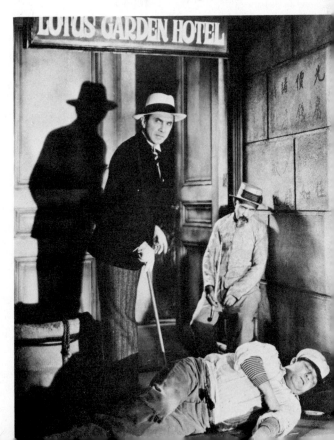

hotel in search of Fields, who finally escapes with Peggy in an autogyro.

The film is both insane and inane, but suffused with a lively, comic air of improvisation. Fields, his usual Dirty Old Self, makes a few comments about a pussy in his car, looks over Peggy Hopkins Joyce as if he were buying a tenderloin in a meat market, and brings a pleasant and honest air of corruption to the whole business. Franklin Pangborn, as the effeminate hotel manager fluttering his eyebrows and hands in indignation as Fields makes a shambles of the hotel, contributes to the fun. Lugosi, too, seems to enjoy his part and, whether as indignant husband or irate pursuer, added considerably to the humor of the picture and showed that he could successfully play "straight" parts when given a chance.

Life was not all movies for Lugosi. In his off-hours he did some reading, walked his dogs (he was quite fond of them), and attended soccer matches. In fact he even bestowed the "Bela Lugosi Award" for the best players. Bela did not socialize much with his fellow actors. English was still a difficult tongue for him, and he preferred spending his time with fellow Hungarians with whom he could laugh, joke, drink, and reminisce about the good old days.

Lugosi was a busy man. Agents called, contracts had to be signed, his house managed, and fan mail acknowledged if not always personally answered. He needed a secretary who could translate for him and who could find the right English words to express his thoughts. He hired Lillian Arch, a girl born of Hungarian parents, who could handle both languages fluently. She typed letters, tried to keep account of his money and appointments, and occasionally drove him around; Bela persisted in not learning how to drive. Lillian earned $16.50 a week in 1932. Slowly the relationship changed, and on January 31, 1933, in Las Vegas the fifty-year-old actor married the twenty-one-year-old girl. This fourth marriage was Lugosi's longest one, lasting a shaky twenty years. A pleasant, attractive, efficient, and obviously devoted young lady, she embarked on an exciting but stormy existence. Lugosi never received very high salaries, but still the couple were financially comfortable. In later years she might worry where the next dollar was coming from. Bela would worry too, but he would not worry enough to take care of his money. He would still live high and trust somehow in fate to see him through. If Lillian did not get her hands on the money right away, Bela might scurry out, treat everybody in a local

Bela and his fourth wife, Lillian.

Hungarian restaurant, and then buy a new stamp for his collection. But in these early thirties his services were still in demand, and life was hectic but fun. Admittedly Lugosi moped about being typecast as a horror star, but he was certainly enjoying the rewards of his profession. In this period he was at the top of his form. He still had his looks, his health, and his fame. Although he had already made serious mistakes in the management of his stardom, he was not yet suffering for his excesses. In fact, the next two or three years would prove the apex of his career, at least artistically. Only in 1936 did his first setback occur. And it would not be his worst.

In February, 1933, Lugosi won the title role in Columbia's *He Lived to Kill*. The name of the picture was soon changed, and in June it appeared as *Night of Terror*. The film was more terrible than terrifying. After conveying the information that there have been twelve killings, with each body having a newspaper clipping pinned to it, the plot really starts to grind away.

Night of Terror (1933).

In a mansion full of the usual accouterments—secret panels, menacing butler, ugly maniac murderer, and comic black servant—there is a lot of prowling around at night and suspicious peeking through doors. This old-house, reading-of-the-will mystery features a touch of pseudoscience by having a man plan to bury himself alive in a suspended-animation experiment. Lugosi plays a mysterious Indian servant who sports a turban and one earring and is given to portentous observations such as "Death is very near!" He lurks a lot. When the master of the house is killed, his will is read, and Lugosi and another servant, a woman who "sees many things" during trances, receive a large amount of money and will receive even more if the others die. At a séance the "seer," about to reveal the identity of the murderer, is killed and Lugosi arrested. But the coffin in which the scientist lies in a state of suspended animation is found to be empty; it is discovered that the killer had used his phony catatonic state as an alibi to do the two murders, and he is apprehended. Meantime, in the cellar a reporter has killed the maniac who had committed the original twelve murders. Then, alone in the cellar, the corpse gets up, walks toward the camera, points at us, and says, "I'm the maniac! If you dare tell anyone how this picture ends, who the murderer is, I'll climb into your bedroom tonight and tear you limb from limb. I'll haunt you. Good night. Sleep tight. Heh, heh, heh." Heh!

Although Lugosi's performance was not criticized, the film was. "Photography only fair, sound not of the best and direction uninspired. Just an all-around miss that still makes a good enough offering for cheap spots," said *Variety*.[26] When the film was first shown, it "drew mirth from the action-loving audience." [27] Needless to say, such a film hardly added to Lugosi's reputation. Nor was Bela happy about his third red-herring role in a few years. Once again he complained in the press sheets for the film about being typecast and bluntly said, "I can blame it all on that play [*Dracula*]." Lugosi stated that he hoped to retire from films soon and settle down on a little farm. The interviewer found the image of the ex-count among chickens difficult to accept.

Lugosi also found time during 1933 to appear in a twelve-part serial called *The Whispering Shadow*, made by Mascot. Lugosi starred as Professor Strang, a magician who operates a waxworks; his costars

[26] June 27, 1933.
[27] New York *Herald Tribune*, June, 1933.

were Henry B. Walthall and Karl Dane. Like most serials, its recipe consisted of chases and fistfights with an occasional dash of death-ray murders thrown in to add to the flavor. Roy D'Arcy, wearing a perpetual leer that he had learned from Von Stroheim in *The Merry Widow*, and Bela, standing often in front of a vast array of electrical equipment, are the prime suspects. Despite the fact that Lugosi was given top billing and that the entire serial lasted four hours, the picture made little use of its master of horror. His sparse dialogue did not give him the opportunity to wrest diabolical implications from his lines. The serial's one virtue was that it kept the audience in suspense. The real villain was not revealed until the last minutes and he, of course, was the most unlikely of them all, and hardly credible if one thought about the previous plotting. The Mascot studio was convinced, and rightly so, that audiences over the three months the serial took to play would not worry about character consistency or motivation.

Universal as early as 1933 was planning a sequel to *Frankenstein*, called *The Return of Frankenstein*, and had vague plans to star Karloff and Lugosi in it, but the project was postponed.

Although Lugosi already seemed doomed to play just horror parts, he had a brief chance to escape the mold. Fox was making another Foreign Legion film called *The Devil's in Love*, directed by William Dieterle. Lugosi, who had appeared in many bit parts for Fox, decided to forget his stardom and return to his former status. He might, indeed, have been an afterthought, for a newspaper clipping of June 23, 1933, states that he "has been added to the cast." [28] His small part was uncredited and has been forgotten, for almost no one seems to know he was in the film at all. Lugosi is an officer who is the prosecuting attorney at the court-martial of a man falsely accused of a crime. Lugosi addresses his questions in the courtroom in an effective manner, smiling cynically as the defendant offers honest but unconvincing answers. Lugosi's facial expressions and vocal inflections radiate his Continental experience and show him as a man of the world who could not possibly believe the defendant. His performance proves that he fitted well into the foreign milieu and could essay roles other than horror ones, but unfortunately his brief bit not only did not convince anybody, it was not even noticed.

With no new films in the offing and anxious to renew his contacts in

[28] New York *Evening Post.*

the theater, Lugosi returned to New York in the last week of July, 1933, and a few days later started rehearsals for a Broadway production, *Murder at the Vanities*, a musical mystery in which he received fourth billing when it opened on September 12. Plans had been made with Paramount for Lugosi to repeat his role on the screen,[29] but they were shelved. Even though the play did not create any enthusiasm among New York playgoers, Paramount made a film of it anyhow and released it in May, 1934, but without Lugosi.

The plot of *Murder at the Vanities* was hardly original. During a performance of Earl Carroll's *Vanities*, a woman is murdered. Inspector Ellery investigates and declares that he will solve the crime between the Saturday matinee and the evening performance. Surrounding the mystery plot were numerous musical and variety specialties such as tap dancers, roller-skating acrobats, and a fan number with "four rows of blonde chorus girls tossing uneasily to languorous rhythms on a strange edifice that fills the center of the stage." [30] The first act concluded with what must have been the apogee of camp: a maypole of neon light tubes.

One critic wrote that "Bela Lugosi walks around the stage in a Lexington Avenue Swami's costume. He has a dagger that he uses every once in a while in a blackout. Women scream and men murmur tosh!" [31] John Mason Brown described Lugosi as "stalking around ominously under a green spotlight." [32] Lugosi remained with the cast until November, 1933. Considering that he was a major Hollywood figure, his decision to appear in this musical showed little more restraint and judgment than his choice of some of his movie roles. Certainly the play does not sound like a production that would enhance his reputation, but it did bring him back to Broadway.

After leaving the cast of *Murder at the Vanities*, Lugosi decided to pick up some extra cash and headed a vaudeville bill at Loew's State Theater beginning on December 9, 1933. He offered "the most thrilling parts" of *Dracula* for his variety vehicle. "His act, somewhat more novel than the ordinary headline piece, should be a treat for variety-goers." [33]

Lugosi was then announced as having acquired for spring production

---

[29] Los Angeles *Times*, July 29, 1933.
[30] New York *Times*, September 13, 1933.
[31] New York *Herald Tribune*, September 13, 1933.
[32] New York *Evening Post*, September 13, 1933.
[33] New York *Herald Tribune*, December 9, 1933.

in Chicago a play by S. J. Warshawsky entitled *Pagan Fury*. "Lugosi's role will be something apart from those he has been doing in the films for several years." [34] He was to play the role of a modern painter. Although the play was scheduled for April, he never did appear in it. Instead, he went back to Hollywood, where in the next two years he created some of his greatest roles.

Universal, where Lugosi returned, had not done well with *Murders in the Rue Morgue,* but the studio decided to take another chance on the strength of Edgar Allan Poe. Back in December, 1932, Universal's writers, Stanley Bergerman and Jack Cunningham, had provided a treatment combining "The Fall of the House of Usher" and "The Black Cat," presumably under the impression that two stories put together were better than one. This concoction was called *The Brain Never Dies.* Two rather strange recluses, Roderick and Madeline Usher, live in an old New England house. They are attended by Dr. Alonzo Metta, who believes that the brain never dies and that it can be put in another body. He plans to transfer the brain of a sickly but world-renowned scientist into the body of an athlete, and the brain of a courtesan into that of a co-ed. For a friend, Dr. Metta has a black cat, whose skull contains half a human brain. The doctor arranges for all his unknowing subjects to stay at the Ushers' place, but the co-ed's boyfriend gets suspicious and arrives with the police just in time to prevent the brain transplant. Metta's cat, developing a sudden hatred for its owner, pushes him into the ruins of the crumbling house and the evil doctor is killed.

This film was never made, but the idea of the black cat seemed to have multiple lives, if not exactly nine, and again tried to claw its way to the screen. This time Universal followed Poe's story more closely and planned to star Boris Karloff as Edgar Doe, a man who, through too much drinking, becomes a sadistic brute who tortures both wife and cat. One night he gouges out the cat's eyes, strangles the animal, and ultimately picks up another cat. Finally he kills his wife and buries her in a wall. When the police come to investigate, Doe shows off the new wall in the cellar. The cry of a cat is heard, the wall torn down, and the body of the wife discovered with the cat perched on it.

Somehow this treatment of Poe's story did not seem very appealing, and so Edgar Ulmer, who was to direct the film, thought up a new plot

[34] New York *Times,* January 15, 1934.

of his own and submitted the script to Universal in the first week of February, 1934.

The scenario was based partially on the activities of Aleister Crowley, a British citizen who had always been interested in magic and the summoning of spirits. Calling himself the Beast of the Apocalypse, he took pains to build a reputation for himself as a symbol of evil. In the early 1920's he and his followers established the Abbey of Thelema in a Sicilian farmhouse. From time to time, newspapers carried sensational stories about outrages committed there during devil-worship ceremonies. At one of them a cat was killed at the altar and its blood drunk by the various worshipers. Sometime after, one of the participants died, and it was rumored that there had been an actual human sacrifice. In 1933 an artist named Nina Hammett published her autobiography, *Laughing Torso,* in which she described some of the weird activities. Crowley, in need of money, sued the author and publisher. The resulting trial was sensational. Crowley himself took the stand, and his revelations caused the press to refer to him as "the wickedest man in the world."

The headlines of Crowley's unsavory activities were current when Ulmer concocted his script. He had come from Germany, where he had once been the assistant of F. W. Murnau, who had directed *Nosferatu, The Last Laugh,* and *Faust.* Murnau had been fascinated by evil, and perhaps this concern rubbed off onto Ulmer. In any case, Ulmer fed as much of his own interests into the film as possible. He decided that the villain should be an architect, and named him Hjlamar Poelzig, in memory of Hans Poelzig, a scene designer who had created the sets for *Der Golem* (1920). Ulmer also helped design the modern Bauhaus-style sets used in the film.

While Ulmer was indulging himself with set designing and scriptwriting, he had only one demand from Universal: that Karloff should have the lead. Soon, however, another bright idea entered. Why not star both Karloff and Lugosi? Bela, who had been in New York and who was guest of honor at the Hungarian Actors Ball at the Pennsylvania Hotel on February 10, returned to Hollywood.[35] Lugosi went to see Ulmer. For a change, language was no barrier, for both could speak German. Lugosi, as he later said, persuaded him that he "could play a romantic or at least a benign role." [36] The script was

[35] New York *Herald Tribune,* February 16, 1934.
[36] Press sheets for *The Return of Chandu,* summer, 1934.

changed and the setting switched from Sicily to Hungary in order to make better use of Lugosi's accent and to avoid any lawsuits with Crowley. The script gyrated a bit more, other writers were called in, and shooting finally began at the end of the month, although somewhat chaotically, for many additional changes were made on the set. Lugosi managed to get himself a larger part than had been originally intended.

Universal took advantage of the coup of its two horror stars together in subsequent advertisements:

> *The Daddy of 'em all!.* The Monster of *Frankenstein* plus the Monster of *Dracula,* plus the "monstrousness" of Edgar Allan Poe—all combined by the master makers of screen mysteries to give you the absolute apex in supershivery! . . . . There are no two ways about it—it's tremonstrous! [37]

The film was by no means so "tremonstrous"; in fact, it had far less effect than *Dracula* or *Frankenstein* in terms of sending shivers down

[37] *Motion Picture Herald,* April 21, 1934.

On the set of *The Black Cat* with Edgar Ulmer, 1934.

the spine. Its main problem (and virtue) is tone. The film, for all of its extravagant action, is basically a serious one, interested perhaps more in depicting the malaise of the survivors of the First World War than in attempting to horrify, even though all the ingredients are there. It refers with furious abandon to a man's pursuit of his rival, a bus accident, "a morbid fear of cats," the killer of another man's wife who has married her daughter, mummified women in glass cases, a mediumistic trance, a heavily mined fort, devil worship, a chess game over the destiny of a woman, and a scene in which a kindly man skins alive the villain and dynamites himself and others with him. Although *The Black Cat* is at times imaginatively directed, with a good visual sense, there are too many failures with the script to have it make much sense or to give its characters some kind of cohesion. One of the advertisements for the film, in light of the story's failings, had a delightful double meaning: "two superfiends in a ghastly plot against each other." Despite the story and its barrage of incidents, the picture provides some excellent dramatic situations and dialogue, and remains one of the best films of its two stars. In later years Ulmer claimed that Universal had cut the film severely. This might account for some of its confusion.

As the film opens, a just-married American couple are riding on a train through Hungary. Into their compartment comes Dr. Vitus Werdergast (Lugosi). When a suitcase begins to fall from the top shelf, Lugosi leaps up and grabs it. "It is, after all, better to be frightened than to be crushed," he says in his own inimitable way. The young husband (David Manners) asks Vitus whether he is traveling to Marmaros for sport. "Perhaps," he replies ominously, "I go to visit an old friend." Later that night the husband sees Lugosi lightly touch the sleeping girl's hair. "I beg your indulgence, my friend. Eighteen years ago I left a girl—so like your lovely wife—to go to war. Kaiser and country, you know. She was my wife." The sound of the train comes through, and Vitus continues. "Have you ever heard of Kulgaar? It is a prison below Omsk." Lugosi looks intense. "Many men have gone there; few have returned. *I* have returned. After fifteen years, I have returned." Few actors could say these lines as effectively. Lugosi's role here is one not unlike himself. He is svelte, polished, intelligent, and melancholy. A curious sadness and resignation are reflected in his characterization, one that is unique in his many Hollywood roles. Lugosi here is a sympathetic character, a man who has been betrayed

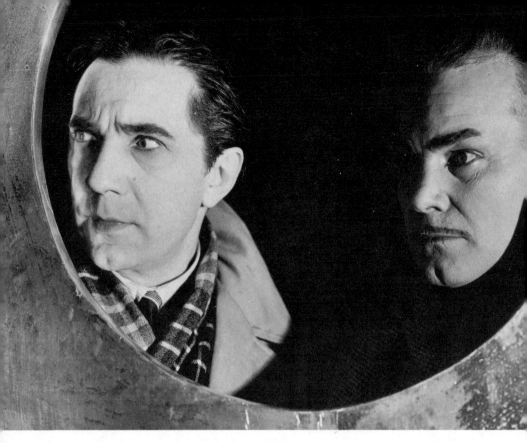

Dr. Vitus Werdergast and his servant, in *The Black Cat.*

by his friend and unjustly imprisoned for fifteen years, a man who has lost his wife and child, a man who is going back to find his past and revenge as well. Despite the fact that Lugosi, for a change, is playing the role of a good person, there are still overtones of the demonic that come through.

As Vitus and the couple leave the train in a heavy rainstorm, Vitus' servant joins them, and they enter a rickety bus. The driver explains that the river ran red with blood as thousands of men died in this famous battlefield of the First World War. The bus slips on the rainy road, the driver is killed, and the couple and Vitus and his servant enter Poelzig's place. On top of the hill where the fort once was, Hjalmar Poelzig (Karloff) has built a Bauhaus mansion. For audiences of 1934 this place was weird, for it was all modern, bright, and clean-lined. As Werdergast later describes it, "a masterpiece of construction built upon the ruins of the masterpiece of destruction—the masterpiece of murder."

With David Manners, in *The Black Cat.*

Vitus dresses the wife's slight wounds and gives her a drug. Later, while Poelzig, the hero, and Vitus are talking, a black cat comes by, and Vitus shrinks back, horrified, and throws a knife and kills it. The cat here seems to have some effect, for the wife enters the room as if in a trance with a look of evil on her face. Werdergast explains that she has perhaps become "mediumistic, a vehicle for all the intangible forces in operation around her." The husband replies, "Sounds like a lot of supernatural baloney to me." Vitus answers in the famous lines: "Supernatural perhaps. Baloney, perhaps not. There are many things— under the sun." Although there is some attempt in the script to suggest that the evil from the cat has now entered into the girl or that she functions as some kind of medium, this aspect is almost entirely dropped; the black cat seems to have entered the film only to justify its title.

The action now shifts to the struggle between Vitus and Poelzig. When Vitus demands to see his wife, Poelzig leads him to the underground sections of the place.

The Black Cat, Lugosi and Karloff.

VITUS: I can still sense death in the air.
POELZIG: There is still death in the air. It is just as much undermined
   today as ever. . . ."

This is an observation that will bear fruit at the end of the film, but it is
also, in terms of the picture's odd theme, a philosophical comment
about the postwar situation.

Vitus is shown his wife, a mummified woman mounted vertically in
a glass case. Poelzig says, "You see, Vitus? I have cared for her
tenderly and well. You will find her almost as beautiful as when you
last saw her." Poelzig explains that she died two years after the
war—and adds "of pneumonia," although his slight blink betrays that
he is lying; he explains that the daughter also died, though in reality she
is quite alive and is, in fact, Poelzig's bride. Vitus is overcome with
emotion looking at his dead wife, and Lugosi, with tears in his eyes,
delivers his lines without the verb that was included in the script: "And
why she, why she like this?" Poelzig replies, "Is she not beautiful? I

wanted to have her beauty—always." Vitus cries out, "Lies, all lies," and takes out his gun. "You killed her, as I am about to kill you." But at this moment the black cat comes by, and Vitus collapses. Then, in probably the finest moment of the film, Karloff and Lugosi mount the stairs, the camera becomes subjective and sweeps over the concrete walls and staircases as Karloff beautifully reads the lines that give the film, amid all its horrors, a certain philosophical inflection:

> Come, Vitus. Are we men or are we children? Of what use are all these melodramatic gestures? You say your soul was killed and that you have been dead all these years. And what of me? Did we not both die here in Marmaros fifteen years ago? Are we any the less victims of the war than those whose bodies were torn asunder? Are we not both the living dead? And now you come to me—playing at being an avenging angel, childishly thirsting for my blood. We understand each other too well, we know too much of life. We shall play a little game, Vitus. A game of death, if you like . . .

It is a superb moment, one with class and *Weltschmerz,* one full of despair and disillusionment, one suggesting the pain and horror and ruined lives of those who fought in the war. This scene has an artistry and sophistication that the rest of the film unfortunately does not have. The maturity of this passage is soon belied by the plot. Poelzig decides to use the girl in his black mass, plays a game of chess for her destiny and wins over Vitus, kills Karin so that Vitus cannot see his daughter, has the servant knock out the husband and place him in a dungeon, and starts the ceremony. Vitus, with the aid of his servant, rescues the girl, but when he finds out that Poelzig has killed his daughter, he fights with Poelzig and ties him to his own embalming rack: "Did you ever see an animal skinned . . . ? That's what I'm going to do to you now. Tear the skin from your body—slowly—bit by bit. . . ." Meantime, the husband has escaped, and when he thinks that Vitus, who helps the girl, is hurting her, he shoots him. Vitus tells them to go. Then to Poelzig: "It's the red switch, isn't it, Hjalmar? The red switch ignites the dynamite; five minutes—Marmaros, you, and I, and your rotten cult will be no more. . . . It has been a good game." As the place explodes, the couple escapes.

The Black Cat is a hodgepodge of incidents and can best be enjoyed by not thinking about the plot's remarkable weaknesses. Vitus' killing of the cat, for example, does not surprise Poelzig in the least, which

The famous chess game.

means that Vitus must have had this strange problem fifteen years previously. Poelzig kills Karin, Vitus' daughter, despite the fact that she is, in Poelzig's words, "the very core and meaning of my life." And he does this without the slightest compunction or regret; it just happens. Poelzig refers to Vitus as "one of the world's greatest psychiatrists," despite the fact that the doctor could hardly have practiced his profession while residing in prison for fifteen years and serving in the army for three.

If the plot does not quite hold together, at least the characterizations must carry the burden. But they too are odd. Admittedly Lugosi wanted to get away from being typecast as a villain, but still he was far more suited to the devil cultist than Karloff. The British actor is curiously restrained and does not entirely suggest the sinister, despite the rather odd makeup. Lugosi was far more apt to design such a building, put attractive mummified women in cases, and commandeer a cult of evil-worshipers. Instead he is given an essentially weak part, but manages to invest it with a wonderful sense of gentlemanly unhappi-

An off-camera shot of Hollywood's gruesome twosome.

ness. A kindhearted man, Vitus is weak; he loses at chess, he seems unable to initiate action and plays second fiddle to Karloff's muted violin. As a result, the film is slow and lacks the dynamic interchanges that the two stars could have had and that would have given it excitement. There are some fine moments, as when the two climb the stairs and Karloff speaks about the living dead, but the film lacks pace and a straight and clear dramatic line of narrative and character conflict. The film seems to show that Ulmer was more interested in set design and mood and postwar disillusionment than he was in the tension between these two archenemies.

Despite its faults, *The Black Cat* remains one of Lugosi's more respectable films. At least he was working with a good director and had a better-than-average cast around him. The air of improvisation that hovers over the picture and occasionally weakens it also prompted the filming of a publicity scene that fortunately has been preserved. During the shooting of the chess game, someone decided to film the two great movie monsters as themselves. They glare at each other over the board, call each other Dracula and Frankenstein, and then break out laughing.

Shortly after the completion of *The Black Cat* Universal made the final revision of the patched-together script of *The Gift of Gab*, and soon shooting began. The studio asked Karloff and Lugosi to play bit parts in this routine musical. Directed by Karl Freund and released in September, 1934, it told the story of a glib radio announcer. As a reviewer put it, "There is more gab than gift to it." [38] In one section of the film a little group acts out a drama in a radio studio. Lugosi appeared as an Apache (a role harkening back to his Broadway success, *The Red Poppy*) and Karloff as "the phantom." The film did not capitalize on their presence in the cast nor should it have. Lugosi was seen for about two seconds standing in a closet! In the *Variety* listing of credits Karloff was twenty-sixth and Lugosi thirty-first of the thirty-one performers identified.

In the summer of 1934 Lugosi was hired by Principal Pictures to appear in a serial of the further multifarious but somewhat ridiculous adventures of Chandu, aptly called *The Return of Chandu*. Since the original idea of a master magician stemmed from the radio serial, it was not difficult for the studio to accommodate its format to a motion-picture serial as well. In 1934 this genre was hardly considered the highest

---

[38] William Boehnel, New York *World Telegram,* September, 1934.

or most prestigious aspect of the cinema, and it is questionable whether Lugosi was wise to become involved with the project. At least Lugosi was now allowed to play Chandu, his former character of Roxor having disintegrated along with the ray. Although his portrayal of the mystic was an improvement over Edmund Lowe's almost catatonic perform-ance, Lugosi does not exactly shine resplendently either. Although no one could by looks and demeanor be a more impressive master of the occult than Lugosi, Chandu, despite his magical powers, comes off as a rather normal fellow, an interpretation that no doubt stemmed from his characterization on the radio program. Lugosi, however, was pleased to get a part that did not make him a villain. He was quoted in the press sheets for the film as saying: "*The Black Cat* was the picture that secured for me my present stellar part in which I am at last permitted to appear before American audiences in a distinctly romantic charac-terization. . . ." Greta Garbo had once complained to Louis B. Mayer that she did not want to play any more "bad womens," and Lugosi probably did not want any more "bad mens" either. Although he won the "good" part in the Chandu serial, the plot is such a welter of complications and ridiculous twists and the direction so weak that the film ends up being one of his most hilarious productions. The master mystic seems unusually bewildered, as if someone had thrust him in front of the cameras and yelled that he do something without telling him exactly what. Indeed, the part is so weakly written that Chandu appears less like the master of events than the victim of them. He wanders around the sets—including the giant gates from *King Kong*—and at every difficulty invokes the aid of Yoga, his great teacher, and asks repeatedly for help in his "hour of need." However, Yoga must have a hearing problem, since despite the fact that Chandu needs his superior's help roughly every hour on the hour, no special aid seems forthcoming. Of all Lugosi's films, this one perhaps comes closest to being pure camp. In any case, the film kept him occupied during the summer of 1934. The following year, footage from this serial was reedited into the features *The Return of Chandu* (released in April, 1935) and *Chandu on the Magic Isle* (August, 1935). *Variety* said plainly that "Bela Lugosi is wasted. Even at that he stands shoulders above the rest." [39] Although he may have been the best, his hopes to escape typecasting came to naught, for he quickly returned to villainy.

[39] April 13, 1935.

A few months later, as a New Year's gift to New Yorkers, the management of New York's Rialto Theater presented Columbia's *The Best Man Wins*. The gift was not entirely appreciated. The plot dealt with deep-sea divers, two pals (one a crook, the other a cop), and an evil doctor (Lugosi) who uses a consuming interest in collecting rare fish as an excuse for his nefarious practice of smuggling jewels. Unfortunately most of the film was devoted to Edmund Lowe and Jack Holt amid swirling seas, bubbling air hoses, and conversations with the female lead.

Lugosi then harnessed his Hungarian accent to his slightly Oriental countenance and portrayed the principal character in *The Mysterious Mr. Wong*. The plot hinges on Mr. Wong's attempt to retrieve the twelve coins that Confucius gave to his friends at his death, for their possession will make him ruler of a Chinese province. Mr Wong obtains eleven of the twelve and then is foiled by a wisecracking and obnoxious reporter (Wallace Ford.) The film is full of ethnic slurs. When someone asks whether the name of Wong is known, the reply is, "They all sound alike to me."

Lugosi has a dual role in a sense. He plays Lychee, an old herb dealer with round spectacles, a weak voice, and a strange and effective but unoriental accent. However, as soon as Lychee walks through the secret panel in the back of his Chinatown curio shop, he becomes Lugosi, the archvillain, with the usual Hungarian accent. Wong is seated in his well-appointed Oriental rooms when suddenly a gong sounds and poor Bela inadvertently jumps at the noise. In fact he seems to react unfavorably every time it rings! Although he finds the gong disturbing, he commits his numerous evil acts with typical amoral flamboyance. Certainly he sacrifices everything to his goal of getting all of Confucius' coins. "One more, and the province . . . will know its rightful ruler!" His niece explains his problem in a great *non sequitur:* "This madness of his is driving all reason from his mind." Lychee, however, is a tough nut to crack. In one scene he is nonchalantly heating bamboo splints to drive underneath his victim's fingernails. His solution to other problems is swift and most direct: "A few hours with the rats will make him speak the truth!" Wong is ruthless in getting his coins. As the Irish cop says, "There ain't been a murder around here in thirty minutes."

Unfortunately the film, despite its murders and mysterious writings

The Mysterious Mr. Wong (1935).

on laundry tickets, doesn't have enough tension and speed to make it exciting, and Lugosi could at times have shaded his evil characterization more gently. As it is, he is too serious while the reporter is too unserious, supposedly functioning as comic relief, though to most people he is more obnoxious than amusing.

Finally Wong captures the reporter and his girlfriend but ties them up in a room where there just happens to be a handy telephone for the reporter to use. The police arrive and Wong tries to escape but is shot. His hand falters on the door handle, and slowly the fingers relax as he dies. Despite the effective death scene, critical appraisal was not too favorable: "It takes more than barbering and costuming to turn out a convincing oriental fiend—so we'll refrain from rating Lugosi's

performance out of deference to his earlier, happier characterizations." [40]

Four years after *Dracula*, Lugosi was given the chance to don his
vampire cape again. Over at MGM Louis B. Mayer and his cohorts
decided to return to the horror genre after their initial forays in 1932.
MGM was the most respectable of the studios because it catered
mostly to middle-class taste, a taste that looked askance at the
imaginative and supernatural realm, where Universal's creatures had
taken up seemingly permanent residence. Mayer's studio instructed its
writers to draw upon a property called *London After Midnight*, which
it had already filmed in 1927 as a Lon Chaney vehicle. This concoction
was "revamped," as it were, and, after being titled *Vampires of Prague*,
was finally released as *Mark of the Vampire* (1935). In some ways the
screenplay was a direct steal from the landscape, characters, and
mythology of *Dracula*, so superficial changes had to be made.
Wolfbane became bat thorn, Transylvania became Czechoslovakia,
Professor Van Helsing became Professor Zelen, Count Dracula
became Count Mora, and, unfortunately, myth became muddled
reality. The film broached the supernatural with vampires, flitting bats,
strange deaths, and logic-defying events and then disastrously explained them all away in the finale as the machinations of all-too-
earthly characters.

MGM chose Tod Browning, who previously had directed *London
After Midnight* and, of course, *Dracula*, and he in turn called upon
Lugosi. The other members of the cast, such as Lionel Barrymore and
Jean Hersholt, were taken from MGM's own impressive roster of
stars, but Browning also chose Lionel Atwill to add to the Continental
atmosphere. Despite vampires, a brace of bats, a conclave of spiders, a
bevy of cobwebs, a fog to end all fogs, and gothic sets laden with
enough dust to be the despair of even the most slovenly denizen of the
dark, the film was only occasionally frightening. Most of its footage
was spent on conversations between the "normal" people as they try to
figure out how Sir Karrel Borotyn had been drained of his blood in the
little Czechoslovakian village of Visoka. Although the local peasants
feel that a vampire must be responsible, the inspector (Atwill), an
experienced hand at dastardly crimes, rejects that explanation. A
learned doctor (overplayed by Barrymore) is called in to help.

[40] Irene Thirer, New York *Post*, March 6, 1935.

Chewing scenery far more than a vampire ever belabored a jugular, he eventually solves the mystery by revealing the motive and method of the all-too-human murderer. The seemingly supernatural beings that hover around the castle prove to be actors hired by the villain. The film is therefore a tease, and its impressive atmosphere and evocation of evil loses validity because of the denouement, one that curdles the mind far more than the blood. All the improbable twists of the plot would have been more acceptable if given a supernatural origin than with the present realistic but lame explanation. As a result, the people who liked supernatural films resented the ending, and people who hated supernatural films could not be placated by the final revelations. The film concluded with a pathetic scene of Lugosi—in his only lines—telling the female vampire: "This vampire business has given me a great idea for a new act, Luna. In this new act, I will be the vampire. Did you watch me? I gave all of me; I was greater than any real vampire!"

But in the film he was not "greater." Lugosi had been used by the studio for his name. He was Instant Vampire, but without any characterization or any dialogue to work with. He just walks through the settings. His fans resented that the film and Lugosi's role did not provide more than they did. Despite these difficulties, Lugosi performed as well as he could. *Variety* considered him "particularly effective" and also praised his companion in blood, Luna, the female vampire.[41] She was indeed one of the more intentionally frightening female creations of the thirties. How this rather young girl (Carol Borland) received the part of Luna adds an interesting sidelight into Lugosi's character. In an interview with this author, Miss Borland explained her friendship with Lugosi.[42] As a teenager she had seen Bela in his stage version of *Dracula* in 1929 and had been inspired to write a sequel, called *Countess Dracula*, which continued the same diary form and the same characters as the novel. Lugosi expressed great interest and came to her home, where she read him the book. Any commercial venture as a play or film could not achieve fruition because Stoker's estate at that time still had control over the property.

Lugosi grew fond of his protégée. An intelligent and lively girl, at sixteen she was already going to the university. "The University," Lugosi would remark, shaking his head in wonder. He was impressed

[41] May, 1935.
[42] Interview with Carol Borland, Hollywood, November, 1973.

Mark of the Vampire (1935).

with this fact and no doubt thought back on his own lack of formal education. Young Carol was also interested in acting, and when the leading lady of the touring *Dracula* company in California proved inadequate, Lugosi engaged her to play the part of Lucy. "He was always full of fun," she said. One day as he strode out upon the stage and extended his Dracula cape around her, he dropped a piece of ice down her back. Lugosi proved the despair of the fire marshals of the theater because he was always taking puffs from his omnipresent cigar and leaving the smoking stub someplace backstage when he had to do his lines.

After the performances he would sometimes take her dancing, often at the Hotel Roosevelt. He liked to do waltzes and other old-fashioned dances. At this time he was reasonably cautious with his finances. He gave her a good time but by no means threw his money around as he did in later years. Quite likely there was little to throw, since the stage *Dracula* was not that lucrative. After the dancing they would stroll down the streets of Hollywood. At Christmastime in 1931 she recalled that Lugosi was having "cat-fits" because various stores had pictures of the famous stars and there was a display of Karloff as the Frankenstein monster and not one of him. At other times they would read plays aloud to each other. They did *Romeo and Juliet*. Lugosi did his part in Hungarian and Carol would reply in English.

Bela was a perfect gentleman with Carol. He was a senior artist and she a junior one, and although the relationship hovered on the verge of romance—Bela was between wives three and four—it did not blossom because he always considered her a teenager. He was quite protective of his young charge and cautioned his fellow actors to watch their language in her presence.

When Carol went back to school, Bela wrote her; these letters, beginning always "Dear Little Carol," were dictated by him to his secretary. "They had his syntax," she said, but the secretary would probably have to fix up some of the sentences. This secretary was probably Lillian (at least in 1932), and one wonders how she felt when Lugosi wrote his young coactor.

In the fall of 1934 Carol saw an article in the trade press that MGM was looking for a female vampire. She found herself an agent and showed up at the studio. They put her in a pale blue nightgown and told her to play the vampire. "They were amazed," she said, "at how I had the same mannerisms and the same timing and the same gestures.

It was incredible; they couldn't understand it." She did not tell them that she had worked with Lugosi and had learned all his mannerisms. The studio was still not convinced. She had long, straight hair, and when she was sent to the makeup department, the staff there was so used to short hair—it was then the fashion—that they could not do anything with her. So she was sent to the men's makeup department, and there a young assistant and she decided to make use of the long hair. They parted it in the middle and used spirit gum to stick back the edges. And from that makeup the classic vampire face was created. The studio then worried about how this small girl and the tall Bela would "scale" together. So she called him up and told him she was trying out for the part and asked whether he could come down to the studio. He said, "Yes, of course." But he cautioned her, "Don't do it, don't do it. If you do, the same thing will happen to you that has happened to me. You'll just be haunting houses the rest of your life." Despite his warning, she thought it was a great adventure, so Lugosi came down to the set, and they were introduced to each other. At her request, he did not let on that they knew each other. He brought his cape with him, and the people at the studio told him that it wasn't needed, since all they wanted was a still photo of the two of them. Lugosi replied, "I never play without my cape." So he scrunched down for the photo and she wore her high heels and everyone was surprised they looked so well together.

The relationship Luna has with Count Mora is an odd one in the film. Guy Endore, who had worked on the script, said that there had to be an origin to the presence of the vampire couple. Bloodsucking was not the only means by which one became a vampire, he told her. Endore explained that "Count Mora and his daughter had committed incest and this was why they were killed" and why they remained the haunters of the castle. At first, she said, this was indicated in the acting, but the studio did not want such an unsavory idea. As a result, all hints of the incest were removed from the film although still photographs do show him approaching her with evil desire.

Carol claims that neither she nor Lugosi saw the whole script until the end of the film. Browning felt that their performances would not have been as good if they knew they were not real vampires. When the two found out that they were only actors, they were disappointed. Both, she says, thought it "absurd."

At the end of each working day Bela's wife, Lillian, would pick them up in the car. They would merely change their clothes and ride home without removing their makeup: Lugosi had a large bullet hole on the side of his temple, and Carol had her hair pasted down. Driving down Sunset Boulevard, Bela in the front seat and Carol in the back, the car stopped at a light. Bela turned to say something to her, and she leaned forward. Next to them, driving a truck full of chickens, was a farmer. He took one look at the two vampires leaning close to each other, with their eye shadow, bullet hole, pasted-down hair, and white faces, and did the most perfect double take Carol had ever seen and promptly drove up on the sidewalk!

Lugosi enjoyed this incident, but he would often complain that all he ever got was "house-hauntings." Miss Borland felt that he could have played the older, Continental gentleman charmer, the kind of role that Ezio Pinza later starred in, but Hollywood did not see him in this light at all.

In the meantime, Universal was trying to continue its relatively profitable production of horror films. *The Black Cat*, in its pairing of the two biggest horror stars, had done reasonably well, but Universal was not unaware of the serious faults in its script. When the studio started on its next project for its two experts in the macabre, it was more careful.

On August 31, 1934, Guy Endore (who had written the novel *The Werewolf of Paris*) submitted a nineteen-page treatment called *The Raven*, supposedly influenced by Poe's poem. On October 1, 1934, two other writers, Michael Simmons and Clarence Marks, made a fuller version and then submitted a screenplay in November. The story was still not satisfactory. Jim Tully took over, wrote two treatments in December, and at the end of January submitted a screenplay. It was again found wanting. Then David Boehm was assigned to the project, and wrote three complete screenplays before the film was put into production on March 2, 1935. The long gestation was worth the trouble, for the film (released in July, 1935) suited itself admirably to the talents and strengths of both actors. Although Lugosi's role would never equal the fame of his Dracula, it was probably his greatest performance. For once the dialogue and action were equal to the charisma of the man.

A fast-paced and inexpensive film, *The Raven* ran only an hour and was not intended to be a box-office bonanza like *Dracula* and *Frankenstein*. Despite this or perhaps because of it, the script of *The*

Raven contained some aspects more interesting than those of the so-called A productions. Unfortunately neither the script nor its filming was appreciated by the critics. The New York *Times* said:

> *The Raven* should have no difficulty in gaining the distinction of being the season's worst horror film. Not even the presence of the screen's Number One and Two Bogymen, Mr. Karloff and Bela (Dracula) Lugosi, can make the picture anything but a fatal mistake from beginning to end.[43]

The Raven, however, has in more than one way survived the *Times.* Like many other films using Poe's titles, it has very little to do with the writer's actual work. The poem, except for the presence of a stuffed raven, did not inspire even one scene or episode, but this does not mean that the film had nothing to do with Poe. On the contrary, it captured some of the essence of this nineteenth-century creator. The film's inspiration was not Poe the critic, or Poe the Southerner, or Poe the magazine editor, or Poe the alcoholic, or Poe the ineffectual husband watching his young wife cough away her tenuous life, but Poe the imaginative and romantic dreamer, the creator of a never-never gothic world of castles, doomed men, and failing and fragile heroines languishing among velvet folds of black drapes. This literary genius countered the indignities of poverty and indifference by creating a lucidly insane world of birds of ill omen, torture devices, and ingenious revenge. He depicted a blighted universe that candlelight could never brighten, where cries in the night stifled the joys of laughter. But Poe's wild imaginings originated in a mind of impressive logic and superb reasoning. Compelled by his audience and magazine markets to work in the form of the short story, he developed a minor aspect of literature (the horror tale) into a number of superbly executed achievements, works that remain undimmed by the century that has passed. The question has often been raised of how such a gifted writer could be concerned with such a limited goal as fright. The psychoanalyst would probably answer that he was exorcising a demon within him—a demon of frustration, of thwarted love, of jealousy, of revenge. Here, then, was a mind of great poetic intensity gifted at solving cryptograms and ciphers, at creating an imaginative landscape of the south pole, and at

[43] July 5, 1935.

extolling the deductive method of solving crime far in advance of Sherlock Holmes.

Universal's scriptwriters were somehow aware of the complexity of Poe's character. Rather than re-create one of his stories or poems, they put their finger on the basic dichotomy in Poe's character—imagination and scientific precision—and so created Dr. Vollin (Lugosi), a genius as a surgeon and researcher, an accomplished musician, and a monomaniacal devotee of Poe. Vollin centers much of his life on Poe's weird imaginings and has sublimated his sadistic inclinations by reconstructing many of Poe's torture devices. Although Dr. Vollin is a sadist, he is not a sexual one but an intellectual one. Torture fascinates him and is no doubt the reason that he chose the medical profession to begin with.

Dr. Vollin has not compromised with the exigencies of life. Retired from actual practice, he now sits among his Poe memorabilia, carrying out his own research. He has found his peace with the world by removing himself from it. Only when he falls in love with a girl does he lose that balance (if not entirely "sane," at least legal and productive; if not normal, at least in equilibrium). Vollin can no longer sublimate his energies into research, but will now more directly release them by literally torturing those who torture him. It is an extraordinary thesis, farfetched but not entirely unbelievable, one that despite the necessities of a horror film's melodramatics, is quite satisfactorily and imaginatively carried out. The script allows Vollin to articulate many of his feelings and is perhaps the most literate (in the good sense of that word) of any of Lugosi's films, portraying a kind of sophisticated though offbeat intelligence seldom revealed in Hollywood productions. Dr. Vollin, like other diabolical characters of fiction, will be ultimately hoisted by his own petard. But his death, for all its horror, is its own ecstasy, although the film does not entirely realize this aspect. Despite the fact that the picture was designed to be thrilling and to capitalize on the presence of Universal's two horror experts, and thus by necessity must succumb to melodramatic excess, it also adheres rather firmly and consistently to its main thesis.

The Raven's original script (dated March 18, 1935) was carefully followed during shooting, although certain significant changes were made. Originally the film began with a scene before a theater on a foggy night where fans seek the autograph of Miss Thatcher, a dancer.

The Raven (1935). On the set.

She is in a hurry, though, and leaves—only to have an auto accident. A note in the script by Boehm explained: "I do not revise these shots although if it's in a fog they will need revising, but I think it should be left up to the Director to use a certain amount of discretion and get the best shots. He can show a crash or skid." Some discretion indeed was used. After ominous chords heralding the titles, the film opens with an automobile racing down a road; it crashes, an ambulance arrives, and at the hospital the doctors decide that the nerves at the base of her brain have been damaged and that no one can help but Dr. Vollin.

The next scene begins with a close-up of a stuffed raven as the voice of Lugosi, deep, halting, and deliberate, recites the lines:

> Sud-den-ly, there came a tapping, as of someone gent-ly rapping, rapping at my chamber door.
> O-pen then I flung the shutter, when with many a flirt and flutter, in there stepped a stately raven—[44]

The voice stops, and then Lugosi tells his listener, a mild-mannered, bespectacled Mr. Chapman, who comes from a museum interested in Vollin's Poe collection, that "the Raven is my talisman."

"Curious talisman," answers Chapman, "the bird of ill omen, a symbol of death."

"Death *is* my talisman, Mr. Chapman," Lugosi answers ominously. "The one indestructible force, the one certain thing in an uncertain universe. Death!"

Dr. Vollin's strange revery is interrupted by a telephone call from the hospital; it is the injured girl's father, Judge Thatcher, asking for Vollin's aid. The doctor resists: "You know that I've retired from actual practice and am doing only research." Vollin finds out which doctors are on the case and says, "They can handle it as well as I," and hangs up. Vollin then tells Chapman that he has built many of the torture and horror devices that Poe described in his tales. Mr. Chapman, the typical bland innocent, chimes in: "Imagine building those things! A very curious hobby." Lugosi stares off into the distance and answers most impressively, "It's *more* than a hobby."

---

[44] Although the various treatments and screenplays departed further and further from the poem, the shooting script still contained a few references; most of these, however, were omitted in the filming. Originally, for example, there was to be the sound of tapping while Lugosi recited the lines; furthermore, the raven was to be perched above a bust of Pallas and a similarity between the Raven and the "birdlike" features or look of Lugosi was to be stressed.

Thus within the first few minutes the film has established much of the exposition, including Vollin's entrancement with Poe, his wish to retire from the world to do research, and his indifference to mere mortals.

Meantime, Judge Thatcher decides to plead with Vollin personally. The film efficiently cuts from a shot of Thatcher riding in a car to the middle of the conversation between the two:

THATCHER: But you can't say no.
VOLLIN: I have said it.
THATCHER: I'll pay you any amount of money, Dr. Vollin.
VOLLIN: Money means nothing to me.
THATCHER: But someone is dying. Your obligation as a member of the medical profession—
VOLLIN: I respect no obligation. I am a law unto myself.
THATCHER: But have you no human feeling? My daughter is dying.
VOLLIN: Death hasn't the same significance for me as it has for you.
THATCHER: You're the one chance she's got.
VOLLIN: [sneeringly] Doctors Cook and Hemenway are "competent" doctors.
THATCHER: Competent! It seems that competence is not enough. Cook, Hemenway, and Halden, they say you are the only one.
VOLLIN: [His face lightens.] So they *do* say I am the only one.
THATCHER: Yes. I beg you for my daughter's life.
VOLLIN: Very well, I will go.

The exposition contained in this scene is remarkable. On the telephone Vollin had said that he had retired to do research. This research is not necessarily for humanity, but for his own satisfaction. He has had enough of untalented meddlers and obviously has had controversy with the staff of doctors at the hospital and therefore slurringly calls them "competent." Vollin does not want money, he wants only to be left alone. When Thatcher reminds him of his obligation to the medical profession, Vollin answers that he is a "law unto myself," a fact that is true even to the point of murder. Vollin is the supreme egotist, but a man whose genius warrants much of his own high estimation of himself. His difficulties no doubt have come from the conflict of his own giant will and talent with those of the "competent" ones who plague his life. Only to show them up, to prove that he is indeed "the only one," does he agree to save the girl's life.

Vollin has exorcised all touches of humanity from his character and is moved by neither pain nor suffering nor death. He is not half in love with easeful death, as Keats expressed it, but fully in love with painful death! By restraining his human tendencies, he has been able to sublimate all his strong passions into abstract work, into research, and so finds release in the fantasy world of Poe. But this astringent paradise will now break down; his solitary Eden will now be blasted, broken by a woman.

After a brief sequence in the operating room (the script describes Lugosi: "Instruments in his hand . . . his stature tremendous—his face like a god or a demon"), the next scene takes place in Vollin's study. He is seated at the organ playing Bach as the girl looks at him admiringly.

> JEAN: You're not only a great surgeon, but a great musician, too.
>   Extraordinary man; you're almost not a man. Almost—
> VOLLIN: A god?
> JEAN: Yes.
> VOLLIN: A god with the taint of human emotions.[45]

Jean naturally has discovered that Vollin is extraordinary, that he is in a way a god. She does not know, however, that he is a jealous god and that when he wants something, he will take it. Vollin, in his reply, reveals his own attitude toward this new development in his life. He is upset by his emotions. They are not redeeming or delightful, but rather a "taint"; they are the clay parts of his self-image, which he will master either by conquering the girl or by eliminating her.

Vollin puts his hand on her neck. "The scar is almost gone," he says. Then he adds with odd enthusiasm, "When I touch it, does it still hurt?"—a remark that betrays his fascination with pain.

> VOLLIN: A month ago I didn't know you.
> JEAN: And now I owe my life to you. I wish there was something I
>   could do.
> VOLLIN: [determinedly] There is.
> JEAN: Tell me.
> VOLLIN: The restraint that we impose upon ourselves can drive us
>   mad.

[45] This passage wasn't forgotten by Universal in 1939 when *Tower of London* was made. Mord (Karloff) tells Richard III (Rathbone): "More than a Duke, more than a King: You are a god to me."

Uncomfortable at this passionate statement, Jean backs off, but thanks Vollin for making her fiancé, Jerry, his assistant. "It means we can be married that much sooner. Now I owe you another debt."

"You owe me nothing. I did it to give him something to take the place of what he's losing."

The shooting script at this point says that Vollin "pulls her toward him in an embrace," and she, "fascinated—attracted—and still resisting," gives him "a quick impulsive kiss" and starts to go. The film omits the embrace and kiss. As a result, the only indication that she is strongly attracted to Vollin appears in her speech about his being almost a god. Unfortunately both the script and the film omit the tension between this brilliant older man and the uninteresting and bland boyfriend. That she is not really concerned with or hardly aware of the disparity between her two admirers is what makes the film more of a melodrama than a study of the human condition.

She starts to leave, but tells Vollin to attend her dance performance because she has a surprise for him. The surprise for him was also a surprise to the director, for the final version of the script said that the content of the scene had not been established, except that it was to be titled "The Spirit of Poe." The script added: "With the dance might be a recital of some of the lines to acquaint the audience with that immortal masterpiece, 'The Raven'!"

At the theater Jean goes through a rather effective, though perhaps campy, performance in pseudoballet of "The Raven," accompanied by lines from the poem. Vollin watches her with great intensity, a look that Judge Thatcher does not miss. Later, in the dressing room, she asks Vollin whether it was a great surprise. His answer, observed by Judge Thatcher, is brief but ecstatic: "Whom the angels call Lenore!"

The next scene opens with Thatcher visiting Vollin, telling him that "Jean is in danger of becoming infatuated with you. Of course I can understand that. You saved her life, Dr. Vollin."

"You think it's only in gratitude she feels?" [46]

Thatcher goes on to say that he doesn't approve. "I came to you once and asked you when death was near to save Jean. I come to you again. But this time instead of from death—"

"You want to save her from me!" Vollin crushes the test tube he has

---

[46] Lugosi's troubles with English never left him. The original script lacks the "in" that Lugosi included.

been holding in his hand. Thatcher is surprised, not knowing that Vollin feels this way.

Vollin says, "Now that you know, you still say that your greatest wish is for her to marry Halden?"

"More than ever. There's no point in saving Jean's life if we're to sacrifice her happiness. You mustn't see her again."

"You drivelling fool. Stop talking," Vollin says commandingly.

"Be careful, Vollin!"

"Not see her again! Listen, Thatcher, I'm a man who renders humanity a great service. For that my brain must be clear, my nerves steady, and my hand sure. Jean torments me. She has come into my life, into my brain."

"Forget it, man. Forget it."

"Judge Thatcher, there are no two ways. Send her to me."

"Do you know what you are saying?"

"There are no two ways! Send her to me!"

"You're mad!"

"I am mad. And I tell you the only way you can cure—"

"I can't talk to you, Vollin. I came here with a perfectly reasonable objection, and I expected you to be reasonable, and instead I find you stark, staring mad. Good day, Dr. Vollin." He leaves.

"Send her, Judge Thatcher, I warn you," Vollin intones to himself.

This scene contains the basic theme of the film. Vollin is not a man who asks, he is a man who demands, and his will shall not be thwarted. "There are no two ways." Since Jean torments him and now that he cannot have her, his love turns to hate, and he will torment those who torment him. Vollin has gone off the deep end, but there is a kind of insane logic to his methods.

Fate too will attempt to help Vollin. Edmond Bateman (Karloff) has heard in underworld circles that Vollin has talents as a plastic surgeon. Although in the existing film Bateman goes from a saloon almost directly to Vollin's house, in the script Bateman is told that Vollin works at General Hospital and waits inside a drugstore until the pharmacist points out Vollin going down the hospital steps talking to Jerry Halden. Bateman goes toward them, but is almost run down by a car and then yelled at by a policeman. His attempt to speak to Vollin thwarted, Bateman shows up at Vollin's house that night. Much of this episode was omitted, probably after shooting, since scenes of Karloff

Karloff and Lugosi on a break during the shooting of *The Raven*.

walking down the street in the daytime are immediately followed by his evening arrival at Vollin's house.

Vollin recognizes Bateman as a notorious criminal and says that he will help if Bateman does something for him.

"Like what?"

"It's in your line."

"Like what?"

"Torture—and murder."

Vollin then recounts some of Bateman's previous actions, how he broke out of prison and turned an acetylene torch in someone's face. Bateman's rather lame reply is almost funny: "Sometime you can't help things like that." But the contrast is quite clear. Bateman is a simple creature of impulse. He kills in anger, but Vollin, on the other hand, is not impulsive but cerebral. He coldly plans his deeds. When Bateman explains that he has done ugly things because he looks ugly, Vollin suddenly brightens. "You are saying something profound, Bateman. A man with a face so hideously ugly—" He stops, caught in the beauty of his new scheme. Then he agrees to help and explains that the operation will take only ten minutes because he merely adjusts the roots of the seventh cranial nerve. "From this come the nerves that control the muscles of the face. If something happens to these nerve ends, it alters your expression." [47] Lugosi's reading of "alters your expression" is diabolical. "In other words, I who know what to do with these nerve ends can make you look any way I choose." And here, of course, Vollin becomes God. "Any way *I* choose."

Vollin performs the operation. "Do I look different?" Bateman asks. "Yes," says Vollin with ill-concealed delight, for one side of Bateman's face is hideously altered. Vollin leaves the room, looks down on Bateman through an iron grate, and causes curtains to pull back from a number of full-length mirrors. Bateman sees his new face, growls, and takes his gun and shoots the mirrors. [48] Vollin howls with laughter.

"You're monstrously ugly. Your monstrous ugliness breeds monstrous hate. Good. I can use your hate."

Bateman pleads that his face be changed again, but Vollin agrees

[47] The scriptwriters did some medical research, for they gave Bateman Bell's palsy, a disease that affects the seventh cranial nerve and results in something like Bateman's affliction.

[48] In the original script Bateman was supposed to growl a number of times. This patent attempt to copy the Frankenstein monster's inarticulate despair was omitted except for one growl. In terms of character consistency it could have well been dispensed with entirely.

The Raven. Karloff: "Do I look different?" Lugosi: "Yes."

only after Bateman has aided him. "I can't use *my* hand to do it. My brain, your hand." And this, indeed, is the distinction.

Afterward Vollin shows Bateman around his museum of torture. He then points out a device from one of Poe's stories, "The Pit and the Pendulum." Vollin starts to enact the actions of the victim: "A man was thrown into a pit—and tied to a slab like this—suddenly he hears some peculiar noise coming from above his head. He looks up and sees a knife flashing, swinging rhythmically as it gradually descends." Vollin then lies down on the slab to demonstrate the device. He indicates a lever that controls manacles that clasp the wrists and ankles. The victim cannot move. "In fifteen minutes the knife reaches the heart."

Bateman watches his tormentor and traps him by pulling the lever. His one functioning eye moves back and forth at the pendulum. Vollin, caught in his own machine, tries to reason with him. He warns Bateman that "should anything happen to me, you'll remain the hideous monster that you are." This statement clinches his argument, because Bateman soon unclinches him.

Later that night Vollin's guests arrive, among them Jean and Jerry.

Bateman (Karloff) needs some persuasion to carry out the tortures.

In the early version of the script Vollin declares, "I have good horses to ride," but budget or perhaps aesthetic modifications took place, for in the film the real horses become just a parlor game. Thatcher appears later to take away his daughter, but Vollin apologizes for what he had said the other day.

As the evening progresses, Jean sees Bateman and screams, although afterward she tells him she was sorry that she reacted to his ugliness. The after-dinner conversation switches to Poe.

In the shooting script Thatcher is far more bitter to Vollin. "Why your extraordinary interest in Poe, Dr. Vollin? Because he was a madman?" This last line was omitted in the final version. Vollin interprets the famous writer along the lines of his own obsessions:

> Poe was a great genius. Like all great geniuses, there was in him
> the insistent will [thunder sounds] to do something big, great,

constructive in the world. He had the brain to do it. But—he fell in love. Her name was Lenore. . . .

Something happened. Someone took her away from him. When a man of genius is denied of his great love, he goes mad. His brain, instead of being clear to do his work, is tortured, so *he* begins to think of torture. Torture for those who have tortured him! [Lugosi's reading of these lines is superb; his voice is deliberate, halting, labored. He then changes his tone, having realized what kind of impression he might be making.] My interest in Poe, the way I speak about torture and death, you people being laymen perhaps do not understand. As a doctor, a surgeon, I look upon these things differently. A doctor is fascinated by death—and pain. And how much pain a man can endure. [With this last comment, of course, his obsession intrudes again.]

Vollin escorts his guests to their rooms, even though Thatcher thinks that Vollin is mad and wants to leave. "And now the ceremony begins," says Vollin to Bateman. Judge Thatcher is captured and dragged down into the cellar and put under the pendulum. Thatcher's frenzied questions allow Lugosi to appear at his sardonic, superior best. Tied to the slab, Thatcher asks:

> THATCHER: What's that thing?
> VOLLIN: A knife.
> THATCHER: What's it doing?
> VOLLIN: Descending.
> THATCHER: What are you trying to do to me?
> VOLLIN: [simply] Torture you.
> THATCHER: Oh, try to be sane, Vollin.
> VOLLIN: I'm the sanest man who ever lived. *I* will not be tortured. I
>   tear torture out of myself by torturing *you!*

He laughs ecstatically and then sobers. "Fifteen minutes," he intones. "There's the clock; you can see it." And then he goes into another revery: "Torture waiting, waiting. Death will be sweet, Judge Thatcher." He laughs insanely. Shortly after, he asks the suffering Judge, "Do you mind if I smoke?"

But Vollin's plans are also for Jean. He pulls a switch, and her whole room—which is really an elevator—descends to the basement. Jerry, hearing her screams, rushes upstairs and opens the door and is more than a little surprised to find the room gone. The premiere audience

Looking villainous, for a publicity shot.

laughed at this point, as the hero dangles in air clutching the doorknob.[49] He tries to wake the other guests, but Vollin goes to a large control panel, and soon iron shutters close over the windows and the phone lines are cut. The guests are isolated, trapped by Vollin, the supreme monarch of his house of torture.

Jean tries to convince Bateman to release her. But Bateman, albeit reluctantly, carries out Vollin's orders, though he assures her, "He won't hurt you." The hardened criminal is softened by a girl with a pretty face and a few kind words. This limited creature, for all his impulsive acts of violence and cruelty, is still basically human. It is Vollin, for all his urbanity, who has denied his own humanity, who has moved on to an abstract sense of what mankind is and is able without even a qualm to plan rather coolly the murder of others. "I'll soon be rid of my torture, rid of it, and I'll be the sanest man who ever lived."

[49] New York *Herald Tribune*, July 5, 1935.

Vollin then orders Jerry and Jean into a room "in which the walls come together" and starts some machinery that will crush them to death. "And now, my gift to you: the place where you will live. A humble place," Vollin says sarcastically, "but your love will make it beautiful. . . . It will be the perfect marriage, the perfect love. You will never be separated, never." As the walls start to go together, Vollin grows ecstatic: "What a torture! What a delicious torture, Bateman! Greater than Poe. Poe only conceived it; I have done it, Bateman. Poe, you are avenged." He laughs.[50]

But Bateman does not want Jean killed and pulls the switch to release them. Vollin shoots him, but Bateman overpowers Vollin and throws him in the room and closes the doors. As Bateman dies, Vollin screams in his own torture device as he is crushed to death. The Judge is released literally in the "nick" of time and all is well. In a kind of epilogue, Jean and Jerry lament poor Bateman, though oblivious of the extraordinary man who had saved her life and who had, quite imaginatively, tried to take it away as well.

The Raven is a melodrama, but not one that is terribly frightening. Although it lacks atmosphere and an air of mystery, it has a swift pace and plenty of action, and a theme that is viable. It could well be studied as a minor masterpiece in pacing. Only sixty minutes long, it wastes no time. Exposition is neatly and efficiently accomplished, and within the first five minutes the film has already started to race to its conclusion. And yet there are moments for sustained dialogue, for good characterization, and for mood setting. The footage of the shots in the seven reels that constitute the film show the buildup:

Reel One:	59 shots
Reel Two:	58 shots
Reel Three:	69 shots
Reel Four:	51 shots
Reel Five:	98 shots
Reel Six:	119 shots
Reel Seven:	115 shots

With the credits, the film averages out to have one shot every ten seconds.

[50] The original shooting script has Vollin, after "Poe, you are avenged," say to himself: "The Raven knocks at the door . . . enters" and in a "low, startlingly low" voice, utters, "The Raven—Symbol of death" and then "in a sing-song" intones: "Nevermore—Nevermore—The Lost Lenore! The Lost Lenore!" These lines, quite wisely, were not used.

Although *The Raven* has a good pace, there is very little imaginative lighting or mysterious atmosphere. The director, Friedlander, who won what little reputation he had in serials, knew how to keep a film going, but he did not know how to invest it with an appropriate sense of gloom or foreboding. In short, he shot the film in a workmanlike manner, but never gave its basic premise much thought. David Boehm, the screenwriter, must have been disappointed with the prosaic treatment of his script. When Vollin and Bateman drag Judge Thatcher down into the dungeon, Boehm described what effect he wanted:

> The scene we should get here should be like . . . one of those paintings that I once saw in a gruesome exhibition of paintings of the Spanish Inquisition.
>
> Candles light up the blackness of the scene, throwing their fantastic gleam on the face of Vollin—who is like a diabolical Spanish Inquisitor—and on the face of Bateman—who looks like an executioner beyond the imaginings of any Spanish Inquisitor.

Friedlander kept the scene, but lost the psychological effect that would have raised the film beyond mere melodrama. What redeems the film, then, is not the direction, but the story and, of course, its two famous actors.

Although *The Raven* provided Lugosi with one of his greatest roles—it is his definitive mad scientist—the picture was not too appreciated, nor is it today by most horror buffs. Most of them prefer *The Black Cat*. Admittedly that film is better at creating mood, but its story is much less effective than that of *The Raven*. Certainly Bela would never be given a better chance to play "himself." Within four years he had provided three perfect performances: Dracula, the sorcerer in *White Zombie*, and Dr. Vollin. Ahead of him lay only repeat performances with weaker scripts and poorer directors. The one challenge that yet awaited him was the crippled Ygor.

Lugosi's future almost ceased to be after *The Raven*, for the film caused at least a temporary halt to his career and to the genre itself. When the picture was shown in England in August, it created such a furor that the British Board of Censors answered a "Nevermore" to future horror films.[51] Earlier, on June 27, the President of the Board of

---

[51] London *Daily Telegraph*, August 3, 1935.

Censors, prompted by a screening of *The Raven*, warned the trade that such films were unfortunate and undesirable. Although the Board did not feel justified in condemning the industry without prior warning, it now stated clearly that future horror pictures would be scrutinized far more carefully than before and quite likely would be banned. Since American studios received a good amount of their profits on horror films from England, they now grew so cautious that the genre soon went into eclipse.

After completing *The Raven*, Lugosi again wandered from the major studios and found himself starring in *Murder by Television* for Imperial-Cameo productions. There was nothing particularly imperial about the film when it was finally released in October, 1935 (the film had been completed by August), nor was Lugosi's role a cameo in any sense of the word. The film was a conventional murder mystery gimmicked up by the then exotic invention of television. The story seems to be woven from the limited thread of *International House*, in which there was another TV inventor, but unfortunately there was no W. C. Fields to wander through the film. A professor refuses all offers for his invention, but some unscrupulous promoters intend to get the secret by other means. The professor is murdered, his plans stolen, his revolutionary TV tube spirited away, and a number of suspects appear all over the place. Among them is Arthur Perry, another red-herring role for Lugosi. The film is not terribly exciting, nor is Lugosi given much to do. It was just another sixty-minute quickie. When the film makes it seem as if Lugosi is the murderer, suddenly he is found killed, yet in subsequent shots shown to be living. Later the character explains that the dead man was his twin brother but that he did not identify him until he made further investigations on his own. Indeed Lugosi is the gifted one in this film. He discovers who the murderer was—obviously the most unlikely person—and shows that the villain had turned on his own equipment at the same time as the professor was telecasting, and so "created the interstellar frequency which is the death ray." Shades of Roxor!

Murder by Television, an independently made film, was not shown very widely; in fact, one print sufficed for all of New York State.

Lugosi received a contract from England to make a film, *The Mystery of the Marie Celeste* (known later in America as *The Phantom Ship*), and took the train to New York prior to embarking. He was therefore able, when *The Raven* was shown at the Roxy Theater in

Murder by Television (1935).

New York on July 4, 1935, to appear on stage and take some bows. A few days later an interview with him was printed in the New York *Times.*[52] The reporter was surprised to hear Lugosi offer him an "eye-opener," for "despite his Hungarian upbringing and his precise, rather formal manner of speaking, [he] frequently intersperses his conversation with Yankee idioms." Lugosi sat in a small armchair, smoking a pipe. "He is a quiet, gentle man who gives an impression of mellow wisdom. Many things amuse him, especially the wry paradoxes of life." Lugosi told the reporter that his fan mail came mostly from women and that he received far more attention as a vampire than he ever had as a romantic lead. "They eat it up," he said, speaking of his audiences. The reference to devouring brought forth another question from the reporter. Did Lugosi believe in vampires, and was he a vampire or a werewolf himself? "I answer them both in the same way," Lugosi replied diplomatically. "I say I have never met a vampire

[52] July 7, 1935.

personally, but I don't know what might happen tomorrow. This saves me from lying, and it does not give away my trade secrets."

One secret that Lugosi did give away was his wish to leave the horror genre a few times a year in order to play straight parts. He emphasized, however, that he took his fiendish roles seriously:

> You can't make people believe in you if you play a horror part with your tongue in your cheek. The screen magnifies everything, even the way you are thinking. If you are not serious, people will sense it. No matter how hokum or highly melodramatic the horror part may be, you must believe in it while you are playing it.

Certainly Lugosi was correct in this observation. If nothing else, his horror roles, no matter how absurd the scripts, were generally believable, for he brought a curiously intense passion to his acting. It was this passion that made some fans suspect that he really was in league with the Dark Forces.

About the same time, a reporter from the New York *Herald Tribune* also asked for an interview. In his hotel room Lugosi sat next to his wife. Lillian was described as a "tall, charming Chicago girl who was Lugosi's perfect secretary before she married the star of weird films." When asked about her, Lugosi replied that she was "a perfect wife, a perfect housekeeper, a perfect woman." He confessed that he admired pretty clothes and would often go out shopping to bring back for his wife a dress, a hat, or a bag and that the articles did not usually have to be returned, either. Then the subject changed. Lugosi made a brief but revealing comment that was, unfortunately, not pursued by the reporter: "Every actor is somewhat mad, or else he'd be a plumber or a bookkeeper or a salesman."

When asked about his new film, *The Phantom Ship*, Lugosi confessed that he was not acquainted with the script "although he always likes to know what the story's about before he goes to work in a picture." And then, in a significant comment, he added:

> However, I'll be truthful and admit that the weekly pay check is the most important thing to me. Of course I enjoy my work. I haven't been an actor nearly thirty years [notice that about five were shaved off!] without getting pleasure out of the profession. And with me it wasn't a sudden urge—acting. I studied at the Budapest Academy of Theatrical Arts for four years [not true], and emerged

with a degree before I finally made my debut in Budapest. And even then I didn't rate important roles. It took several years more of hard work in small parts before I attained stardom. Of all the roles I've done on the stage, I'm partial to Cyrano de Bergerac [no record of his having played this part can be found] and I hope that some day I'll have the opportunity to do a screen version. I understand Charles Laughton is slated to film it this year. Well, maybe I will sometime, when they stop casting me in horror pictures.

Although I'm afraid I'm typed by now, I'd like to quit the supernatural roles every third time and play just an interesting, down-to-earth person. One of these days I may get my wish! Meanwhile, I'll take any story if it's good.

His wish, of course, would never be granted. A horror star he was and a horror star he would remain.

Soon after arriving in England, Lugosi began on *The Phantom Ship*. It was based on one of the most puzzling incidents of the history of the sea. When the *Marie Celeste* was discovered in 1872 floating on the waters with absolutely no one on board and with no apparent reason for its abandonment, it created a mystery that was never solved. The British scriptwriters adjusted the real-life situation in order to give a reason for the abandonment. The film told of a seaman (Lugosi) who had been thrashed so thoroughly by a first mate that he became a physical and mental wreck. Six years later and unrecognizable, he has the opportunity to sail on the same ship under the same first mate, and so begins his revenge. There are some effective scenes, including storms with the wind blowing in Lugosi's long white hair, but the film is more dramatic than horrifying. It was praised mostly for "its fine sea atmosphere." [53]

The Phantom Ship was first shown in England on November 14, 1935, and later released in America in February, 1937. The actual shooting of the picture did not take very long because on August 26, 1935, Lugosi arrived in New York by ship and in another interview made this revealing comment about his career as a horror star: "It's a good business; so I can buy steamship tickets, give tips and invite the boys for a drink. If I wouldn't make such pictures—maybe trash—I couldn't do it." These words have a trace of the world-weary despair that Lugosi exudes so sensitively in his screen roles; they are

[53] *The Film Daily*, February 15, 1937.

Lugosi and Lillian aboard ship.

observations that could easily have been made by Vitus Werdegast in *The Black Cat*. In the same interview Lugosi commented on Hollywood, and it was evident that working in England had reminded him of the seriousness and artistic sincerity of his Hungarian filmmaking days. "Hollywood doesn't let authors, writers, exploit and deliver their talents and imaginations. It has to go through the mill, not be passed by one individual talent, right or wrong." [54]

Lugosi and his wife then took the train back to Hollywood, where they bought a $30,000 house in the Hollywood Hills. There he also had two automobiles, two dogs, and—as he said in a later interview—"money in the bank." None would last very long.

His career burgeoning, and for a change his economic situation more than solvent, Lugosi decided to form his own company and to film *Cagliostro*, a story about an eighteenth-century wizard that had previously been made as a historical spectacle in France in 1929. "Lugosi has wanted to play the role for some time, but no studio has seen fit to buy the property from him. He will be starred in the version written by Andre de Sous." [55] His attempt to break loose from the Hollywood mode and do a film the way he wanted was very audacious in 1935, when independent production was extremely rare. His plans fell through, however, when he could not find backing.

In late September Lugosi began work on a film called *The Invisible Ray*. First known as *The Death Ray*, the story was purchased by Universal in May, 1935. Perhaps no one remembered that a film called *The Invisible Ray* had been made in 1920. It told of a mineralogist who discovered the ray and how a band of scientists seek to employ its untold powers for a worldwide criminal scheme. [56] The new script was about Koh, a Belgian, who goes to Africa, finds a meteorite, and becomes radioactive. He goes to the expedition doctor, Dr. Morceau, who gives him an antidote that lasts eight hours. If a treatment is not taken, he will kill whomever he touches and die himself. Meanwhile, Koh's wife, rebuffed by her husband's indifference, falls in love with a member of the expedition and leaves with him. Later Koh dresses another man in his clothes, kills him, and then vows revenge on the six people of the expedition. He murders some of them, but when the

[54] Asa Bordages, New York *World Telegram*, August 27, 1935.
[55] New York *Times*, September 29, 1935.
[56] *Exhibitor's Trade Review*, February 28, 1920.

The Invisible Ray (1936). Karloff explains his theories.

opportunity comes to kill his wife, he can't. Forgetting his poisonous state, he embraces her and she dies. Too long supercharged himself, he also succumbs.

The script underwent some modification during the summer and early fall of 1935. The initial setting was changed to the Carpathian Mountains. Koh's name became Janos Rukh (Karloff), and Dr. Morceau's part was enlarged and his name changed to Dr. Benet (Lugosi). Otherwise the plot remained pretty much the same, except that the wife did not die at the end.

The Invisible Ray was the third major pairing of Universal's greatest horror stars. Well produced, with good, sets, fine special effects, a somewhat logical premise, a literate script, and good direction, it was released in January, 1936, but it was still disliked by the critics; the public was not too fond of it either, probably because it was not terrifying enough.

Janos Rukh, an astronomer, theorist, and inventor claims that he can capture the light rays of Andromeda and see events taking place on earth millions of years before. He demonstrates his discovery to a number of eminent scientists, among them Dr. Felix Benet (Lugosi). Although at first skeptical, Benet agrees that Janos is correct and invites him on an expedition to Africa. Janos there discovers a new element (Radium X), which can disintegrate matter. In the process he somehow poisons himself. When the lights are low, he glows in the dark. Janos goes to Dr. Benet, who finds an antidote, which at least stops him from glowing and killing those he touches. But, as Benet says, there is no way of knowing how the poison and strong antidote will affect the brain. Janos had always been intensely secretive and monomaniacal about his experiments, and now the paranoid tendencies he had exhibited earlier in the Carpathians come to the fore. He wants the invention for himself, whereas Benet wants to give it to the world. Janos is interested mainly in Janos; he does not find or use the element for the benefit of humanity as much as to prove his theories. Benet, on the other hand, has no such egotistical view. He gives due credit to Janos, but wants to use the element to heal as many people as possible and not to keep it a secret.

Janos, with his dark, curly hair, moustache, large-brimmed hat, and rather shabby cape, resembles more a misunderstood artist than a scientist. In contrast, Dr. Benet, as portrayed by Lugosi, is dapper, neat, social, and "adjusted." Benet lives in a palatial apartment in Paris, Janos in a spooky gothic building in the mountains. Benet is reasonable, part of the establishment. Janos is unreasonable, in opposition to the scientific world that had rebuffed him, though far more gifted. In many ways, then, Karloff's character resembles one of Lugosi's mad scientists, but he brings to the part a kind of "hangdoggish" quality. Although his intellect is superb, his personality is not very impressive. He is a pitiable person and, despite his monomania and paranoia, lacks the flamboyance, the excitement, and even the intense hatred and resentment that Lugosi would have brought to the role.

Janos echoes some of the lines of Roxor, his scientific predecessor in *Chandu the Magician*, when he says that he has harnessed the power of the ray: "I could crumple up a city a thousand miles away. I could destroy a nation." Karloff's delivery of the lines lacks the magnificent glee that Lugosi always gave to such literally earth-shaking lines.

Janos does not break away from society because of his radiation poisoning, but is already alienated in the beginning of the film and progresses steadily to complete isolation. Perhaps the film would have been more poignant if his awareness of being a pariah and poisonous to

The Invisible Ray. An informal moment.

the touch (save for his medicinal antidote) caused him to turn into a madman. The script is partially to blame here, but so is Karloff's playing. When he stares in the mirror and sees his glowing face—a scene so rife with symbols and overtones—and finds that he is a stranger, "even unto himself," this should have been the moment that definitely switches him from a member of the human race to a completely separate creature, and ultimately a law unto himself. Because this is muffled by Karloff's calm reaction—he is not appalled or later incensed enough—his deeds of revenge are not as passionately motivated as they could have been.

Karloff, with his British sense of decorum, perhaps felt that a madman need not rave, but as a result of his underacting, the film lacks the verve that it would have had if the two stars had switched roles. Lugosi's temperament was far more suited to Janos (just as he was more ideally Dr. Vollin in *The Raven*), but Universal, feeling that Karloff was the bigger star, gave him the larger role.

Dr. Benet's part, *as written,* represents more the scientist that would come in science fiction films of the fifties; he is concerned with research, but not to an insane degree. Even though faced with a rather bland role, Lugosi managed to raise it above the level of a mere theoretician-technician good guy. Although the film shows that he could play a straight part and do it quite well, at times he seems to be straining at the bit by putting in some hand gestures and intonations that belie his benign character. In one of the African scenes Lugosi treats and cures a sick baby and hands the child to its mother. "The little creature is going to live," he says, acting as if he were getting rid of a bundle of wolfbane. Later, in his Paris clinic, Benet dismisses with a polite but chilly gesture a little girl whom he has cured of blindness. Lugosi was hardly "all heart," even in this straight role. He also brought to the part a mild touch of monomania. Throughout the film he extolls the efficacies of *his* theory: astro-chemistry, a term that rolls over Lugosi's tongue with less than liquid eloquence in lines like: "This proves, I think, that human organisms are only part of astro-chemistry, controlled by radial forces from the sun."

The radioactive scientist goes on a rampage of killing, and in an effective scene encounters Benet:

> BENET: Do you intend to kill us all?
> RUKH: Yes.
> BENET: I felt it was better to let things alone when you were first poisoned. I warned you about your brain.
> RUKH: It began to affect my brain almost immediately. I could feel it coming, crawling for cells.
> BENET: Aren't there ever moments when you think as you used to think? When you're human?
> RUKH: Not often now, not often.

Both actors keep a straight face during this rather odd exchange and even bring pathos as well as drama to their scene. Rukh approaches Benet and gives him the lethal touch—one of the few times that Lugosi's death in a film was a tragic one—and soon after, the radioactive Rukh himself perishes.

Although the film had some good scenes and special effects, Lugosi fans were disappointed, for their hero was placed in a role that left him obviously champing at the bit. Lugosi as a mild and reasonable scientist was wasted. Still, he tried as much as he could to rise above his material. In certain scenes he engages in the good old habit of scene

stealing. At one point in the film, while Karloff is in the forefront going through significant action, Bela stands in the back playing with his pith helmet. He must have gone home happy that day, having pulled a fast one on the director and on Karloff, but he must have wondered—as viewers still do today—why he had received the lesser role in the first place.

Neither Lugosi nor Karloff could have known that by the end of 1935 the highest points of their careers had passed and that the demand for them as horror stars would fade. Their names could still draw at the box office, but both would rarely appear in productions as intelligently scripted, carefully photographed, and skillfully directed as those of the previous few years. In short, the Golden Age of Horror was over. It would be followed only by pale echoes, not only in imagination but also in such mundane but important factors as production values. Except for *Son of Frankenstein* (1939) and one or two others, their remaining films were to be hastily made low-budget productions with little of that uncanny feel for the grotesque and spooky that makes a horror film triumph over its melodramatic plot and extravagant action.

The year 1935 had been one of Lugosi's most active and creative; but the following few years would be disastrous, due less to the actor than to the decision of the British Board of Film Censors regarding horror movies. Faced with the loss of that large foreign market and the fact that such films were not doing well in America, Hollywood decided the genre had run its course and stopped production.

After Lugosi completed *The Invisible Ray*, he shifted to Republic Studios to begin *House of a Thousand Candles*. He grew ill, and on January 24, 1936, he had to leave the picture. His scenes were reshot, and Irving Pichel took over the role. Lugosi recovered, but his job opportunities did not. Finally he accepted a part in a poorly made film, *Postal Inspector,* a Robert Presnell production released by Universal in August, 1936. Taking third billing under Ricardo Cortez (the Inspector) and Patricia Ellis (the heroine), Lugosi played Benez, a nightclub owner who employs the heroine as a singer. When she innocently tells him about a large sum of money being shipped through the mails, he plots a daring robbery that takes place during a flood (which was shown via newsreel shots of a real disaster from the previous spring). *Variety* accused the film of containing "giddy lines, inane situations, and ofttimes makeshift direction" and felt that the picture would "have difficulty standing alone." It did.

A couple of months later—in October, 1936—Lugosi turned up in an undistinguished serial, *Shadow of Chinatown,* distributed by Victory Pictures. He played a mad inventor who, evincing no particular prejudice, was determined to eliminate both the Oriental and the white races. After completing this picture, Lugosi impatiently waited for another offer. Used to high living, he and his wife, Lillian, reluctantly started to cut down on their expenses. Finally he was hired to appear in another serial, *S.O.S. Coast Guard,* as Bornoff, another mad inventor, who is determined to sell his disintegration gas to the European country of Morovania. He has a problem, though, because a metal that he requires can be found only in the United States and is controlled by the government. As a result, he comes up against the intrepid Ralph Byrd, as a Coast Guard officer. The twelve chapter titles include "Barrage of Death," "The Gas Chamber," and the evocative "The Fatal Shaft." Released in August, 1937, the twenty-five reels of film were eventually recut into a sixty-nine-minute feature that appeared in 1942.

Shadow of Chinatown (1936). Lugosi as the villain, in disguise.

From the middle of 1937 through most of 1938, Lugosi did not appear in any films at all. The horror blackout was almost complete. According to Lugosi, who described this period in a 1942 interview, "The mortgage company got my house. I sold one car and then the other. I borrowed where I could, but who considered a jobless spook a good risk? By the end of 1937 I was at my wit's end. I was forced to go on relief." [57]

In the midst of Lugosi's financial troubles a mixed blessing arrived on January 5, 1938: a seven-and-one-half-pound boy named Bela, Jr. Lugosi was of course proud of his fatherhood, but here now was another responsibility. In the following years the marriage began to falter for a variety of reasons, and the son was caught between the factions. The relationship between the father and his son would not

[57] Interview with Frederick C. Othman, unidentified source, August 31, 1942.

prove particularly strong. His paternal feelings were lavished on others, among them Don Marlowe, his agent at various times, to whom he once signed a photo "Dad." He was also fond of his younger fans, as this writer can testify.

What was Lugosi like in this period? He was a mixture of many motives and drives, like most human beings. On the one hand, he was extremely happy that he had won such fame and easy money. He had gone a long way from being a locksmith. On the other hand, he also felt he deserved this fame, and even a higher standing than being a horror star. Basically, however, he was a rather simple man, albeit a flamboyant and emotional one. The money had come in easily and gone out the same way, even though his wife did provide a restraining hand. When all of a sudden the steady demand for horror parts vanished he scurried around looking for work and tried to console himself. But Lugosi thought big. If his screen roles had him conquering the world, his own wishes were more modest, but still grandiose. He liked to live big, and the character traits he showed in Hungary persisted. Bela never quite grew up—it is the charm and downfall of many a man—and when his career, so prosperous and rewarding in 1935, disappeared, he could not account for it.

It was during this period that Lugosi's looks changed. Whether the transformation was the result of mental depression, additional weight, or just age—he was now in his middle fifties—is not clear. But the lean face of Lugosi soon began to grow a little puffy, and the "handsome" years of his life grew to an end.

Some people might feel that drugs were the cause. In 1955 Lugosi declared to the media that he had been taking dope for twenty years. As a result of this statement, most people have employed a little arithmetic and come to the conclusion that he therefore must have begun his addiction in 1935. Lugosi, as usual, exaggerated mightily. "I don't know why he said that," his wife, Lillian, told this writer in 1973. "It wasn't true." Lugosi's problem began years later, sometime in the 1940's.

By late 1938 Lugosi's career was in severe difficulties. In 1936 he had appeared in a play called *Tovarich* in California. In it he played a dignified but down-on-his-luck aristocrat. Reality seemed no different. He had not appeared in a motion picture for a long time, and his future and that of the horror film seemed bleak. Universal had changed ownership, and the new regime was not too interested in the type of film that had made the studio famous. Still, it could not ignore the potential profits of a new Frankenstein picture and so in September, 1938, began to think about another chapter in the monster's unhappy life.

Universal's story department again mulled over Mary Shelley's novel, but could find nothing more of use. Scriptwriter Willis Cooper decided to strike out on his own and on October 20 submitted his screenplay. In the meantime, *Dracula* and *Frankenstein* had been rereleased to outstanding box-office success. Perhaps, reasoned the studio, if enough money were lavished on a new Frankenstein film, even greater rewards might be obtained.

In Cooper's initial plot, the late Dr. Frankenstein's will stated that his son Wolf would not inherit the estate until twenty-five years had elapsed without a reappearance of the monster. After this requirement is met, Wolf, with his wife, Elsa, and their young son, arrive during a stormy night. Unknown to them—and for no explicable reason—the monster emerges from the laboratory and kills a policeman and also a peasant family of three. When Wolf's butler disappears, both Wolf and the police chief, Neumiller, suspect the monster, and they are thoroughly convinced when the child tells them that a giant came through the wall and took away his picture book. Wolf goes to the laboratory, where the monster grabs him, begins to strangle him, declares that he is lonely and wants another wife. The monster threatens to kill both Elsa and Erwin if his connubial needs are not met. Wolf reluctantly agrees, but he is not a Frankenstein for nothing and soon becomes entranced with his work.

Neumiller, in the meantime, questions little Erwin, learns of the secret passageway, discovers the body of the butler, calls in a troop of soldiers, and has the castle placed under guard. Wolf, fearful of the monster's threats, tells Neumiller nothing (a far clearer motivation than in the final version) and returns to the laboratory, where the monster has brought the body of a soldier he has killed. But the man's brain has been ruined and therefore cannot be used, so the monster abducts the son and himself attempts to put the child's brain in the body of his new mate. Wolf arrives and repeatedly stabs the monster, but to no avail. Suddenly Neumiller and the soldiers enter and shoot the monster, who falls into a deep well. Neumiller then throws a grenade down the well, destroying the creature.

The problem of writing a worthwhile Frankenstein picture was not easily solved. In the first film the monster had been a limited creature capable of only grunts and howls. Universal cured this communication difficulty in *Bride of Frankenstein* (1935) by giving him the ability to speak and also to smoke cigars and drink wine. But this new monster was almost comic at times and far less fearsome because of his newly developed powers. The studio wanted him returned to his former inarticulate and simple-minded stage. Even if Universal could somehow make his regression acceptable to faithful horror fans, what would they do with a dumb brute as a protagonist? Not much, they thought, so the next contribution to the saga was to give him a companion in evil. Why not develop the crippled assistant who used to help Dr. Frankenstein? Why not give him a fuller characterization and make the servant—now evil rather than merely slavish—the mouthpiece and indeed the motivator of the monster's actions? (Actually Dr. Frankenstein's assistant in *Bride of Frankenstein* had already taken on some of these nasty traits and committed much murder and mayhem, but almost all of those scenes were cut from the final print.)

Cooper's initial screenplay was sent back for major revisions. His original story had borrowed heavily from *Bride of Frankenstein* in its main motivation, the creation of a woman. When it was submitted again, the script had been drastically altered. All the business about the brain transference was cut (though the monster's desire to use a child's brain reappeared a few years later in *Ghost of Frankenstein*), and a new character was born: the unforgettable Ygor (Lugosi). With Karloff as the monster and Bela as Ygor, the film would have the box-office advantage of having the two most famous horror stars on the marquee.

Universal was willing to spend time and money, but it wanted to be quite careful that the results would be horrific. *Bride of Frankenstein* had been a real tour de force by its director, James Whale. The images were strikingly handsome and at times grotesque, the sets and makeup and acting superb, but the film was marred by a certain tongue-in-cheek humor. Whale did not take the sequel to his 1931 masterpiece entirely seriously and so undercut the film's original intention: to frighten the public, a public, incidentally, that wanted to be frightened. Such a mistake would not be made with the third film in the series, *Son of Frankenstein*. Perhaps for this reason James Whale was not used. Instead, Rowland Lee was given the task.

As the film opens, the villagers of Frankenstein discuss the return of the son to the ancestral castle. One man mentions the family's accursed urge to experiment, saying, "It's in the blood, you know." And indeed it is. The Frankensteins are all intensely passionate men, dedicating their lives to science, not for evil, but out of curiosity.

The next scene shows Wolf (Basil Rathbone) and his wife and son (now called Peter) aboard a train, coming to regain the ancestral home. Through the train window can be seen a singularly gaunt and spare landscape full of twisted trees against a most forbidding fog and rain-filled sky. The wife's tactful comment to her husband, "Strange looking country," is quite to the point.

At the station the mayor makes quite clear that he is meeting them, not greeting them, and takes them to the castle. Wolf goes to the library and beneath a painting of his father opens the box of papers the mayor had handed him. In them the father offers his son "the sum total of my knowledge" and a statement reaffirming his all-consuming scientific curiosity. With a glass of brandy, Wolf salutes his dead father.

Inspector Krogh (Neumiller in the earlier version), played by Lionel Atwill, arrives to offer his help, not "if," but "when," it is needed. The Inspector had had his arm torn off by the monster as a child and thus his future military career was ruined. Now he is a bitter and frustrated police officer. Atwill milks his role for all it is worth by creating lots of "business" for his false arm. He salutes with it, cranks it behind him to hold his hands behind his back, places his monocle within the gloved fingers while polishing it with his good hand, slips a box of matches onto the finger, and later while playing darts sticks them in his forearm to hold them. Perhaps modeling his character on Erich von Stroheim's German officer with a broken spine in the previous year's *La Grande Illusion,* Atwill provides one of the most singular cameo performances in the whole Frankenstein series.

It is around Wolf that the dramatic theme of *Son* is constructed, for the film goes beyond the basic monster plot to show the change that events cause in the scientist. Wolf enters the film as a self-satisfied man with an objective, scientific outlook, but he lacks the ability to be impressed by nature and the unknown. He fears nothing. Though his wife is bothered by the gloom of the castle, he finds it "exciting, exhilarating!" He is skeptical about the fear the townspeople still have of the monster.

He describes to his wife the thunder and lightning that is stirring up the night:

It's magnificent! Nothing in Nature is terrifying when one under-
stands it. . . . My father drew that very lightning from Heaven and
forced it to his own will, to bring life to a being that he created with
his own hands. Why should *we* fear *anything?*

This intellectual arrogance, this refusal to be awed, is soon to be
shaken.

The next morning Wolf goes to the laboratory, where Ygor tries to
kill him by pushing a boulder down on him. Wolf pulls out his gun and
orders Ygor to climb down.

With his broken neck, snaggle teeth, matted hair, crippled walk, and
hoarse voice, Lugosi is unrecognizable. Not only through makeup but
also through voice and movement, he has completely subjugated the
Count Dracula image and become instead a rather low and malevolent
being. Ygor is probably Lugosi's greatest character role and overall one
of his finest performances, proof that he had a far greater range than
was revealed by the vampire and mad-scientist roles to which he was so
often reduced. Although he has only a few simple lines, he manages to
infuse them with a Lugosi sense of evil. Universal was intelligent
enough to realize this, and so revived Ygor as well as the monster for
the film's sequel, *Ghost of Frankenstein.* Since that script gave Lugosi
far more opportunity to talk and act, it might be said that his
performance there is even better. In both cases Lugosi's facial
expressions and his vocal timing and inflections and especially his use of
the long pause perfectly create a sense not only of low cunning and
peasant shrewdness but also of black humor. Ygor is marvelously
cynical about mankind and its motives, and he acts upon his convictions
with conscienceless glee. Ygor tells Wolf that he used to steal bodies
for his father—long pause—"they say." He then leads Wolf down a
secret passageway to the tomb of his father. On the coffin someone had
chalked in "maker of monsters." Wolf, framed by the camera with a
coffin on either side of the room, walks forward into a close-medium
shot, and then the camera backs up farther to reveal the huge but
prostrate body of the monster filling the screen. Wolf is astounded to
see the creature lying on top of a coffin and almost screams when he
sees the monster's hand move. Ygor explains that his friend was hurt
one day by the lightning while he was out—long pause—"hunting."
Wolf decides to vindicate his father by helping the monster. Taking a

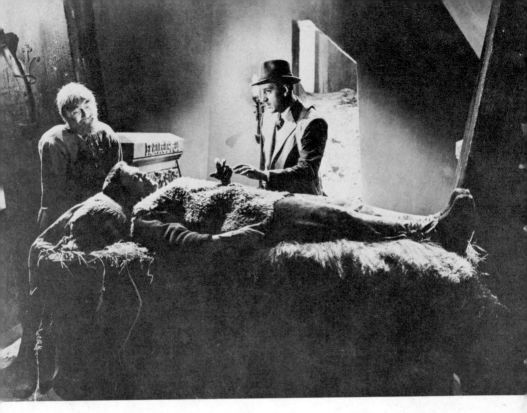

Son of Frankenstein. Note the obvious expressionistic influence.

torch, he scratches out the last word of "maker of monsters" and writes in "men."

Soon after, one of the most effective moments of the film occurs. The unconscious monster is tied to a wooden table and hoisted through the floor of the laboratory. The shot of the monster rising is most impressive and is admirably concluded when the body is placed on its back, the camera shooting between his two huge feet, filling each side of the frame, onto its ugly and unconscious face. Indeed, the monster is more than a man with makeup; he is here a kind of monolith.

Wolf hooks up the electrodes; in this case it is a kind of shock treatment to get him out of his coma and not technically an electrical recharge. For a moment the monster regains consciousness and starts to attack Wolf's butler but then relapses. Wolf thinks he has failed.

Later Wolf's son tells of how a giant came through a wall and took his fairy story book. Wolf hurries to the laboratory, but no one is there. Then, from behind him, crawling up the ladder next to the sulfur pit, comes the monster, who stealthily approaches Wolf and puts his hand

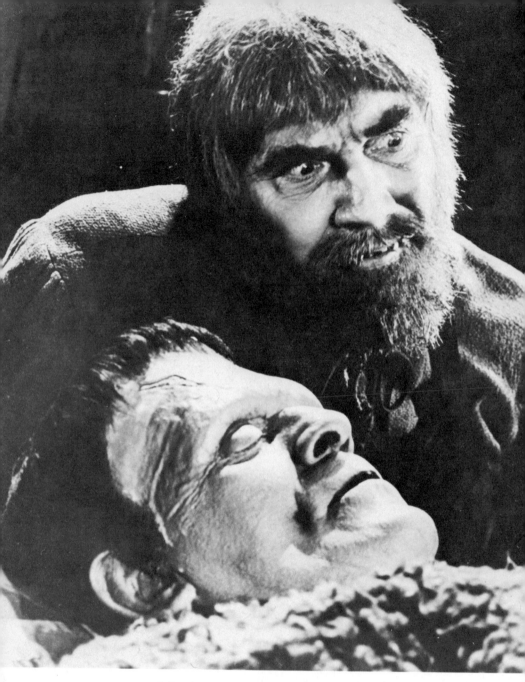

A barely recognizable Karloff and Lugosi.

Son of Frankenstein.

upon his shoulder and turns him around. Arrogant Wolf has finally met fear. Unlike the monster of later films, this one is lithe and quick-moving, and cannot be outrun or easily eluded. He is an insane creature of immense strength, as quick and alert as any human, and this is what makes him the most frightening manlike creature that Hollywood ever invented. The monster sees his reflection in the mirror and moves Wolf over to compare the two faces. He growls at his own ugliness. In him there is a kind of primal good or innocence, despite his murderous activities. Ygor arrives, turns the mirror around, and leads the monster away. He makes clear, however, that he does not want Wolf to attempt to cure his friend any further. He likes him just the way he is, the powerful tool of his own revenge.

One of the more intriguing aspects of the film is the master-servant relationship between Ygor and the monster. Both are outcasts. Ygor, who has survived the experience of being hanged, feels a kinship with the creature, since he himself is officially dead and the monster was made from the dead. Ygor also likes the monster because before lightning struck him, he "did things for me." Of course, what he did was kill all the people Ygor did not like, namely the jurors who decided that the grave-robber should be hanged. Ygor is hardly one to forget a grudge, and the monster is a convenient engine of destruction, yet there is also an affection, strong but perverse, between these two gargoyles.

Wolf is trapped, caught in a kind of blackmail. He is unwilling to tell the police that the monster is alive, for he still wants to vindicate his father, yet he does not know how to control Ygor, who in turn controls· the monster. When the butler suggests that Wolf tell the police, Ygor overhears and soon has the adviser killed. Then, eager to pursue his revenge, Ygor has the monster kill a few more of the people who were responsible for Ygor's hanging. The village is outraged and the police inspector arrives, but Wolf keeps his silence.

Wolf then goes to the laboratory, where Ygor attacks him. Wolf shoots Ygor and runs off to look for the monster. Soon after, the monster crawls up the side of the sulfur pit, sees his dead friend, and howls with agony and then rage. He throws everything he can into the boiling sulphur below. Then he picks up the fairy story book, calms down for a moment, and then with revenge motivating him, he crushes the book and goes off in search of the child. These scenes are the most frightening of all, due to the sheer rage and power of this man-giant with a simple brain. Here he becomes the nightmare figure—the ogre. It is not insignificant that the child gives him the fairy tale book, for the monster is the most frightening fairy tale of all. Yet for all his insane fury, he is not inhuman. He has a heart, and this touch of humanity brings his deeds to the verge of tragedy. When the monster lumbers off in search of the child, the film becomes all action, with almost no dialogue. The monster takes the child back to the laboratory and almost tosses the child into the pit, but the boy is unafraid and climbs the ladder and gives a helping hand to his giant friend. Meanwhile, the inspector has gone through the passageway and confronts the monster, who grabs his arm, and in a moment of both terror and black humor, the arm is ripped off again. Just as the monster is about to kill the inspector and the child, Wolf climbs up the side of the laboratory, swings on a cable à la Tarzan, and pushes the monster into the boiling sulfur pit. The last scene shows the Baron saying good-bye to the villagers and leaving on the train.

This would be the last film in which the monster was still a normally functioning creature with blood pressure, breath, and ailments. In later films he would be more powerful, less human, more like an unkillable robot. No creature could survive being immersed in boiling sulfur of 800°. From here on, he cannot die by so-called normal means but can be destroyed, the films tell us, only by dissection (*Ghost of Frankenstein*) or by reversing the electric poles (*Frankenstein Meets the Wolf Man*), though neither method was used. But by the time of *House of Frankenstein* and *House of Dracula* he was, for all his travails, unkillable. The monster was doomed to a kind of suspended animation and except for *Ghost of Frankenstein* was awakened or revived only long enough to kill a few people in the last reel and to "perish" again. In *Ghost of Frankenstein* he was burned alive, in *Frankenstein Meets the Wolf Man* he was washed away and drowned in a flood, in *House of Frankenstein* he sank in quicksand, and in *House of Dracula* he was burned again. Certainly a monster's lot is not a happy one.

At times, *Son of Frankenstein* resembles a German expressionist film from the twenties. A stylized castle, the fancy woodcut lettering of "Frankenstein" on a gate, the long shots of village houses, the angular, almost Caligari-esque window that Ygor peers through while playing his shepherd's pipe, the nearly primitive wooden staircase inside the castle (looking much too constructivist for a medieval structure), the low ceiling beams and heavy arches, and the conical, almost beehivelike laboratory reminiscent of Attila's buildings in *Kriemhild's Revenge*—all are quite imaginative, if derivative. Unfortunately the outer, more expressionistic sets do not always mesh with the interiors, nor are the movements of the actors sufficiently stylized to blend with the expressionistic sets. Despite these problems, *Son* was obviously the delight of Universal's art department and was the last Frankenstein film to contain really elaborate and imaginative decor.

Given a reasonably high budget and allotted an "A" running time (ninety-three minutes), the film is the longest of the series. This, however, is not entirely an advantage, for the plot takes a long time to get going and thereafter too much time is spent on Rathbone's facial expressions and occasional overacting, and not enough on Ygor and the monster, both of whom are far more interesting.

Despite its worthwhile production values, *Son*'s identity as a horror movie caused most critics to look down on it automatically. The first-string critic for the *Times* avoided it, and the review was written by the not-yet-promoted Bosley Crowther. His tone was one of ignorance, strained condescension, and mockery.

> If . . . [*Son of Frankenstein*] isn't the silliest picture ever made, it's a sequel to the silliest picture ever made, which is even sillier. . . . It must have been all the actors themselves could do, in this day and age, to keep straight faces. . . . Imagine, if you can, a picture so tough that Basil Rathbone plays a sympathetic part in it, so mean you feel sorry for Lionel Atwill, so ghastly that Bela Lugosi is only an assistant bogeyman. . . . Anybody who'd like a nice, un-sunny place to be haunted in couldn't do worse than rent Castle Frankenstein for the season. . . . With a pit of boiling sulphur in the basement and Bela Lugosi living there as a combination monster-nurse and janitor, what could be cozier? Yes sir, Castle Frankenstein is the showplace of the neighborhood.

In May, 1939, only five months after *Son of Frankenstein* was released, Lugosi appeared in *The Gorilla*, for Fox, and received seventh billing after the three Ritz Brothers, Anita Louise, Lionel Atwill, and Patsy Kelly. This comedy-mystery, directed by that veteran from the silent period, Allan Dwan, was based on a play that had already been filmed twice.

The story takes place in a mansion filled with sliding panels, lurking shadows, reverberating thunder, and bright flashes of lightning. A gorilla is at large, killing people. Lugosi, as Peters the butler, walks around stealthily and casts evil looks at people and becomes a likely suspect for the source of the villainy. But (surprise!) Lugosi is used as a red herring. Actually the real bad guy is someone else, who had been committing nefarious deeds dressed up in a gorilla suit. The Ritz Brothers are private detectives hired to see that Atwill is properly protected after that gentleman receives a note signed "the gorilla" establishing midnight as the hour of his doom. "It's all supposed to be either very funny or shockingly thrilling, depending on how you look at it. We couldn't see it either way," said the New York *Times*,[58] while *Variety* claimed that this "combo of broad slapstick, surprise situations and eerie chills is well-mixed, at a speedy pace."[59] Even *Variety*, though, could not take the Ritz Brothers.

[58] May 28, 1939.
[59] May 24, 1939.

The Gorilla (1939). Lugosi tries his best to ignore the Ritz brothers.

Lugosi's typecasting had come to the point when characters in the film have only to look at his unmade-up face to react unfavorably. "I don't like your looks" and "He gives me the creeps" are just two of the reactions. Lugosi plays his part reasonably straight, although he bestows a few suspicious looks and menacing glances in his small amount of screen time in order to remain a prime suspect.

Lugosi then received an offer from Britain, and on March 24, 1939, he sailed with Lillian to England to film *Dark Eyes of London,* released in that country in November; Monogram distributed it in the United States in March, 1940, under the title *The Human Monster.* Dr. Orloff (Lugosi) is both the kindly head of an institute for the blind and a figure of evil who first insures his victims and then collects on the policies when he has them killed. He is aided by Jake, a huge, ugly, blind fellow who rather unceremoniously drowns the victims in a tank of water and then throws them out the back window into the Thames. Lugosi's role as the insurance man is peculiar. At times he is quite pleasant and kind, but at other moments he suddenly becomes completely sinister, a transformation that his patrons do not seem to notice. His nefarious schemes are spoiled by a British detective who eventually discovers that Orloff is the criminal but who does not know yet that Orloff and the head of the institute are the same person. The film indulges in some rather gratuitous horrors. When a blind and dumb person, Lou, is liable to squeal, Lugosi hooks tubes to his ears and makes him deaf as well. When the police are going to question him via braille, Lugosi takes the helpless creature and drowns him in a tank of water. This act is not one to endear him to the audience, nor does it please Jake, who was the victim's friend. Enraged, Jake, in the usual pattern of horror films, attacks his master and, although shot, manages to throw Lugosi into the engulfing mud of the Thames.

The script of the film was adapted from a novel by Edgar Wallace and was well directed. Lugosi's role was not really dual. The part of the head of the institute was played, at least at times, by another actor, especially during all the dialogue scenes. Lugosi could hardly have lost that accent of his or his intonations and thus could not convincingly have fooled anyone. A London-based reviewer noted that "the macabre element is competently sustained and should send thrills creeping down the spines of the unsophisticated"; in his opinion, "British thrillers seldom offer such full measure of horrors." [60] The film would have been better with fewer horrors and more suspense, but it had good production values, moved along rapidly, and by no means was as bad as the Monogram films that were to follow.

Lugosi returned to California and appeared in Universal's *The Phantom Creeps*, probably his best serial. *Variety* reported that it

> . . . gains considerable box-office life from the presence of Bela Lugosi, arch-villain of horror features. It also contains certain popular appeal through pitting a mad scientific genius against American military intelligence service, with the foreign nations also struggling for his secret formulas.[61]

Although the review praised it for avoiding a lot of hokum and for being plausible, the film had more than its fair share of outlandish inventions. Dr. Alex Zorka (Lugosi) must have allowed himself little leisure during his lifetime. Besides extracting a new radioactive element from a meteorite (courtesy of the plot and some of the footage from

[60] *Motion Picture Herald*, November 18, 1939.
[61] August 9, 1939.

Human Monster (1939). Planning to dispose of another heroine.

The Invisible Ray), he has developed a mechanical spider, a ray gun, a devisualizer belt, and a giant robot. The spider pursues victims and induces suspended animation, the ray gun dispatches a few people, and the devisualizer allows him to dissolve in and out of various scenes, but the robot proved a poor investment. Although about eight feet tall and blessed with a monstrously ugly face, the robot actually accomplishes nothing. Even Lugosi's dumb assistant perceives its fatal flaw ("I don't see what good it is") and notes that such a creature roaming around the streets would hardly go unnoticed. Lugosi counters, "What could the police or anybody do against an army like that?" He neglects, however, to build more than one, so throughout the film the robot stays behind a secret panel, and except for one minor instance it performs no other function than to frighten the assistant. When finally it could be of use, the assistant sabotages it, and it blows up immediately.

Most of *The Phantom Creeps* centers on foreign agents, American counterspies, Zorka's assistant, and the great scientist himself scurrying around after a box containing the element. The film is packed with all kinds of frantic action: car chases, racing boats, airplanes, falling high-tension towers, gigantic fires, and miscellaneous and sundry explosions. Universal ransacked its stock-footage vaults, sometimes successfully, sometimes not. A slight fire in one room, intercut with exciting but old fire-truck scenes containing telltale vintage cars, eventually causes a conflagration that wrecks an entire city. Dramatic shots of a plane taking off and flying around in the foggy night are ludicrously interspersed with sunlit footage as the relentless search for the box goes on. Most of this fuss could have been avoided if Zorka had not, in a moment of hubris, chosen to reveal the box's location to his assistant. Considering the problems of trying to get back his element, Zorka would have done far better to invent a faster and newer car than a gangly robot. The old car, however, exists so that stock footage of chases and crashes could be inserted.   Although the plot (as in most serials) is a busy one, it prevents Zorka from enjoying his inventions until the very end. He spends most of his time getting in and out of his old car, roaming around his cheap laboratory, and having to contend with his woefully dumb and consistently disloyal assistant. Lugosi, however, enters fully into the spirit of his part as "the world's greatest genius" and plays it with even greater enthusiasm than is usually his wont. He explains that his inventions "could crush all opposition and make me the most powerful man in the world." He demonstrates some of his power. "They called me a dreamer, a fool, but now I have it," he says with satisfaction. A moral scientist who witnesses the experiment tells Zorka, "My only fear is what you will do with it." Zorka replies, "I shall do with it as *I* wish, not hand it over to the government, as you would have me." When the scientist asks the doctor whether he knows to what dreadful ends his inventions might be used by foreign powers, Zorka answers simply, "Of course!"

This dialogue from the first chapter reveals the biggest weakness of the story: There is little suspense. Lugosi is obviously the villain, and viewers waited patiently for him to get his meteorite back through eleven chapters of foreplay so that he can carry out his climactic, monomaniacal plans. The last chapter, aptly titled "To Destroy the World," features Lugosi flying around in an airplane gleefully dropping little test-tube portions of his rare element upon cities, ships, and anything else that strikes his evil fancy. At one point he spies a dirigible and drops a bomb on that too so that real-life footage of the explosion of the *Hindenburg* could be included. During all these moments he chuckles happily. No one ever enjoyed being mean as much as Bela! Throughout the film, despite all the outlandish events, Lugosi remains convincing and shows that *The Invisible Ray* (with substantially the same story line) would have been a far more exciting film if he, not Karloff, had played the mad scientist.

In the summer of 1939 Lugosi returned briefly to MGM, where he played Comrade Razinin in the classic Ernst Lubitsch comedy, *Ninotchka*. It is Razinin who is responsible for sending Ninotchka (Greta Garbo) to the West, and thus for exposing her to the appealing decadence of Paris and Melvyn Douglas. At the end he again sends her off, this time to Turkey and, unknown to him, a final reunion with her lover. *Ninotchka* provided one of Lugosi's rare appearances in a nonhorror film, but his role was one-dimensional, an image of a cold, efficient Russian, the sole villain of an otherwise good-natured film. His big scene consists almost entirely of the following monologue:

> If I told you what's going on in Constantinople right now, you wouldn't believe me. They are sitting there, those three, for six weeks, and haven't sold a piece of fur. This anonymous report was sent to me. They are dragging the good name of our country through every cafe and nightclub. [He reads:] "How can the Bolshevik cause gain the respect among the Moslems when your three representatives Buljanoff, Ivanoff and Kopalski, get so drunk that they throw a carpet out of their hotel window, and complain to the management that it didn't fly." Unbelievable! It's an outrage. . . . Don't waste my time, Comrade. Do your duty. Goodbye!

Lugosi started in the second week of November, 1939, on RKO's latest installment in the Saint detective series, *The Saint's Double Trouble* (released in February, 1940). George Sanders as usual starred as the detective, Simon Templar, and Lugosi was given fourth billing. The film received poor reviews ("the whole thing is pretty messy"), with Sanders in particular roasted for indulging in "a field day of overacting." [62] *Variety* called it "one of the slowest and most absurd" of the Saint films. "Bela Lugosi doesn't have much chance as the diamond-smuggler from Egypt." [63]

And thus the thirties came to an end. It had been a busy and

[62] New York *World Telegram*, February 13, 1940.
[63] February 14, 1940.

Greta Garbo encounters Lugosi. *Ninotchka* (1939).

confused decade. The world had gone from the Depression into another war; the movies had moved from the freewheeling early thirties into a tightly censored production-code era; Universal had stopped doing films like *All Quiet on the Western Front,* and its classic horror series, and became even less of a first-rate studio. And Hollywood, as a whole, although it had been berated by critics, did not know that a really creative and lucrative era had passed. The next half decade would prove more profitable, but less artistically impressive. And from then on, both earnings and art would decline. Perhaps only in the 1960's did American production regain some of the excitement and activity it had offered in the twenties and thirties. And Lugosi, whose future had appeared so promising in 1931, was far less radiant with hope as the new decade opened. But if he had by this time given up a career as a multifaceted actor—the handwriting on the wall continually spelled horror films or nothing—he was at least working. The nature of the employment, however, was another matter. The choice was not that of Milton's Satan: "Better to reign in hell than serve in heaven." He served in what grew to be more and more a hell as the years drew on.

❧ 5 ❧

The Early Forties

THE LATE 1930's had not been Bela Lugosi's happiest period, but the 1940's became in some ways even worse. True, he worked more steadily up through 1945 and was financially better off, but he was hopelessly typecast and unable to show the range of his abilities.

Universal, long the most productive horror studio, had almost completely abandoned both Lugosi and Karloff and chose Lon Chaney, Jr., to be its horror star. Chaney was given leading roles as the wolf man, the Frankenstein monster, and even, insult of insults, the Count in *Son of Dracula.* An unexciting actor—a pall of dull sincerity hung over him—Chaney created characters that were more to be pitied than respected, more cringing than aggressive, more plebeian than aristocratic. If ever a star lacked charisma, it was Chaney, Jr., but Universal somehow did not see it that way. Perhaps Chaney's relative youthfulness was the reason. Perhaps, too, Universal felt that the poetic intensity of Lugosi was old-fashioned and that Chaney's prosaic personality was more suitable to the reputedly unselective audiences that attended the low-budget, second-feature horror films then being made.

Universal did not drop Lugosi entirely. They gave him a few minor parts, as in *Black Friday* and *The Wolf Man,* and only one really good role: a return engagement as Ygor in *Ghost of Frankenstein.* In some films Lugosi was used merely as a red herring who had only to look sinister enough to divert suspicion from the real villain, as in *Night Monster* and the second version of *The Black Cat.* It is ironic that this aristocratic Hungarian, having played numerous counts, seers, doctors, professors, and scientists, would now often be cast as butlers and handymen. The Hollywood-style "reasoning" behind this change probably proceeded in this fashion: since Lugosi had made an effective

Ygor in *Son of Frankenstein* and later *Ghost of Frankenstein*, he was therefore capable of being something besides a man of innate though insane dignity and so was solidly retyped as an assistant. The frustration and even insult of being demoted from a count to a no-account servant did not escape this sensitive man; but he felt, perhaps rightly, that it was better to serve than to starve.

Although Lugosi no longer appealed to Universal, he did arouse the interest of Sam Katzman, who with Jack Dietz ran Banner Productions. Katzman decided that there was still money in cheap horror pictures, so he produced a number of them for Monogram. Economically astute but artistically deprived, he eventually became one of Hollywood's most notorious purveyors of *schlock,* and Lugosi helped him along the path to this dubious position. Katzman's scripts generally had the coherence of a madman's dream, though little of its imagination. The resulting films plodded and plotted their way through primitive sets, casual lighting, dull camera work, and third-string actors with the efficiency and indifference of a large discount store. Lugosi struggled manfully with impossible roles and infantile dramaturgy, and through the magic of his own skill and personality managed to elevate the reprehensible to the barely palatable. Although occasionally Lugosi did leave Monogram and Katzman to appear in pictures for other companies, he would never again (except for Columbia's *The Return of the Vampire* in 1943) be the main lead in a major studio production.

Back in September, 1939, the wheels at Universal had again started to grind, and an idea for another film with Lugosi and Karloff, to be called *Black Friday*, developed. Curt Siodmak and Eric Taylor conceived what could have been an interesting film. Briefly, they imagined the story of Dr. Huxley (Karloff), a gentle professor of English literature. In a small upstate college town, a car containing gangster Red Banning is shot at, and Huxley is crushed in the resulting accident. The ganster has a broken spine and the professor a damaged brain, so Dr. Sovac (Lugosi) puts Banning's brain into Huxley's body. The patient recovers and reveals by his actions that Banning's brain is taking over. Sovac takes extensive notes on his friend's activities, checks into newspaper files to learn more about Banning's career, and then puts Huxley into situations that will stimulate his criminal memories. Huxley finally "becomes" Banning and kills some of the gangsters who had double-crossed him. At this point Huxley's family arrives and the professor partially regains control.

Sovac, fascinated by the dual nature of his friend, again coaxes the Banning brain to the fore. From here on, many more of the mob are killed. Jean, Sovac's daughter, who knows about the operation, becomes suspicious of the results and convinces her father to end his experiments. Eventually the Banning personality attacks Jean, and Sovac has to kill Banning-Huxley in order to save his daughter. For this he is incarcerated in a state hospital for the criminally insane. The plot ends as he appeals his case, claiming that the experiment was a step forward for science; the question of whether or not he is freed is left up in the air.

This potentially good script (evocative of Siodmak's novel, *Donovan's Brain*) gave Lugosi a fine role and Karloff a meaty double one, but for some strange and foolish reason the casting was drastically changed so that the roles that were created for both stars were shifted. When the film was released in March, 1940, Karloff was in Lugosi's part of the doctor, Stanley Ridges had taken Karloff's role of Huxley-Banning, and poor Lugosi, with almost nothing left, had become the gangster hunted by Banning. Although the roles were switched, no one bothered to change the names or any of the personal details about the characters. Thus Karloff kept the name of Sovac and despite his British accent and manner was supposed to be a European refugee. Lugosi had almost nothing to go on and was not terribly convincing any more than James Cagney would have been a believable Count Dracula. As a result of somebody's dabbling with the reasonably good script, what could have been one of the studio's best gruesome-twosome pictures instead became an unexciting crime melodrama that gave the best role to an actor that no one really wanted to see. The publicity department created some hoopla when it had Lugosi hypnotized so that the scene in which he is locked in a closet would appear genuine. The weak episode hardly merited the services of a hypnotist, except perhaps to convince Lugosi that the part was worth taking at all.

When *Black Friday* resulted in less than a bonanza at the box office, Universal did not blame its peculiar miscasting of the roles, but decided instead that Lugosi and Karloff had lost their appeal. It seemed incapable of realizing how well Karloff's quiet menace and Lugosi's flamboyant passion complemented each other and how some effective scripts could have made the team as inevitable to horror as Laurel and Hardy were to comedy. Although the studio continued to make horror films and occasionally made use of each star separately, *Black Friday* proved to be the last time Universal paired its famous men. For Lugosi there was at least one advantage: he would no longer have to endure the afternoon tea breaks that his British rival demanded.

Lugosi then went to New York and joined Ed Sullivan's *Star Dust Cavalcade* stage show, in which he played a short scene from *Dracula* with Arthur Treacher.

His next movie role was in *You'll Find Out* (November, 1940), a simple-minded mystery-comedy that was relatively popular with the public. Probably its biggest liability is Kay Kyser, a bandleader-comedian whose musical and personal gifts are difficult to appreciate.

The plot is a simple one: Kyser's band plays for a young heiress' twenty-first birthday party at a spooky old mansion absolutely crammed with secret passages. The girl's aunt believes in spiritualism and has Prince Saliano (Lugosi) conduct an occasional séance to communicate with the spirit of her dead brother. Saliano, with the family lawyer (Karloff) and a phony professor (Peter Lorre), plans to

Bela hypnotized by Manly Hall. *Black Friday* (1940).

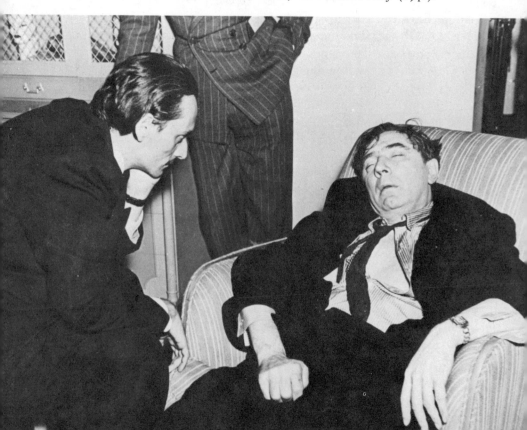

kill the girl that night because at the age of twenty-one she will inherit the family fortune, and their nefarious schemes for bilking the old lady will be at an end.

For part of the entertainment Ginny Simms sings a song. Bela smiles during the performance and then goes up to her and says how "splendid" she was, kisses her hand, and speaks of the fine quality of her voice. He brings his fingers to his mouth and kisses them in a Continental gesture of approval, but then, as his face darkens, he adds that "it's criminal to waste it on such trash." It is tempting to interpret this remark as Lugosi's own reaction to appearing in *You'll Find Out*.

Finally the Prince is prevailed upon to conduct a séance. He asks for some appropriate music and hopes that Kyser's "musicians [he sneers at the very word] will oblige." Bela now intones, in words that barely get through the accent barrier: "Presently I shall assume a state of trance, in which the outer mind merges with the astral portion of the human ego." During the séance a chandelier falls, barely missing the girl, and despite other attempts to kill her, she of course survives the evening.

Three wasted villains in *You'll Find Out* (1940).

Kyser runs around dark passageways, discovers the Prince's séance paraphernalia, and exposes the plan to kill the girl for the inheritance. Suddenly all three villains enter, throw a bomb in the room, and run out; but a dog carries it after them, and after an explosion the dog returns, the villains presumably now only astral selves.

The villainous roles, although immersed in a pseudocomedy setting, are still played straight by each of the heavies. Kyser functions as the foil. One of the drawbacks is that the film did not have a few scenes of the three villains plotting together. With Bela's accent, Karloff's lisp, and Lorre's peculiar whine, a delightful confrontation could have been created. Bela might have grandiloquently offered some cosmic villainy, Karloff a more decorous and dignified solution, while Lorre could have dredged from his faintly controlled psychosis a particularly sadistic and loathsome demise for the girl. The critics, however, did not miss these potentials. *Variety* felt the picture to be "solid comedy entertainment,"[1] and the *Daily News* gave it three stars.

Lugosi's next film, *The Devil Bat*, although a cheap production, returned him to a more typical role. Released by Producers Releasing Corporation in January, 1941, the film contains the *Ur*-myth of his screen personality. Here he plays Dr. Paul Carruthers, a research chemist embittered by the fact that one of his formulas has brought a fortune to his employers but nothing to himself. Bristling with passionate resentment as only Lugosi can, he seeks revenge by breeding giant bats and giving his enemies a shaving lotion that attracts the creatures. Lugosi advises his victims to put the lotion "on the tender part of your neck" and then intones a very pregnant "Good-bye." His parting remark becomes a kind of running gag. Toward the end of the film he omits the "Good-bye" and instead tells his victim, "I assure you, you will never use anything else!"

The script puts its heavy thumb on man's basic wish for vengeance and retribution. Such an emotion is not limited to medieval Italy, modern Sicily, or the Hatfields and McCoys of a few generations ago. Lugosi, the brilliant chemist, wants revenge—to which, in a sense, he is entitled—and he proceeds to get it. His ruthless determination appeals to the public's Walter Mitty mind. Most people resent the various outrages perpetrated against them, but since they can seldom do anything, they try to forget. But not our mad scientist. He not only

[1] November 14, 1940.

The "Prince" endures Kay Kyser. *You'll Find Out.*

Lugosi and his lethal shaving lotion. *The Devil Bat* (1940).

broods, he breeds. His giant bats carry out his revenge, and even though he is finally punished—shaving lotion thrown on him causes his bat to kill him—the story still provides the audience with primitive and basic satisfaction. Lugosi's scientist will do anything to get his innings, and he doesn't give a damn about what society thinks or what the law demands. He is not above the law. He *is* the law.

The ideas of the film are far more interesting than their realization. The sets are few and cheap, the dialogue flat and unwieldy, and scenes of two newspapermen trying to solve the mystery are visually dull and go on far too long. Unfortunately Lugosi is not featured enough in the film, nor is he given many effective lines. There are, however, a few enjoyable moments beyond his wonderful "Good-bye." In one, a professor explains over the radio that there could not possibly be a devil bat. Lugosi, working away in his laboratory, listens to the self-assured and pompous professor and mutters "imbecile" and "feeble mind" at him. *Variety* summed up the film with "This is pretty terrible" and added that it "hardly can pass muster on even the most lowly dual situations." [2] Still, for all its drawbacks, the film is kind of fun.

If the critics thought *The Devil Bat* was poor, they had yet to see the Monogram series. Lugosi had been faced with the choice of receiving small parts in B productions or winning star billing and major roles in Monogram's C and D films. In the beginning of 1941 Lugosi made his decision and began his ignoble association with Sam Katzman. The results proved profitable to the producer but disastrous to Lugosi's reputation. Bela's first film was to be called *Murder by the Stars* and was eventually released as *The Invisible Ghost*. This split-personality tale was based on an actual case, but its treatment is too farfetched to be believable.[3]

The Invisible Ghost told the story of Dr. Kessler (Lugosi), a kindly man who occasionally goes berserk and unknowingly kills people. Even though the doctor's wife had run off with his best friend years before, he still honors her memory. As the film opens, he is having dinner with his daughter and her fiancé and lovingly addresses the empty chair of his missing wife. Meanwhile, out in the kitchen, Jules, the gardener, is raiding the refrigerator and taking food to Mrs. Kessler. Because she suffers amnesia from an auto accident, the

[2] January 22, 1941.
[3] New York *Morning Telegraph*, February 26, 1941.

gardener feels she would be too much of a shock to the doctor and therefore keeps her hidden, in the hope that she might soon recover.

As the boyfriend leaves the house, he encounters the new maid, his former girlfriend. The two have an argument that is overheard by the butler. Later Mrs. Kessler wanders forth and appears outside a window. When the doctor sees her face, he becomes hypnotized and starts shuffling around the building in search of someone to murder. He enters the maid's room and kills her. The evidence points to the boyfriend, who is jailed, tried, convicted, and executed. Then his brother (played by the same actor) arrives from South America and stays at the house. That same night Kessler again observes his wife's face at the window, and this time he kills Jules, who is still at his favorite occupation, ransacking the refrigerator. Soon afterward Mrs. Kessler goes out for yet another stroll, her wanderlust seemingly unimpaired, and stares once more into the window. This triggers the usual response: Kessler goes up to his daughter's room and is about to kill her when he is awakened by lightning. In the morning a portrait of Mrs. Kessler is discovered ripped and a policeman found dead.

With Jules' death, her filched fare has ceased, so the wife ventures forth to the much-raided refrigerator herself, but she is caught by the police. When Kessler sees her, his eyes widen with the usual response, and he automatically starts to strangle the nearest neck, that of a policeman. The wife thereupon collapses and dies—a plot device unworthy of even a grade-school author—and after her husband returns to normal, he is told that he himself is the murderer. At this point Lugosi provides a moment far more inspired than anything else in the picture. Turning toward the camera, he soundlessly pronounces the word "me," and then brings those beautiful, eloquent hands up before his face in a gesture of despair. The technique here may be reminiscent of Lugosi's earlier days in the Hungarian theater, but has a distinction far beyond the "film acting" by which he is surrounded. Finally Kessler says, "Nothing can part us now," and is led away, presumably to his eventual execution.

Lugosi's role did not offer or demand much, but it is one of the few occasions when he portrayed a warm, kindly human being. He is friendly to others, devoted to his daughter, compassionate concerning the boyfriend's execution, and properly outraged and appalled at the killings. The Lugosi menace does not even inadvertently lurk in the background of the characterization to mar his performance as a "nice" man. In fact, the scenes of him acting normally are more memorable than those in which he is a killer, as when the daughter tells Kessler that she is in love and he is pleased at the news. He clearly was capable of playing a straight role without the ominous expressions and gestures associated with his villains.

Considering the script, *The Invisible Ghost* is not too badly directed by Joseph H. Lewis, who uses more close-ups than are usual in such cheap pictures, and in the killing of the maid shows considerable imagination. She is in bed, listening to music from a radio, and shots of her, of Kessler advancing with his bathrobe held out, and of the radio are intercut. Then there is a shot of a black screen, which turns out to be Kessler's robe; he lowers the robe until we can see his eyes over the top, with the rest remaining black. Then he raises it until all the screen darkens and the scene ends.

The film's illogical plot, however, held it back from receiving any critical praise. *The Invisible Ghost* was deservedly disliked by every reviewer. One cracked that its "story is invisible, too," [4] and another opined, "The kindliest thing that one can do when Hollywood turns out a little monstrosity like this is to pretend you didn't see it." It is impossible to disagree with these opinions, since the script and production values were so poor that even Lugosi's charisma couldn't redeem them. These reviews might have been enough to discourage most producers, but Sam Katzman simply looked at the profit sheets and sent his untalented writers off to concoct another unmemorable plot.

Meanwhile, Universal released *The Black Cat* in April, 1941, although it had probably been filmed before *The Invisible Ghost*. This new picture used the same title as the 1934 film, but it was no closer to Poe than the other attempt had been. Lugosi plays a rather scraggly-looking caretaker who lurks menacingly about and has only a few lines to speak. Typical of these half dozen or so statements is his immortal observation that the gates of the mysterious mansion had been closed ever "since car killed cat." Lugosi's dark-webbed eloquence as Dracula had become pidgin English.

It took the combined efforts of four scenario writers to change Poe's highly original story into a familiar tale of murders and wills. The film told of a rich old woman who lived in a mansion with her housekeeper,

[4] New York *Daily Mirror*, May 9, 1941.

her servant Eduardo (Lugosi), and a vast number of cats. Several greedy and, for the most part, rather unpleasant relatives come to the house, and after a few rancorous discussions about her will, the old lady is killed. A number of murders follow, until the tale concludes in a crematorium, where the dead cats had been incinerated.

According to *Variety*, the film was not even a good B production, and Lugosi spent his time "constantly leering in windows." [5] This can be taken as a definitive description, because that was about all that he did in his few short scenes. Yet, despite the insignificance of his part, he was billed fourth under Basil Rathbone, Hugh Herbert, and Brod Crawford. Another small role in the film was played by a young Alan Ladd, whose career, in contrast to Lugosi's, was on its way up.

After this ignominious appearance as a servant, Lugosi paused for a few months and waited for work. None appeared. Sinking to a new low—he could not resist the temptations offered by Sam Katzman—he performed with the East Side Kids in *Spooks Run Wild*, released in November, 1941.

The East Side Kids are given a two-week holiday at a camp for underprivileged boys and hear over the radio that a vicious killer known as "the monster" is at large. Meanwhile, Lugosi, accompanied by a dwarf assistant, drives up to a gas station with a trailer carrying three coffins and asks directions to a deserted mansion. The attendant tells him that the house has been vacant for the ten years since the last owner was murdered. Lugosi asks, "Is there a road to it?" The attendant replies, "Yes, but, uh—" Lugosi says, "Good night, my friend. Thank you," and drives off without ever asking where he can find the road. Such logical oversights are par for the Monogram course. Another man, a bearded professor, then drives up in pursuit of the killer. The professor requests secrecy, explaining: "at night the monster's strong—and the police would be helpless against him."

That night the boys take a shortcut through a graveyard. Disregarding a watchman's cry to stop, the boys run away, and one of them, Pee Wee, is shot. The others take the wounded boy to the nearby mansion, where Lugosi is found reading a newspaper with a headline about the killer. The black youth, reacting to the mysterious atmosphere, says, "I'm so scared, I'm turning white now." Lugosi treats the wound and says to the others: "You will notice this is a very old house—in some respects, a very strange one." The boys agree to stay the night while Pee Wee recovers. One of them describes the bedroom as "a very charming room in a repulsive sort of way."

Various scenes of haunted-house comedy follow as the boys are scared out of their limited wits by dark hallways, trapdoors, secret panels, and other obligatory devices of old mansions, as they search for Pee Wee, who is wandering around in a trance. The boys learn from a book that the monster can be defeated only with "silver bullets and blessed iron," but lacking these necessary ingredients, they decide to amend the recipe by planning to "get tough." The boys hide under a sheet, hold up a skull, and accuse Lugosi of murdering the estate's owner, charging, "You scared the health out of me." Lugosi protests that he has never been there before and, after falling down a flight of stairs, is knocked out by the thrown skull. The boys tie him up, locate Pee Wee, and eventually discover that the professor is the real killer and that Lugosi is just an innocent magician who came to the house to practice some new routines. In an epilogue he demonstrates his skills by performing for the boys. As in *Mark of the Vampire*, Lugosi turns out to be a theatrical performer and not the monster he appears.

Most of the time *Spooks Run Wild* tries to follow the Dracula myth.

With the East Side Kids in *Spooks Run Wild* (1941).

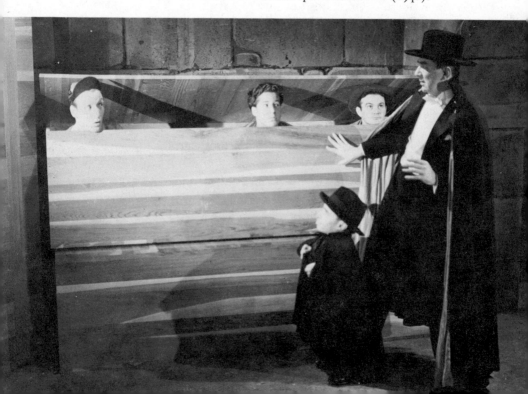

Lugosi wears a tuxedo, has an assistant, brings coffins with him, is pursued by a Van Helsing type, supposedly sleeps by day, and can be hurt only by certain things. Even the dialogue suggests the earlier film. "This is a very old house" is reminiscent of the Count's "very old wine." And a scene in the cemetery echoes "The children of the night—what music they make" when Lugosi hears wolflike sounds and blandly says to the dwarf: "The City of the Dead—do they hear the howling of the frightened dogs?" Yet never once is the word "vampire" used in this film; the villain is always referred to as the monster. And Lugosi has suffered another change since *Dracula*. In that film women found him attractive, whereas in this one just his face frightens the kids, as if he were some kind of repulsive and ugly creature.

The only place where a good word could be found for the film was in its press sheets, which contributed the immortal caption "The Merchant of Menace vs. Those Tenement Terrors" and described the film

> as about the most uproarious picture of its type that has reached the screen in many a moon. . . . Last night's audience literally rocked in their seats.

The source of this rocking was supposed to be hilarity, although cynical viewers might consider other reasons. In any case, the film made a profit, as did almost everything that Sam Katzman had a hand in. As someone once observed, no one would ever go broke underestimating the taste of the American public.

With a new horror cycle building up speed at Universal, Lugosi returned to appear in *The Wolf Man* (released in December, 1941) as Bela, the Gypsy who one night bites Lawrence Talbot (Lon Chaney, Jr.) and so spreads a lycanthropic curse that would endure through several films. *The Wolf Man* or at least the potential of its story is far richer than most of the horror films of the forties. Written by Curt Siodmak, it draws upon the old werewolf myths, which even the Catholic Church had once believed. Despite the difficulties of such a subject, Siodmak gave a sense of tragedy to the personal dilemma of his afflicted protagonist, but this was undermined by Universal's rather crass wish to establish nothing more than a new bogeyman.

Lugosi could not have felt much resentment at being denied the title role, since the character was tailored for Chaney and is far different from what Lugosi played or what he could possibly play, but he probably was unhappy that his part was not larger. He played a moustached fortune-teller who gets upset by a bundle of wolfbane that the heroine has brought with her. He becomes even more disturbed when he reads her palm, for he jumps back in horror and implores her to leave. He has seen in her hand the pentagram, the sign that reveals her as his next victim. Moments later, in the woods, she is attacked by the wolf—which rather inconsistently looks like the real thing, and not like the hairy semihuman that Chaney later becomes. Hearing her cries, Chaney arrives and clubs the animal to death with his silver-headed cane. Thus the early demise of Lugosi's character.

Although *The Wolf Man* is flawed, it does stumble upon the elements of an infinitely sensitive and meaningful myth, one that could have made a superb and frightening allegory about a man on whom is thrust a fate he neither wants nor comprehends.

Universal continued to mine its treasure trove of horror and in the spring of 1942 released *Ghost of Frankenstein*, reuniting Ygor (Lugosi) and the monster (now Lon Chaney, Jr.). It was a well-directed, fast-paced, melodramatic but somewhat plausible sequel that has satisfactorily survived the years and by no means deserves the vast number of insults leveled against it by critics at the time. Although a lesser work than the previous Frankenstein films, it is by no means a travesty. Perhaps the major complaint is that the film is not frightening. However, it told its story with skill, took itself seriously, and was the last time that the monster was given the budget (about $500,000), direction, and script that he deserved.

The film opens in the much-harassed village of Frankenstein, where the townspeople (engaged in another of their confrontations with the mayor) want to blow up the castle and thus once and for all rid the world of Ygor, who for some reason had not died from Dr. Wolf von Frankenstein's bullet. They also want to remove any possibility that the monster might still be alive. The crowd, torches in hand, runs toward Frankenstein's ancestral home. This castle is no longer the expressionistic set seen in *Son*, but a solid stone building of massive but unstylized proportions. Ygor appears on the roof and, like Quasimodo, pushes part of the fortifications down on his tormentors. In the meantime, some of the dynamite is set, and as Ygor runs down the steps, the castle explodes. Ygor, always lucky, lands in the cellar, where he notices the silhouette of a hand moving on the wall and turns to see that the monster is still alive in the now-hardened sulfur pit. Delighted that the sulfur has "preserved" his friend, Ygor leads him out of the castle just before it is blown up entirely.

What Ygor leads away is no longer the alert and lithe Frankenstein monster; it is a slow-moving, brutish creature more mechanical than human. Although the sulfur preserved him, it also drained him of his former vitality. Lon Chaney, Jr., who plays the role, lends the creature his usual taciturn nature. But still, his was the best portrayal of the monster after Karloff left the series. The versions that would follow—including Lugosi's own interpretation—were to be far worse.

A thunderstorm, obligatory to the genre, quickly develops. The monster pushes Ygor away. Although a bolt had previously hurt him—in fact it had put him in a coma, just prior to *Son*—it here has a more fortuitous effect. As the monster raises his arms to the heavens, lightning strikes him on the electrodes, and as chords of music climactically crash on the sound track, the monster regains his strength, though not his Karloffian agility. Ygor cries out exultantly, "Your father was Frankenstein, and your mother was the lightning!"

Soon after, Ygor leads the monster to the town of Vasaria in search of Ludwig Frankenstein, a brother of Wolf (the doctor in *Son*). Ludwig (Cedric Hardwick) has followed the family's medical profession and is a specialist in diseases of the mind. With his daughter (Evelyn Ankers) he has put aside the past, and no one knows that it was his father who had created the monster. A practicing scientist, he is aided in his experiments by Dr. Bohmer (Lionel Atwill), who has taught Ludwig all he knows. Bohmer had made some dreadful but unspecified error years before that spoiled his career, and he is now bitter that his pupil has won greater recognition.

While Ygor asks directions to where Ludwig lives, the monster wanders off. A little girl is being teased by some boys who have kicked the ball with which she was playing high onto a roof. They run away when the monster appears. He lumbers up to the little girl, and is shown from a low angle; the child, from a high angle. "Are you a giant?" she asks. The monster likes her, one assumes, because she is not afraid of him and treats him kindly, and also because he empathizes with the mistreatment she receives from the "others." As a favor, he carries her onto the roof to retrieve the ball. Meanwhile, the villagers arrive, and one threatens to shoot the monster. Another runs up after the creature and is pushed off the roof for his trouble. Despite the promise of the girl's father that if the monster puts the girl down no one will hurt him, he is attacked by the crowd and captured. Helpless, Ygor goes to see Ludwig and, threatening to reveal the family's past, blackmails him into asking the police to hand the monster over to the doctor.

Ludwig goes to the town hall, where the monster, looking very imposing indeed in a low-angle shot, sits in a witness chair while the prosecutor asks him questions. There is a lynching-party mood to the crowd, reminiscent of a similar scene in *Bride of Frankenstein.* Curiously, the "people" come off rather badly in horror films, as opposed to their golden virtues in "message" pictures. After all, the people of Vasaria are the "folk" just as much as are the Okies in *The Grapes of Wrath.* It just may be that horror films are more honest about man's motives than the films praised for their so-called reality. In the Frankenstein series the people are often more villainous, more full of bloodlust, than the monster and perhaps are even more evil, because they act in the name of justice and self-righteous anger. The monster, in fact, is (in his own peculiar way) the hero: more sinned against than sinning. Yet he is never so bland as not to be menacing also. Unlike the wolf man, he has considerable conscious control over his actions; therefore he demands a kind of respect that the wolf man, who invariably whines after he dines, never evokes.

While the monster is seated quietly in the witness chair, Ludwig enters the courtroom, and the monster nods his head in recognition. When the judge comments upon this action, Ludwig replies that he never saw "this [pause] man" before in his life. This reply enrages the monster (the script assumes that they had met, although there is no evidence in the previous films), and he breaks loose and attacks Ludwig. But the doctor stands his ground, and the monster, hearing Ygor's shepherd's pipe, escapes with his friend.

The monster enters Ludwig's mansion and immediately murders Kettering, one of the doctors there. The monster here is the uncontrollable engine of fury reminiscent of the Karloff portrayal. Ludwig subdues the rampaging creature by turning on the gas in the corridor and then decides to kill him by means of dissection. He asks Dr. Bohmer's aid, but when the older man refuses, Ludwig decides to do it himself. But at this point a double-exposed image of the father (actually Hardwick) appears—the "ghost of Frankenstein"—and advises his son not to destroy the monster but to give him another brain.

Ludwig agrees and turns on the electricity to give the monster sufficient strength for the operation. The noise awakens Ygor, who hurries in to see Ludwig and says: "You've agreed. You're going to help me, doctor. [With great enthusiasm:] You're giving him life?" Ludwig answers that he is giving him Kettering's brain. "The monster will cease to be an evil influence and will become everything that is good."

"No," says Ygor, "you cannot take my friend away from me. He's all that I have. Nothing else. You are going to make him your friend, and I'll be alone. . . . Ygor's body is no good. His neck is broken, crippled, and distorted, lame and sick from the bullets your brother fired into me. You can put my brain in his body. . . . You can make us *one*. We'll be together always. My brain—his body—together!" (Lugosi delivers this line with all his skill.)

Ludwig replies: "You're a cunning fellow, Ygor. You think if I put your sly and sinister brain into a body of a giant—? Hah. That would be a monster indeed."

Ygor visits the monster, in the underground room, and in a superb scene flings out his arms in malevolent joy, telling him, "A new brain, a new brain." Soon after, Ygor goes to Dr. Bohmer and mentions that Dr. Frankenstein, whom Bohmer had taught "everything he knows," will put Kettering's brain in the monster. Ygor wants his own brain to be inserted. "You fool, you'd die," says Bohmer.

"Die!" Ygor answers. "I will live again, only this crooked body will die. I will live forever. My brain in that body would make me a leader of men. We would rule the state and even the whole country. You do as I say and you will have everything you want."

Here Ygor seems to join with Lugosi's mad-scientist roles, at least in the evil wish to "rule the state."

At this point the monster escapes and goes to the little girl's home and carries her away. But he knocks over a lamp in her room, and the house burns down, covering her disappearance. Returning to the doctor's place, the monster pantomimes that he wants the girl's brain in his body. Ygor says:

No, no. You do not understand. It would kill her. You wouldn't want to kill your little friend! But Ygor has a better idea. You will see. You will have the brain of your friend, Ygor. Tonight my brain will be in your body. Tonight Ygor will die for you.

In these strangely moving words, Ygor explains his plan to the monster—but the creature still has a primitive sense of what is good, so he does not want Ygor's evil brain. The two struggle, and the monster partially crushes Ygor behind the heavy laboratory door. The monster now goes upstairs to Ludwig's room and indicates that he wants the girl's brain. The confrontation is tense, but Ludwig takes the child's ball and, dangling it before the immense creature, lures him downstairs to be operated on.

Bohmer warns Ygor, lying on the operating table, that—"this operation may not be successful. This may be the end of everything." Ygor says weakly: "Better death than a life like this, now that I have seen the promise of a life forever." In these curious overtones of Christian theology, Ygor sheds his own body for the artificial one of the monster. This is not the eternal life of the spirit but the eternal life of the flesh, the same kind of immortality that the vampire has.

The villagers, in the meantime, have been getting restless. Two weeks have passed since the house burned down, but no bones have been found. The girl's father and the villagers decide to storm Frankenstein's mansion to "choke the truth out of him." A policeman heads them off and, placating the villagers for a few minutes, goes to talk to Ludwig, who leads the policeman to the cellar and shows him the monster, telling him, "I have replaced an evil brain with a good one. I've made amends for the great tragedy that my father and my brother unintentionally brought to this community. [This is not true, since Vasaria was not the scene of the creation.] I have restored the good name of Frankenstein."

"You recognize me?" Ludwig asks. The monster nods his head and says, "You are Dr. Frankenstein." The voice sounds strange (it is Bela's dubbed onto Chaney's lip movements), and Ludwig has a horrible suspicion. "But you are—you are Dr. Kettering," he says. "I am not Dr. Kettering, I am Ygor!" The doctor exclaims, "What have I done?" The monster continues, "I am Ygor. I have the strength of a hundred men. I cannot die. I cannot be destroyed. I, Ygor, will live forever!" The doctor realizes that he has "created a hundred times the monster that my father made." Ludwig accuses Bohmer, but the monster tells Ludwig to leave him alone. "He is my friend. I should kill you, Frankenstein, but after all, your father gave me life, and you gave me a brain."

The villagers now break in. Ygor tells Bohmer to turn on the gas and kill all of them. Ludwig tries to interfere and is knocked down. The villagers find the child and set fire to the house. Suddenly the monster cannot see. He yells out for Bohmer and holds him. Ludwig, wounded, says, "Your dream of power is over, Bohmer. You didn't realize his blood is the same type as Kettering's but not the same as Ygor's. It will not feed the sensory nerves."

"Bohmer, you played me a trick. What good is a brain without eyes to see? What good is a brain without eyes—" The monster throws Bohmer onto the apparatus, electrocuting him. Then, berserk, he moves around the laboratory as it bursts into flames. Close-ups of the monster's face show his flesh burning, and blisters appear. Hollywood's motive for such a gruesome detail is curious. The monster—and even Ygor—have had much of the audience's perverse sympathy, but to expiate that kind of allegiance the dual creature must now suffer. All the main characters perish except the daughter and the policeman, who walk away and watch the building consumed to ashes.

The scriptwriter has created some interesting characterizations. There is, of course, the monster, a relatively simple and unthinking creature who, like a giant child, is a victim of his passions. He is ready to kill when aroused, while at other times he is placid. He wants to be liked, thus his affection for the little girl; this innocent child, as in "The Emperor's New Clothes," is the only one who can see beyond the ugly exterior to the essentially simple soul beneath.

But the monster is so often betrayed by others that he becomes vicious. Some of Mary Shelley's original concepts, though sentimentalized in the child, still remain. The monster is a kind of *tabula rasa*, an ugly but somewhat noble savage who has been treated badly by a nonunderstanding world. His main antagonists, as usual, are the townspeople. Rightly, they do not like a monster running around killing; on the other hand, they are invariably shown as a vindictive, unreasoning, vicious group—as monstrous in their own self-righteousness as the monster is in his elemental brutishness. Furthermore, to most horror fans the villagers are really the enemy. They are the censoring force that prevents complete enjoyment of the fantasy of monster and mad doctor committing murder and mayhem.

Ludwig is a man who has put all memories of the past behind him and has struck out anew, but he is still in the same profession and has, indeed, the same inclinations. Like his brother and father before him, he cannot resist experimenting with this creation and trying to vindicate his father's activities. But, as with the whole family, good intentions are not enough, and the monster continues to plague its restorers.

Ygor, the other member of this interesting group, is, in the words of Wolf, a "sly and sinister" person, a "cunning fellow." Ygor likes the monster because he "does things" for him. The creature is the puppet, the instrument by which Ygor gains power. In *Son*, Ygor has him kill off those who condemned him to death. In *Ghost*, he wants the doctor to make the monster strong, so as to be a fit instrument for Ygor's continued evil-doing. Ygor does not—in spite of the blackmail threat—have much power over the doctor, because the doctor is basically good. But he does have a strong effect on Bohmer, who has been nursing his resentment for years.

Ygor is a lonely person; he has no friend except the monster, another outcast from society, and he does not want the monster to be made mentally well, for then he would not be his friend. Later, when he gets the superb idea of transferring his own brain into the monster, his "will to power" arises. No longer will he have to rely on the occasionally difficult monster; instead, he will have everlasting life and rule the state himself. Certainly the role of Ygor provided Lugosi an opportunity to expand one of his meatiest roles and again proves that he was far more versatile than his limited repertoire allowed.

Meantime, horrors more frightening than Universal's entered the news. After Pearl Harbor was attacked on December 7, 1941, the "Japs" rapidly joined the Nazis as the world's prime villains, and Lugosi's accent was drafted. Cashing in on the new international developments, Monogram concocted a topical script (probably on New Year's morning) and in April, 1942, released *Black Dragons*. The story involved several Japanese members of the Black Dragon society who, before the war, had had their faces altered to the Occidental features of certain American businessmen by Dr. Melcher, a Nazi plastic surgeon (Lugosi). The Japanese, while appreciating Melcher's contributions to international espionage, jail him so that he cannot tell anyone about his alterations. Undeterred, he escapes from his cell by performing a quickie face-lifting job on himself and comes to America—his spirit of revenge overcoming his dedication to the axis war effort—to settle accounts with each of the Dragons. It is at this point in the plot that the film begins, with the background eventually revealed in some awkwardly placed flashbacks.

The mysterious doctor, now calling himself Colomb, has moved in with Dr. Saunders, one of the altered Japanese, and has put him under a hypnotic spell. Meantime, the other industrialists are being found dead with small American flags in their hands. Dr. Saunders' niece, Ann, has for a fiancé an FBI agent who has been ordered to probe the strange deaths of the businessmen. When Saunders eventually dies, the last industrialist is taken to Dr. Saunders' house as bait for Colomb. Through a ruse, Colomb manages to get the FBI out of the room and murders the man, but Colomb is killed by the agents before he can make his escape.

Occasionally, in the midst of the film's almost incoherent dramaturgy, Lugosi is allowed to be lucid and even personable. During one conversation, Colomb suggests something other than mundane villainy by telling the niece, "You are very sweet—and a beautiful young woman." This is hardly a profound or even distinctive line, but Lugosi delivers it with his usual grace and also with a tinge of regret at an aspect of life that is now beyond him. Therefore it is understandable that the girl later describes Colomb to her boyfriend as "an interesting man." One night, when she tries to engage him in conversation, Colomb regretfully sets up a barrier between them; the situation is full of moody and suggestive possibilities, but the scriptwriters were so busy constructing their unwieldy plot that they did not bother to create appropriate dialogue for Lugosi. As a result, he has to conclude the scene with the mundane warning, "Curiosity killed the cat." The only characterization possible is in Lugosi's facial expressions and his odd inflections of mediocre and unrevealing dialogue. When someone asks him, "Will we see you again?" Lugosi, in a surprising moment of charm and with a touch of his Continental *Weltschmerz*, replies with a smile, almost as though joking: "Who knows, in this crazy world?" The line is flat and ridiculous in print, but when said by Lugosi it suggests the world-weary aristocratic stance that was so much a part of the man and his image, combined with an unexpected sense of humor.

The New York *Post* found this film "a hard-to-believe item" that succeeds only in putting "unwary Americans to sleep." [6] *Variety* called

---

[6] April 22, 1942.

it "probably the most incredible of the film productions which has come out of Hollywood since the outbreak of the war" and added that its denouement "baffles all logic, science, and respect for the average picture-goer's intelligence." [7] One of the advertisements for the film contained a bogus little letter, signed "B. L.," which read, "I defy movie-goers not to gasp when they see *Black Dragons.*" Indeed, many of them did gasp.

About the time that *Ghost of Frankenstein* and *Black Dragons* appeared, Lugosi confessed in an interview that he was able to release at least artistically some of the Jekyll and Hyde in his own personality:

> To portray a maniac offers a compelling challenge. I find, however, that once I have completed such a role, my interest in it immediately abates. As a matter of fact, chill drama holds no lure for me as a spectator. On the contrary and apparently as a release from my workaday life, I personally gain my theatrical diversion most delightfully from the frothiest of screen nonsense. A travel subject or a cartoon short, well-made and free from realistic thrill stuff, is frequently my choice on the film bill.[8]

When he made this statement, Lugosi was working at Monogram in *The Corpse Vanishes*, which was released in May, 1942; its story deals with the apparent death of seven brides at the altar. Each has been sent a deadly orchid by Dr. Lorenz (Lugosi), who later shows up as an undertaker and removes the girls to his underground mortuary, where he extracts various vital fluids. He then imparts these to his aged wife, who accommodatingly but temporarily becomes young again. This series of deaths obviously upsets the community, and one of those inquisitive cub reporters (Luana Walters) investigates and almost becomes the eighth victim. Lugosi's scheme, as usual, is spoiled.

The film repeats many of the flaws found in other Monogram films: it combines a dull mystery with unconvincing science, while expecting the mere presence of Lugosi to evoke fear with no help from story, dialogue, or direction. For example, the girl reporter discovers that the doctor sleeps in a coffin. He replies, "I find a coffin much more comfortable than a bed. Many people do so, my dear. Is it so strange that I accept one while waiting for my eternal rest?" The scene is not

[7] April 29, 1942.
[8] Unidentified clipping, March 8, 1942.

properly set up to create any suspense or dread, and although the substance of Bela's reply is certainly odd, its phrasing is unwieldy, and even Lugosi could not give such a turgid mouthful the proper elegance. As critic Archer Winsten said, "Mr. Lugosi smirks and menaces in his best style, but the game is familiar." [9] And *Variety* rightly, but familiarly, said, "It insults the average intelligence," adding that "Lugosi does most of his acting with his eyes. His sleeping in a coffin is about the most horrible thing he does." [10]

About the same time as *The Corpse Vanishes* was released, another Lugosi film reached theater screens, but this was just a feature version of the 1937 serial *S.O.S. Coast Guard*. His next new film was another Monogram masterwork called *Bowery at Midnight*, which appeared in October, 1942. It featured Lugosi as Professor Brenner, a teacher of psychology who leads a double life as Kurt Wagner, the seemingly beneficent proprietor of a Bowery beanery who greets new arrivals with, "Here you will find food for your body, as well as comfort for your troubled mind." In this skid-row location, Lugosi hands out food, watches for criminals, and then inveigles these recreants into helping him commit robberies. It turns out that his standard operating procedure is to leave the dead body of an accomplice at the scene of a crime, even though this means cold-blooded murder. The wife of Professor Brenner knows nothing of this other life, however; she thinks that he is spending his nights off researching a book.

Also employed at the Bowery mission is a shaky, alcoholic doctor, who eventually proves to be a genius in disguise. Instead of burying the bodies of Lugosi's victims, this fellow resuscitates most of them and keeps them patiently waiting in the subcellar, presumably for the fortuitous moment when Lugosi will fall into their midst. At the end of the film Lugosi tries to escape from the police through the cellar, but the "doctor," with an unholy laugh, unleashes his corps of vengeance, and the professor is done in.

One of the film's main flaws is an excessive number of characters and situations. There are the scenes at the mission, with the criminals who arrive there and the "doctor," as well as those at the home of the professor and his wife; later, a new strand is added concerning Wagner's nurse and assistant at the mission, whose mother worries

[9] New York *Post*, May 27, 1942.
[10] *Variety*, June 3, 1942.

about her safety. This girl's rich boyfriend just happens to be one of Professor Brenner's students, and when he gives up doing a project on "Thoughts Just Before Death" as too difficult to research (it is topics like this that probably caused the poor professor's mental breakdown), he decides instead to investigate the psychology of the underprivileged and, dressed as a bum, ends up at Wagner's mission. Still another subplot involves a young uniformed policeman and an older detective, who get involved in the case by following criminal Frankie Mills.

Though Lugosi's character is not a mad scientist, he is equally ruthless and kills both enemies and "friends" when they get in his way. Probably the actor's best line occurs when one awed gang member says, "Who woulda thought that I'd be workin' with Frankie Mills on a first-class job?" and Lugosi ironically replies, "Yes—each day brings its little surprises." The most "meaningful" scene occurs in class, when a student recites to Professor Brenner a description of a hypothetical paranoia victim as someone with a "superiority complex . . . delusions of grandeur . . . persecution mania." This individual, he continues, would be willing to use force and indulge in antisocial conduct. As if to make sure that we have made the desired connection, the writers have Brenner inquire, "They might even have a life of crime?"

The film is hardly a noteworthy contribution to the art of the horror film, but even so, the Brooklyn *Eagle* somehow gasped: "Not since his portrayal of Dracula has Bela Lugosi appeared in finer fettle than in *Bowery at Midnight.* Don't go to see it unless you've had your vitamin pills." [11] Maybe a Brooklynite would need such pills, but most audiences found the film mild and by no means terrifying. It had more plot than characterization, more incidents than mood, more explicitness than suggestion, and Lugosi's "fettle" seems, in the perspective of time, not as fine as was stated. It is too bad that the whiskey doctor did not resuscitate the script as well as Lugosi's victims.

Released at the same time as *Bowery at Midnight* was another film made by Lugosi for Universal. This was *Night Monster*, which had some suspenseful moments, but made poor use of Lugosi. He received top billing, but made only a brief appearance as Rolf, the butler. The role was not only small but also unflattering, with one character commenting that Rolf "looks like something you'd find under a wet rock." Why Lugosi allowed his name to be featured when he had such

[11] November 21, 1942.

One of Monogram's publicity photos.

an insignificant part will never be known, but it was not a wise move. Lugosi fans were disappointed, and even the press mentioned that "old hands at the game like Bela Lugosi and Lionel Atwill are simply present for atmosphere purposes." [12]

Lugosi's next film, also for Universal, was made at the end of 1942 and released on March 1, 1943. This was *Frankenstein Meets the Wolf Man*, a confrontation that had a curious background. An article in the May 23, 1942, issue of *The Saturday Evening Post* spoke about the revival of the horror genre:

> The story of how this tidbit of terror was hatched is illuminating in the ways of Hollywood. *The Wolf Man*, the recent successful horrific in which Lon Chaney, Jr. fell into the habit of lycanthropy—werewolf by night and Welshman by day—proved to be an instant grosser, bringing in nearly $1,000,000 to date. One of the executives of Universal pleasurably totting up the countryside b.o. records called up a large exhibitor.
>
> "Wolf man was good, eh?" he said.
>
> "Terrific" said the enthusiastic exhibitor. "Don't see how you can top it!"

[12] New York *Herald Tribune*, November 30, 1942.

"Well," said the executive, "we might give you Frankenstein and the wolf man together."

"Colossal," shrieked the exhibitor. "Stupendous! I can see the marquees now. Wolf man meets Frankenstein."

The title, intact, was turned over to Curt Siodmak, veteran horror writer. It presented difficulties that would have made a less ingenious writer blow his brains out. The wolf man's head had been bashed in by his own father in a Welsh forest. Frankenstein's monster had last been seen crushed under huge timbers in a burning house somewhere in the Balkans.

"Whipped cream is good and herring is good," moaned Siodmak, "so they think they should be better together."

The whipped cream (that is, the continuation of the wolf-man story) was not bad, but the herring (the Frankenstein part) remained unfortunately pickled. The film began with the wolf-man story, enriched the character of poor Talbot, improved his werewolf makeup, and even had him move in a more lithe fashion. The working title, "The Wolf Man Meets Frankenstein," was more accurate than the final one because the story follows the wolf-man's travails and has him meet Frankenstein, not the other way around. The confusion about whether the name Frankenstein refers to the monster or to the family was sidestepped, too, because Elsa Frankenstein, the daughter of Ludwig, does in a sense encounter Chaney.

Curt Siodmak had to change the wolf-man myth by forgetting all about the silver bullet and the silver-headed cane that are supposed to kill the lycanthrope. He transforms the wolf man into an eternal thing, reactivated by moonlight. In terms of suspense and mood, the first half of this film is one of the most frightening of the series. But as soon as Talbot gets to Vasaria in search of Frankenstein's secrets of life and death, the whole film becomes absurd, not only in plot development but also in acting. And a basic fault in terms of the finished film is unfortunately Lugosi's interpretation of the monster. Surely he did not relish the irony of playing the role that he had once balked at in 1931, a role that the now more successful Karloff would no longer perform. If Lugosi, whose resentment of Karloff had long rankled, hoped to vindicate himself by showing how the monster ought to be played, he failed. For a variety of reasons he succeeded only in being the worst of the whole series, certainly a far less effective creature than Chaney's of the preceding film. The question could well be asked how the director,

Roy William Neill, who managed to wring a good performance out of poor Chaney, seemingly allowed Lugosi to portray the monster so badly. The answer lies deep in Universal's vaults, but a few facts have been unearthed; they show that Lugosi's seemingly awful interpretation was not his fault.

Originally Chaney was to play both roles, through the use of doubles. When that appeared too expensive and complicated, the studio decided to use Lugosi because the monster at the end of *Ghost of Frankenstein* had Ygor's brain and was speaking with Lugosi's voice. Thus the film was shot with a talking but blind monster. The results, however, seemed most peculiar. The basic fault of *Bride of Frankenstein*, that of a speaking monster, had been repeated. Furthermore this new monster was not a simple creature but an intelligent being with Ygor's evil brain and Hungarian accent. Having this big hulk come out with literate statements about how, if he were given new strength, he could then control the state seemed too humorous. What did Universal do? After the film had been completed, it cut out all the dialogue (*The Saturday Evening Post* had described the monster as running "off at the mouth for nearly a dozen sentences"). When these scenes were removed, the monster's part grew shorter, and, even worse, all his

Bela as the monster. *Frankenstein Meets the Wolf Man* (1943).

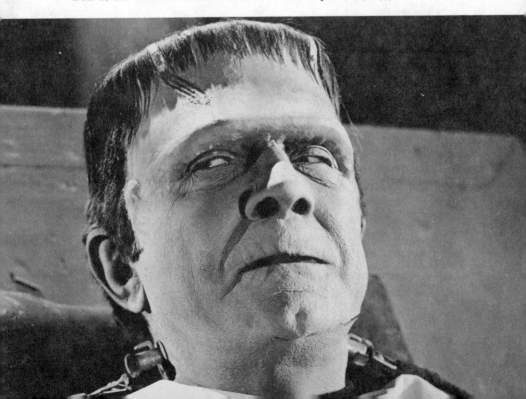

motivations disappeared, including the explanation of his blindness. As a result of these omissions, some scenes now appear ludicrous. The worst one shows the monster, with arms outflung, stalking into the village like a stiff windup toy.

Lugosi had played the monster as if (logically) it had Ygor's crafty brain. The strange, evil smile of triumph at the end of the electrical recharging scene stems from the fact that the monster has regained his eyesight and strength and now can carry out his maniacal plans. Unfortunately the rehabilitated monster wakes up only to fight with the wolf man. Most of this action was not done by the aging Lugosi but by Eddie Parker, a stunt man.

No wonder, then, that *Frankenstein Meets the Wolf Man* is a disappointing film. The strong first half would have been balanced by a well-plotted and motivated second half, but with the dialogue cut, the monster seemingly with sight at some moments and without it at others, plus the stunt man's different appearance and acting style, the finished film is a mess. Bela cannot really be blamed; he had acted his role in good faith. Perhaps some people at Universal, seeing what looked like a poor performance, decided that Lugosi's future services could be dispensed with. Except for one special instance, *Abbott and Costello Meet Frankenstein* (1948), he would never again be used by Universal.

Certainly *Frankenstein Meets the Wolf Man* further debased the monster. Ironically it was Lugosi's blinded and staggering creature that became the prototype for all of Universal's subsequent monsters. This stiff-jointed, mechanical hulk in a semicomatose state was a far cry from Karloff's more frightening conception.

About the same time as *Frankenstein Meets the Wolf Man* was released, Monogram issued *The Ape Man* under the assumption that if Universal's wolf took a good bite out of the box office, why couldn't Monogram's ape? The results from an aesthetic point of view were abominable. Lugosi plays Dr. Brewster, a scientist who, as a consequence of having experimented upon himself, has become permanently bent over in a rough (very rough) approximation of an ape's stance. He has also, though seemingly just more from the want of a razor, the facial hair of an ape.

Lugosi's makeup is, in fact, similar to what he wore in *Island of Lost Souls*. Dr. Brewster is understandably distressed at the results of his

The Ape Man (1943).

experiments and spends his time being willingly locked up with an ape, for he is afraid of the dangerous tendencies he is developing.

To resume his normal appearance, Dr. Brewster needs fresh human spinal fluid and although at first reluctant has become, naturally, anxious to get it. The problem is that such a dose of spinal fluid means death for the donor. A fellow doctor who has been assisting Brewster refuses, saying, "You realize what you're asking me to do? Murder!" Brewster replies, "Oh, call it what you like." Exasperated, frustrated, and weary of lumbering around his laboratory and sleeping with a giant gorilla, Brewster sneaks over to the other doctor's house, kills his butler, and forces the doctor to inject the fluid. As a result, Brewster is able to straighten up again, though he still does not avail himself of a razor. The cure, however, is not permanent, and he soon reverts to his former stance. Willing to do anything to regain his human appearance, he and his gorilla go out and kill people for the precious fluid. But the other doctor refuses to give Brewster the injection and so Brewster— with the usual logic of a Monogram script—kills the doctor. In the midst of this unpalatable and literally primitive plot enter a wisecracking reporter and a hard-voiced female photographer. Eventually the doctor grabs the girl and takes her down to the cellar laboratory, where, in a classic instance of role reversal, he is going to extract her fluid! There is a scuffle, the girl pulls the lever that releases the gorilla from his cage, and Brewster is done in by his ape (as in *Murders in the Rue Morgue*), and the ape, in turn, is killed by the police.

The tortured situation of Dr. Brewster, who feels himself tending to join the animals and wants to be locked up so he will not do misdeeds, is similar to that of Larry Talbot in *The Wolf Man*, just as the two films have parallel titles. But this situation is so badly handled that neither pity nor even compassion is felt for Brewster. And in his role of scientist he is not worthy of respect, either, for he does not give even the briefest explanation of his sufferings and what he tried to achieve. The script is incredibly inept, and Lugosi is simply lost in the stupidity of it all. He is photographed in long medium shot or long shot, and his facial expressions (those visible beneath the hair) are too far in the distance. Neither is he given much of a chance to speak. Instead, he just lumbers around—and not very well, either. At times he seems almost shy and embarrassed shuffling around the laboratory, as if he wished that no one would have to see him.

That a great scientist could be reduced to such an ape creature ("He's going to let me go through life like this") was no worse an instance of debasement than Lugosi being forced to play in such a foul film. Although the competition is keen, it is probably his worst Monogram picture. Besides its poor direction, photography, and basic story, what lends it its final distinction is an amateurish gag in which a dumb-looking fellow is shown looking in windows, giving advice to characters in the film, and otherwise acting suspiciously throughout the narrative. At the end, sitting in the reporter's car, he is asked who he is. "Me?" he answers. "I'm the author of the story." Turning to the camera, he adds, "Screwy idea, wasn't it?" Then he rolls up the car window, which has the words "The End" written on it. The *Daily News* summed it up, "Monogram's writer didn't have to wipe the dust from Bela Lugosi's *Ape Man*; he had to rake the mould off." [13]

Lugosi, again under the aegis of the indefatigable Sam Katzman, appeared in *Ghosts on the Loose* (June, 1943), another encounter with

[13] March, 1943.

the East Side Kids. As the film opens, the boys are preparing for the wedding of Huntz Hall's sister, whom they decide to help by fixing up her new home. Unknown to everyone, the building is also desired by Emil (Lugosi), a German spy who lives next door in a seemingly deserted house that has the reputation of being haunted. The boys decide to clean and decorate the little love nest, but get the wrong address and enter Emil's house instead. Since it is empty, they "borrow" some furniture from the house next door (the right house), which they plan to pay for later. Meantime, Emil arrives with two of his men, and when he sees what is going on, he says, in frustration, "Why do I have such idiots around me?"—a question that must have often resounded in the actor's own mind.

Emil plans to scare the boys away, but being New Yorkers, they are not too impressed. There is a trick portrait on one wall. The painting swings back on hinges, and Emil sticks his own face into the frame and looks around the room, watching the black boy dusting. When Emil sneezes, the boy registers the appropriate fear. Finally the group finds a printing press in the cellar, along with pamphlets titled "How to Destroy the Allies" and "What the New Order Means to You." After further mixups the traitorous villains are apprehended One of the boys knocks out Emil with a mop as he comes through a door trying to escape. At the end of the film Huntz Hall is discovered to have German measles—little swastika marks appear all over his face—and as a result, the married couple is quarantined with the boys.

The film won two stars from the *Daily News*, but received a "phooey" from *Photoplay*. Lugosi received fourth billing under Leo Gorcey, Huntz Hall, and Bobby Jordan, a place that was not too surprising considering that the film was basically an East Side Kids picture and that Lugosi was given very little footage in it.

In the spring of 1943 Lugosi accepted the offer of play producer Harry Oshrin to appear in *Dracula* on the stage. The play was booked for three weeks in Boston, with engagements in Washington and New York as well.[14] It was also announced that Lugosi would return to the coast to film *The Tiger Man*, "a voodoo story." This property finally transformed itself into *Voodoo Man*.[15] Lugosi also contributed to the war effort by appearing at army camps, among them Fort Meade,

[14] New York *Morning Telegram*, April 13, 1943.
[15] *Ibid.*

Maryland, in a performance of *Dracula* at twenty-five cents a head. The army recruits liked the play. It also appeared in Buffalo, where, however, the reviewer for *Variety* found the performance of boot-camp quality:

> Bela Lugosi's portrayal . . . just doesn't add up to contemporary conceptions of the epitome in fiendishness. His delineation is slack and blurred and lacks the sharp edges of characterization essential to credence, while his accent and bearing add almost a paternal note to the supposedly gory and goose-pimply role.[16]

The play then went to Cleveland and other cities and showed up for a week's run in Washington, D.C. Shortly after, Lugosi returned to Hollywood, bloody and bowed.

During the summer of 1943 both Universal and Columbia, perhaps prompted by Lugosi's reappearance on stage in *Dracula*, looked into the possibility of making a vampire film. Universal examined the handsome profits on its recent works of horror and decided that since the Frankenstein series was doing well, the time had grown ripe for the resurgence of the monster's famous twin, Dracula. Curt Siodmak was told to create a new story, and soon *Son of Dracula* emerged. The obvious choice for the Count was of course Lugosi, but Universal ignored him and instead starred Lon Chaney. Lugosi was not only hurt but also enraged that the plebeian Chaney was given his aristocratic role. Indeed, Universal's avoidance of its original Count remains a mystery, one that Lugosi must have puzzled over many a night.

Meantime, over at Columbia, Harry Cohn also decided that the horror genre was profitable and that his studio ought to offer the world its own version of the vampire. Work was started on the screenplay in June, 1943; its content was closer to the spirit of the original *Dracula* than *Son of Dracula*. Unfortunately the writer, Griffin Jay, could not make use of the word "Dracula" (Universal owned the rights to that), so he named his vampire Amand Tesla and called the film *Vampires over London*. Before shooting started, however, it was retitled *The Return of the Vampire*.

Columbia knew that a vampire film without Dracula in its title would need some additional box-office strength. Therefore it chose Lugosi and built the screenplay around his persona. He was eager to

[16] June 9, 1943.

play the part—after all, it was a genuine lead—and the overall production promised to be far better than Monogram's poverty-row talents. Lugosi was in a good bargaining position. He was well aware that his name in a vampire film was helpful on theater marquees, but he was afraid that perhaps someone would come by and take the role from him, so he settled for $3,500, the same amount he received for *Dracula* thirteen years before. *The Return of the Vampire* was begun on August 21, 1943, and was completed in sixteen shooting days. Its entire cost was $138,545.54.[17]

The Return of the Vampire opens in 1918 with a sequence showing how Lugosi, a Rumanian scientist turned vampire, is killed by having an iron stake driven through his heart. At the time he had a hairy assistant, Andreas, whom he controlled. Apparently Tesla's evil influence was able not only to master the man's limited will but also to create a few months' growth of hair on Andreas as well. Indeed, he strongly resembles a wolf man.

Years pass, and it is now the time of the Second World War and the London blitz. A German bomb hits the graveyard, and the vampire's body is exposed. Two cemetery laborers pull out the stake, and Tesla lives again. He wants revenge on Lady Jane Ainsley, who figuratively and literally had had a stake in his interment. After the vampire was killed, Lady Ainsley, no sluggard at social and moral improvement, "cured" Andreas; he is now clean-shaven and a helper around the laboratory. But when Tesla returns to life, it does not take long for him to reassert his demonic powers. He confronts Andreas:

> ANDREAS: I am no longer your slave. Dr. Ainsley has cleansed me of all the evil you have forced upon me. You can't bring it back. I won't let you.
> TESLA: You are a fool, Andreas, a complete, utter fool. Your fate is to be what you are as mine is to be what I am, your master. Come here.
> ANDREAS: I won't.
> TESLA: Look at me, Andreas. Look at me! Andreas—come here!
> ANDREAS: Master, you've come back.

And another thing has also come back—Andreas' facial foliage. At the end of the film Lugosi, as usual, is killed—Andreas, in a bid

---

[17] Hollywood studios are unwilling to provide any information as to salaries and costs. Therefore I am indebted to Lou Phillips, Earl Gains, and Michael Nolin of Columbia for unearthing the above information.

for his own independence, has done the job—and for the first time in a vampire picture the audience sees the dissolution of the face take place.

Shooting of the film ended on September 9, 1943, and the picture was soon readied for release. In November, however, Universal issued *Son of Dracula*. Columbia, afraid that its own film, despite the name of Lugosi or maybe because of it, might be swallowed up by the more famous title or perhaps confused with it, held back its picture for a few months and released it in January, 1944.

The critics were not kind. The New York *Herald Tribune* declared that people "who are partial to this type of entertainment will be glad to know that *The Return of the Vampire* is just as dreadful as all its predecessors." [18] This supercilious remark is unjust. The film was not as good as the original *Dracula* but far better than many of Lugosi's other films. It contained some excellent atmospheric effects, especially in the graveyard, but unfortunately it had more incident than mood and more adventure than fright. Although the wolf-man creature was not very believable, Lugosi was quite impressive as the vampire. Alas, new life could not be infused into his career. *The Return of the Vampire* would be the last film that Bela starred in for a major studio. The rest of his lead roles would be for Monogram and independent outfits.

In February, 1944, *The Voodoo Man* was released by Monogram. A curious combination of *White Zombie* and *The Corpse Vanishes*, it provided Lugosi with one of his better parts in this period and is probably the best of the Monogram series. Although the script has its absurdities, and is by no means horrifying, it does tell a fairly entertaining story. But more than the story, it is Lugosi who carries the film. He brings to it his demonic intensity and yet also his human warmth, so that the performance is curiously powerful and indeed even touching. He has the opportunity, for a change, to act a more complex character and is convincingly a sympathetic husband, a kindly doctor, a strong-minded villain, and a voodoo mystic. Because the master of zombies had a beard and a moustache in *White Zombie*, Monogram felt that he should have them again. The appendages are quite becoming, for they lengthen Lugosi's round face and ironically seem to shave off the mounting years.

As in *The Corpse Vanishes*, here Dr. Marlowe (Lugosi) is a good and faithful husband: his wife had died twenty-two years before, but he has

[18] January 29, 1944.

been keeping her alive in a zombilike state and is now looking for the right young girl to give her "the will to live." To this end he and his assistant, Nicholas (George Zucco), capture girls and try to transfuse their mental vitality into his wife. Previous experiments have not succeeded, and though the women victims did not die, they have lost their souls and now stand in glass cases (à la the first *The Black Cat*) in a somnambulant state. Lugosi may seem evil to the world and certainly violates the civil rights of girls who happen to pass his way, but he is not really a bad man. He is sacrificing everything and everyone to his one goal: to bring his wife completely back to life. But, *in extenso,* his goal or sin is greater than this: it is the age-old dream of vanquishing death, in this case not by science, not by means of a ray, but by a return to the voodoo gods and, in particular, to Ramboona, who in Zucco's marvelously modulated English accent is "all powerful."

The story begins by having a scriptwriter leave his Hollywood job for a few days to go to a wedding. He stops for gas at a small station on a lonely road where he meets a girl who, it turns out, is the bridesmaid. The attendant (probably the most unlikely gas vendor one will ever meet) is the dedicated and always sinister George Zucco. He telephones Dr. Marlowe and tells him that the girl is alone. Marlowe's henchmen, as is apparently their custom, put up road blocks that cause the car to detour down an even more lonely path, at which point Marlowe turns on an electrical machine to kill the car's ignition—a device that Zucco could well have used at the station to increase business. But in this case the plans go awry. Zucco has not had time to put in the gas, so that when the writer drives off he soon runs out and is picked up by the bridesmaid. When the surviving car's ignition fails, he goes to get help. The girl is apprehended by John Carradine and some other inefficient helpers, and brought to Lugosi's house, where the following delightful dialogue takes place:

MARLOWE: Emily, my dear, I brought a young lady to help.
GIRL: Is your wife ill?
MARLOWE: She's dead.
GIRL: Dead?
MARLOWE: She has been dead for twenty-two years.
GIRL: How can she be dead and—
MARLOWE: She's dead only in the sense that you understand that word. [Then, with great enthusiasm] I'm on the threshold of bringing her back to complete life and you may be able to help.

GIRL: What do you want of me?

MARLOWE: Your will to live. Your mind.

GIRL: Oh, no, no. Don't look at me like that.

MARLOWE: Come to me.

And, of course, like all women in Lugosi's movies, she comes to him!

Shortly after, Marlowe begins the ceremony. With Zucco intoning in the background the magic name of Ramboona and Carradine on the bongo giving it his all, Marlowe turns from the seated girl to the "dead" wife and begins the transference, saying in his heavily accented and sincere voice: "Mind to mind; soul from body to body; emotion to emotion; life to death." These phrases are repeated again and again. The wife starts to stir and recognizes her husband.

MARLOWE: You're alive again.

EMILY: How did I get here?

MARLOWE: I have brought you back to me, my darling. Now we're together again.

EMILY: Together again. Togeth—

The Voodoo Man (1944).

She falls back, returning to her former somnambulant state, and Marlowe, convincing in his sorrow and frustration, says sadly, "We failed again." Zucco, indefatigable, answers quickly, "She was not the right subject." Then Lugosi, with beautiful intonation and great passion, says, "Somewhere there must be a girl with a perfect affinity. I must find her. I must find her."

He does. But meanwhile, the sheriff visits him in his dark house. "Cheerful place you have here," he notes. Dr. Marlowe, sensing the irony, explains that he uses very little light because of his eyes. The sheriff then says that he is looking for girls. "You don't say!" replies Marlowe. After a pause the sheriff asks the doctor whether he has seen anything suspicious. Marlowe answers negatively: "I'm quite off—the road," he explains (the humor not quite succeeding here).

Unfortunately for Marlowe and his plans, Carradine simple-mind-edly pushes the wrong button on a glass case and the latest subject wanders off to be discovered and taken to her friend's house. Marlowe eventually traces the girl there and poses as a sympathetic physician advising "rest and quiet." But, sure that she has the proper "affinity," he summons her back by means of a voodoo session with Zucco and company. The film, unlike many of the 1940's, accepts the power of the supernatural with no so-called logical explanations. When the girl returns, Marlowe is delighted, and Zucco replies with satisfaction, "Ramboona never fails." They once again begin the transference ceremony, with Marlowe saying to Zucco, "It must succeed this time, Nicholas, it must." His co-worker replies: "It will. The failures we've had were due to the subject; they were not the right ones. But remember, Ramboona is all-powerful!" Marlowe answers (although perhaps a bit unsurely), "Yes, yes, I know." Unlike most of Lugosi's roles, this part allowed him to be strong and in control but also to be humbled enough by his past failures to be slightly doubtful that he will ever succeed. Lugosi also brings to the part a human warmth, a compassion for his wife and even, in a sense, for his victims that provides more than the usual one-dimensional quality. With the order "Proceed," the ceremony begins. It goes well, and Emily returns to life, but when the police, who had been contacted by the suspicious hero, arrive and interfere, Marlowe is shot. His final words have sad, almost tragic overtones: "Darling, soon we will be together."

In an epilogue the scriptwriter hero attempts to sell the story to his studio. When asked who would play the part of the doctor, the writer says, "Why don't you try to get that actor, Bela Lugosi; it's right up his alley." Indeed it was.

Lugosi then made *Return of the Ape Man*, and although it was completed by May, 1944, it was not released until July. Monogram had done well with *The Ape Man* and decided to capitalize on its success by making a slightly related sequel. Although the result was better than the usual Monograms, it was Lugosi's last for that firm. Professor Dexter (Lugosi) and Professor Gilmore (John Carradine) successfully thaw out a drunk they had found in the park, after keeping him on ice for four months, and decide to go to the North Pole to search for a prehistoric man who might have frozen to death. Gilmore—docile, normal, and willing to give up—says, "Come on, Dexter, we've been up here for seven months and have found nothing."

> DEXTER: You go if you want. I stay here.
> GILMORE: You know I can't leave you, Dexter—but I'm married.
> DEXTER: I'm married, too.
> GILMORE: Married?
> DEXTER: I am married to science!

This rather obvious dialogue effectively characterizes both these men. Gilmore just does not have that monomaniacal drive to prove himself or his ideas that Lugosi's characters usually possess. Refusing to halt his search, Dexter struggles on and shortly after finds what he was seeking. He exults, "One chance in a million, and we've won!"

After their return to America Gilmore wants to hand over their hairy find to the scientific Establishment, but Dexter insists on conducting his own experiments. Using a blow torch, he melts the ice surrounding the creature, whom he then gives an injection; the man comes back to life, grunts as a primitive man should, and shows signs of being menacing. Dexter fends the creature off with the blow torch and herds him into a cage. Dexter, it turns out, wants to know what our primitive ancestor is thinking and decides to give him half a human brain so that he can explain himself. Gilmore, however, disapproves of the idea, for it means murder. Dexter replies in favor of sacrifice for science: "Murder is an ugly word. As a scientist, I don't recognize it."

The argument is tabled when Dexter and Gilmore go to a party given by Gilmore's wife. She thinks that Dexter is mad, and even Gilmore tends to agree with her. The party is the best scene in the film, and although it could have been much better, it still has marvelous

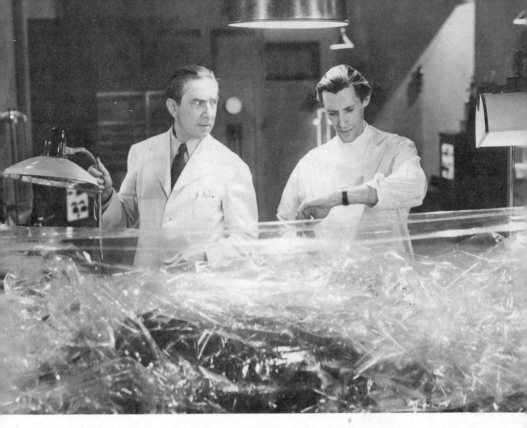

Return of the Ape Man (1944). This low-budget film used cellophane for ice.

individuality. Dexter is shown sitting in a chair, calmly puffing a cigar as he observes the other guests and endures their inane conversations. At someone's request, Gilmore plays "Moonlight Sonata" on the piano. When a guest says to Dexter that he is quiet, the doctor replies, "I enjoy studying people." Then he adds, "You know—some brains would never be missed." His eyes search around the room as he looks for the subject of his new experiment. When he chooses the fiancé of one of Gilmore's relatives, Dexter turns on all his charm, is convincingly friendly, and gets the man to drive him home. Dexter offers his new friend a toast: "To your happiness." The guest unwittingly replies, "To the success of your experiment." This is followed by Gilmore finishing at the piano, Dexter drugging the man's drink, and then Gilmore leaving to look for Dexter. By this time Dexter has his victim downstairs on the laboratory table, but Gilmore enters and, holding a pistol, forces Lugosi to revive and release the man. Gilmore calls Dexter's plan contemptible, concluding that he is a "dangerous man" and that the "hideous thing," the creature, should be destroyed. The two doctors decide to split up, and when Gilmore leaves, Dexter says to himself, "Fool! You'll pay for this!" And pay he will, for Lugosi's scientists are not people who forget.

Though its best sequence is over, the film continues to present a delicious parallel between the mundane world of Gilmore's party, wife, and relatives and that of Dexter and his scientific mission. The ape creature escapes and kills a policeman. The next morning, sipping his coffee, Gilmore reads about the murder. But before he does anything about it, Dexter calls, asking for help in disposing of the creature. Gilmore arrives right away and says, "As a public-minded citizen, I must still report to the police how the poor man happened to be killed." But Dexter has set a trap for Gilmore and paralyzes him with electricity. "So, my self-righteous friend was going to tell the police! You trusting, stupid fool." Feeling that probably his associate is so full of unimaginative middle-class morality that he could offer only about half a brain anyhow, Dexter decides to make him the "volunteer."

> The ape man, after I finish with him, will no longer have the primitive instinct to kill. He'll be a righteous citizen just like you are. You know why? Because part of your brain—the *righteous* part—will be in him.

Gilmore, a gentle and guilty-feeling liberal to the end, says that it is better for him to be the victim than an innocent person, since he considers himself partly responsible for the situation. Such soul-searching does not bother Dexter, however, who sneers, "Spoken like a true scientist." Minutes later, he is operating. When the transference is completed, Dexter gloats, "It is a success. I have advanced his mind 20,000 years in a few hours."

The creature, now half ape man and half Gilmore, escapes and returns to his home. He sits down by the piano and plays and then goes into his wife's room and strangles her for no apparent reason, thus ruining the situation's possibilities. He returns to Dexter's laboratory and grunts his way through this unintentionally funny scene:

> DEXTER: Did you kill somebody again?
> GILMORE: I killed Hilda.

DEXTER: [Astounded] Mrs. Gilmore? Why did you kill her?
GILMORE: I didn't mean to.

Considering the parties, concerts, and advice she was always plaguing him with, perhaps underneath it all he did! Although Dexter is pleased that he "brought him to life," even he sees that his experiment is not going very well. Still, when the police arrive, he tries to hide the creature, but it escapes and kills him. His dying words to a policeman are, "You must destroy that thing," and when told that bullets do not stop it, he says, "There's only one way . . . fire." Gilmore escapes and wanders back to his house, where he meets his niece. "Very pretty," he says. "You will come with me." And he tosses her onto his shoulder and carries her back to the laboratory. Finally the creature pulls some of the electric cables loose, setting the place on fire, and perishes in the flames.

The well-performed confrontations between a devoted scientist and his wishy-washy associate full of middle-class values have a verve beyond the usual character conflicts in such quickie films. The scriptwriters either let out their own resentments or else caught the real essence of Lugosi's dangerous charm. In any case, Gilmore was certainly right, but it would be a rare member of the audience who would side with him emotionally. These ethical debates, plus the scene at the party when Dexter looks for a victim, redeem some of the tired twists of the plot, and much of the foolishness of the ape man, who is so poorly acted that he conveys no sense of the primitive at all. Although *Return of the Ape Man* was criticized for using the old formula of the mad scientist, it was better than many of Lugosi's other Monogram pictures.

Meantime, Lugosi's personal life was in turmoil. His wife decided that the marriage ought to come to an end and filed for a separation in August, 1944. She claimed, according to the court records, that he caused her "great bodily pain and mental anguish, impaired her health, destroyed her happiness or any happiness in the home of the parties hereto, and made the same miserable and discordant." At this time she stated that he was making $2,000 a month and asked for $500 a month support. She further claimed that "if not restrained," her husband "threatens to and will dispose of certain personal property." At Bela's request, however, the divorce action was postponed to October. A reconciliation took place, and in March, 1945, the action was dismissed.

The following years would prove equally stormy, but she stayed with him for almost another decade.

About the same time his wife was deciding to separate, Lugosi switched to Paramount, where he appeared in a comedy, *One Body Too Many*, released in October, 1944. Receiving third billing under Jack Haley and Jean Parker, Lugosi played a suspicious-acting butler. Haley was an insurance salesman who decides to sell Cyrus Rutherford (an eccentric believer in astrology) $200,000 worth of insurance. But Rutherford dies, and the family gathers at his mansion to hear the will. It directs that his relatives remain in the mansion until his corpse is interred in a glass crypt that will allow him to see the stars, which were of such portent in his life. The rest of the film consists of disappearing bodies, Haley's fears, and a couple of murders. All in all, it is moderately amusing entertainment.

Lugosi's role as butler does not give him much to do, but he tries his best to enrich the part with his inflections, facial expressions, and usual Lugosi pauses. He is shown early in the film with the maid as they prepare coffee. He takes a bottle of rat poison off the shelf, saying, "There are too many rats in the house. They should be done away with." He glances at the tray and tells the maid, "You haven't put out enough cups." When she starts reciting the names of the guests, he looks at her intently and says ominously, "All of them." Later Lugosi offers the lawyer some coffee, but he refuses it, saying that it keeps him awake. Lugosi intones, "I assure you this coffee will not keep you awake." Throughout the film, in a kind of running gag, Lugosi is offering everyone coffee, but no one drinks it. A few pick up a cup, but then put it down as some piece of action interrupts them. When Haley is offered a cup, he asks whether it is percolated or drip. When Lugosi answers percolated, Haley retorts that he is the drip kind. At the end of the film, after the murderer is caught, Lugosi and the maid drink their own coffee, the rat poison, of course, being misinterpreted by the audience. Obviously Lugosi functioned as a red herring again and did not have much to do in the film, but it was another job.

And then, for the last time, Lugosi appeared with his old rival, Boris Karloff, and significantly was put to death by him. Produced by Val Lewton, who made a number of intelligently done horror pictures, *The Body Snatcher*, released in February, 1945, was a low-budget but well-done film dealing with the difficulties that medical schools had in obtaining bodies. The head of one school (Henry Daniell) is a good man who is tormented by John Gray (Karloff), a procurer of bodies. Gray was once sent to jail instead of the equally guilty Daniell and now refuses to leave the professor alone. His knowledge allows him to "have something" on the learned and upper-class man, and he enjoys this power immensely. He is also unscrupulous and at one point kills a young girl in order to supply a body. Later, when the doctor's foreign handyman, Joseph (Lugosi), tries blackmail, Gray plies him with drink and ultimately delivers his corpse, too.

Bela's role was small. As *Variety* put it, "Lugosi is more or less lost, probably on the cutting [room] floor, since he is only in for two sequences."[19] *Variety* was kind in its thinking. Lugosi unfortunately was used merely to add his name to the roster, but not for his real abilities as an actor. In fact, his portrayal of the handyman is not a good one. Playing second fiddle to Karloff, his career in the doldrums, and in an uncongenial role, Lugosi could not give much of his potential. The film itself, on the other hand, was an artistic success: indeed, it holds up well as one of the best horror films of the forties.

A few months later, in April, 1945, RKO released *Zombies on Broadway*. Two press agents (Wally Brown and Alan Carney) are publicizing a new nightclub and promise to exhibit a zombie. When the gangster backing the club finds out he will be ridiculed unless he has a genuine zombie, the boys are forced to go to the Caribbean to find one. After some semihilarious adventures, they arrive at the old house of Dr. Paul Renault (Lugosi), who has devoted his whole life not only to the study of zombies but to their creation as well. He examines a bottle of his new formula and says, "This has got to work." Meanwhile, in the backyard some digging takes place. "They are covering up my latest experiments," the doctor explains. He knows the natives can make zombies—indeed, he has one for a servant—but he wants to create his own. He captures a girl and exults to his assistant, "Her beauty will be preserved indefinitely."

The fellows arrive, after escaping from incensed natives, and meet the doctor. Lugosi is the authoritative scientist, inspired, intelligent, and a perfect foil for the two comedians. When the boys, to ingratiate themselves, say they are friends of another professor, Lugosi's face works furiously: "I hate him!" When one of the fellows asks whether he can help in the laboratory, Bela replies sardonically, "There may be

[19] February 21, 1945.

something—[pregnant pause] later." And indeed there is, for the boys are directed to dig their own graves.

Carney is made into a zombie and the girl is about to join him in that unhappy state when the doctor's great experiment is ruined by a little monkey who takes away the hypodermic needle. Lugosi's victims try to escape, and he orders his native zombie to kill, but the creature misinterprets the command and does in its master instead.

Brown returns with the girl and his pal, now a zombie, and proudly presents him to the gangster. At opening night, however, the zombie looks at a pretty girl fixing her stocking and reverts to his former self. What to do? The enraged gangster is about to kill the fellows when the girl grabs a needle and turns out the light. A few minutes later the nightclub act opens with the gangster as the zombie. Brown is pleased but sits down on the needle, and he too turns into a zombie.

Although the film is rather foolish, it does have a few amusing moments. Bela is well directed and carries off his small part with all his old power and dignity. The scary scenes, of course, wouldn't upset anyone, but they intentionally provoked humor because of the reactions of the comedy team. The critics, however, were not impressed. The New York *Herald Tribune* called it "an appalling little film." [20]

RKO was concerned with box office, not critics, and was pleased enough with the results to concoct another picture with the comedy team and Lugosi called *Genius at Work*, released in July, 1946. It may have been at work, but it surely wasn't in evidence. A radio program called "The Crime of the Week," starring the two comedians, features the activities of the Cobra, a master criminal who has been terrorizing the city. The writer of the show, a girl, is helped in her research by an amateur sleuth, played by Lionel Atwill. The girl not only uses some of his insights but also has added some of her own and thus is close to figuring out the identity of the Cobra (of course it's Atwill himself). One would think that this master criminal would be Lugosi, but instead he plays Atwill's servant and accomplice. His part has none of the powerful or mystical overtones of the usual Lugosi characterization. Furthermore, his lines are innocuous and lack the diabolical or ironic portent in which Lugosi's usual pauses and evil inflections can flourish.

[20] April 27, 1945.

Atwill at one point calls Lugosi a "careless fool," a line that he himself had often directed to others.

Later Atwill invites the radio actors and the girl writer to his home, where he shows them his "hobby room." "Some people collect stamps or old china, but I find these much more interesting," he says, indicating a number of torture devices. (Shades of Dr. Vollin in *The Raven.*) When Atwill's guests look surprised, he assures them he prefers sitting in a chair, reading one of his books. At this point the scared radio actor gulps when he picks up Atwill's book, *Murder and Torture Can Be Fun.* After the almost obligatory scene of the two inept actors getting caught in a torture device and Lugosi staring through peepholes at them, the girl forces the two to help her trap the Cobra. Their promise to reveal the murderer's identity over the radio prompts Atwill and Lugosi to arrive at the studio in disguise, Atwill as an old woman and Bela in beard and glasses. They snoot poison darts at the actors with a blowgun, but the scheme does not succeed; to escape, the two villains climb out on the ledge of the high building and after much suspense and comedy plummet to their death.

The film is fast-paced, has some good lines, and the frightened mugging of the two comedians provokes a little amusement; in fact, the film is entertaining, although the plot has enough holes in it to satisfy any fresh-air fiend. The pity is that Lugosi is not allowed to relish some good lines or to radiate his peculiar personality. Instead, he is just another member of the cast in a part that could have been played by anybody.

In July, 1947, an obscure outfit named Golden Gate Pictures finally exhibited *Scared to Death*, which had been completed in April, 1946, under the title *Accent on Horror*. Confused or Bored to Death would have been a more accurate title. Filmed in poor color, the picture was probably considered almost too inferior to release. As *Variety* said, "*Scared to Death* never lives up to its title or story promise. . . . It's a dull, poorly put together melodrama that fails to generate goose pimples expected by a Bela Lugosi vehicle." Furthermore, it was "directed with uneven hand," "badly edited," and given an incomprehensible script.[21]

Lugosi's film career had virtually ended. His remaining years were

[21] July 16, 1947.

to be hungry, desperate ones, and the contentment and self-satisfaction that are supposedly part of one's final years—after all, he had already reached the traditional age of retirement—would be denied him. He wanted to appear in more films, for he liked to act, and of course he liked the money. Unemployment would not have been pleasant in the best of circumstances, but Lugosi's final years would be plagued by another problem: his drug addiction.

Sometime in this period Lugosi began to suffer from sciatica. It affected the nerve running from the pelvis down to the foot. The ailment was almost impossible to cure, but the pain could be alleviated by a standard treatment: morphine. When his doctor feared that he was growing addicted and refused further prescriptions, he went to other doctors. After a while they too would guess the problem, and Lugosi had to obtain the drug illegally.

Much has been made of his addiction, thanks mainly to his indiscreet public statements and to the press, which could not resist the dramatic irony of one of Hollywood's leading horror actors caught in a situation as frightening as any of his films. The gory tale has grown better with each retelling. By 1972 a newspaper called *Midnight* headlined a piece with "Bela Lugosi Spent 40 Years as a Hopeless Drug Addict." [22] Written by David Hanna, who, the paper said, "reveals many secrets of America's top stars—secrets so shocking that they could not be revealed during their lifetime," the article traces Lugosi's habit back to his days in the Hungarian army. The actor had come from "an upper-class family, had an excellent education and fitted perfectly into the world of the military aristocracy." So much for his "facts!"

Lugosi was not the first Hollywood star to indulge in drugs, but he was the only major figure to give himself up voluntarily and to allow the press to feast upon his troubles. Pleased to get attention, whatever the awful reason, Bela exaggerated his woes by stating at the time of his confession in 1955 that he had been taking drugs for twenty years. Narcotics were still a rather exotic subject, and most Americans envisioned Lugosi as a crazed addict with glazed eyes, plunging needles in himself every few hours since 1935. It was not an ennobling image. Suddenly his whole career was seen in a different light and his fantastic characterizations were interpreted in retrospect as if they had been created more by drugs than talent.

[22] August 14, 1972.

Lugosi gave so many conflicting reports that the truth is difficult to discern. From his various accounts one can legitimately place the beginning of the addiction in 1935, 1938, 1944, and 1948. He had taken drugs, respectively, for 20 years (his statement to the press and court),[23] 17 years (his estimate in an as-told-to article),[24] 11 years (shortly after his wife asked for a divorce),[25] 7 years (after three years of addiction he went to England in 1951).[26] Lillian, his wife during this period, told this writer that Bela had much exaggerated his addiction and that he had begun drugs only in the 1940's.[27]

In an account he gave at the hospital the day after he gave himself up in 1955, he said that three years after he had begun taking morphine he went to England to revive *Dracula*.[28] Since he appeared there in 1951, this would place the start of the addiction in 1948. Some commentators have felt that Lugosi meant his 1939 trip, but he did not appear in *Dracula* then. Furthermore, he said that on his return from England, he had brought a box of methadone with him. This drug was developed during the Second World War by the Germans when morphine was no longer available. Originally called Dolophine in honor of Hitler's first name, it was imported to England after the war, and Lugosi was able to obtain it without difficulty, since no prescription was necessary. The drug is not addictive in the same sense as morphine, but one can become dependent on it.

On his return to the United States, his addiction worsened:

> When I switched to methadone I injected two cubic centimeters of demerol [a drug increasing the effect of the narcotics], and I also took barbiturate capsules so I could sleep for eight or ten hours.
> So—and so only—I could work.[29]

He said further that his wife helped him to stop the habit by tapering off his shots and that he had had fair success. But when she left him in 1953 and he was depressed about the dissolution of his home and the loss of his son, he returned to the drugs with a vengeance: "I used to

[23] Los Angeles *Examiner*, April 23, 1955; New York *Daily News*, April 23, 1955.
[24] Bela Lugosi, as told to Lloyd Shearer, "How I Beat the Curse of Drug Addiction," an unidentified 1956 article.
[25] *Ibid.*
[26] Los Angeles *Examiner*, April 23, 1955.
[27] November, 1973.
[28] Los Angeles *Examiner*, April 23, 1955.
[29] *Ibid.*

inject the methadone in my legs, but I lost 50 pounds—from my 180 pounds to 130—and my limbs became just strings of muscle. When I could no longer find a place to inject, that was the end." [30]

These horrors remained in the future for him. He had no reason to think as the postwar period began that his professional opportunities and his domestic situation would disintegrate so badly. The future always beckons with promise, and surely Lugosi thought that his life would continue with some degree of satisfaction. But that was not to be.

[30] *Ibid.*

❦ 6 ❦

The Last Years

LIFE WOULD BE different after the war. Everyone in the country said so! And so it was, not only for the movie industry but also for Lugosi. There was a new national mood, but the mood wasn't a favorable one. The public seemed to have had enough of the type of horror film that he had been appearing in for fifteen years. After all, the atomic bomb of 1945 was a far madder invention than anything that Dr. Lugosi had ever devised. Furthermore, the ominous Russians and the so-called Communists in our own government were villainous enough to satisfy the public's appetite. Although the horror genre had weathered other inflations and recessions, it was now encountering something it could not vanquish: familiarity and the contempt it brings.

The horror film was not the only aspect of the movies to suffer; the whole industry experienced a decline. The millions of men returning from the war were busy obtaining educations, building nest eggs, and getting married, while the populace as a whole relished unrationed gasoline, new cars, and a general economic boom. Furthermore, the federal government's ruling against block-booking—long a bone of contention in the courts—by which the major producers and distributors were able to force theaters to take poor films in order to get good ones spoiled the profitability of low-cost films. Universal, which between 1941 and 1944 had been releasing between fifty and sixty features a year, started to slow down, making 46 in 1945, 42 in 1946, 33 in 1947, 35 in 1948, and a mere 29 in 1949.[1] The horror film was dropped not only by Universal but also by all the other studios.

Television too had reared its bulbous head. This new medium had no appreciable effect in 1946, when there were only 6,500 sets in the country. But by 1948 there were more than one million, by 1950

[1] Michael Conant, *Anti-trust in the Motion Picture Industry* (Berkeley, University of California Press, 1960), p. 123.

To my friend
arthur
Bela Lugosi

eleven million, by 1953 thirty million, and by 1956, the year of Lugosi's death, fifty-two million.[2] These sets satisfied the needs that had previously been met by films. During the war years people had "gone to the movies," not to see a specific film, but just to go out and be entertained. Television changed this. Unless a film was of exceptional interest, the people were content to watch what was being given away free between commercials in the comfort of the home.

As a result, almost no horror films were made from 1946 through 1948. Lugosi, caught in this antihorror "crunch," searched desperately for work. There was none to be had. When the horror film picked up again, in 1949, the industry had changed vastly, and so had the nature of the menace. Science fiction became the new mode. The villain was no longer an individual—a monster, a vampire, a wolfman, or a mad doctor—but a creature from another planet or mutations from atomic radiation. A vegetable man feeding on blood (*The Thing*, 1951), a messenger from outer space (*The Day the Earth Stood Still*, 1951), creatures landing in the Arizona desert (*It Came from Outer Space*, 1953), and giant ants (*Them*, 1954)—all kinds of beings invaded the theaters. They had plenty of room, for there were few people in the theaters anyhow.

Hollywood, concentrating on villains of an extraterrestrial nature, failed to realize, when *Dracula* and *Frankenstein* were rereleased in 1951 to a terrific box office, that there was still a craving for such old-fashioned, earthly villains. If Hollywood remained obdurate, Hammer Films in England did not. After their production of *The Curse of Frankenstein* (1957) proved to be a success, even though the monster looked like Jerry Lewis with acne, the studio went on to make *Horror of Dracula* (1958) and then set about realizing a whole revival.

After Lugosi's stint at RKO in 1945–46 and his appearance in *Scared to Death* he could not find any work. And he needed work badly, because financially he had not been a cautious man. Like his fictional counterpart of the mad doctor, he was impulsive and larger than life in his expenditures as well as his dreams.

When no movie offer materialized, Lugosi grew desperate. His last expedient was to return to the stage. Broadway was not interested, but the straw-hat circuit was, and so in the summer of 1947 he toured in *Dracula*. It was at this point that this writer, as a young boy, finally met

[2] *Electrical Merchandising*, as quoted in Conant, *op. cit.*, p. 13.

his cinematic hero. He made a pilgrimage to see Lugosi at the John Drew Theater in East Hampton, Long Island, in the week of July 14, 1947. It was not a large theater, nor was it crowded, but it harbored Lugosi in *Dracula*. With a great deal of nervous anticipation, the boy waited for the first act to begin. Lugosi's performance did not prove, even to the young admirer's worshipful eyes, that the Hungarian was the greatest of stage actors, but it was a genuine thrill to see the Master Villain in the flesh. The play by this time creaked rather badly, and Lugosi's performance, although effective, was perhaps a bit too deliberate and heavy-handed. Although it was hammy, a certain amount of ham was necessary, since without a larger-than-life, sinister presence the play would be nothing at all.

The writer remembers vividly his excitement after the first act as he got up from his orchestra seat, walked down the aisle toward the exit door near the stage, and ventured down a corridor leading to the dressing rooms. The boy sensed a figure standing immediately by the door, turned, and looked up. It was the tall, magical, great man himself, smoking a cigar. After the proverbial skipped heartbeat and a juvenile series of stammerings, the boy expressed his devout appreciation of Lugosi. The actor was most cordial and agreed after the play to talk with the boy at greater length. The second and third acts moved as in a euphoric dream. Lugosi acknowledged the applause of the small audience with a flourish of his cape, a crinkling of his Slavic eyes—and then the curtain came down. At about equal speed, the boy exited down the aisle and a few moments later arrived at the dressing room.

Lugosi was there with his wife, Lillian, and both proved most kind and not at all like the stuck-up "stars" that Hollywood people were reported to be. Lugosi was genuinely pleased that he had such a worshipful fan, a fan who knew the titles of all his films and who had brought along a collection of lists, stills, and booklets pertaining to the actor's long career. The boy showed him two photos that he had once received in the mail after writing Lugosi. Bela looked at them and declared that they had been signed not by him but by his wife; she nodded her head in agreement. After glaring at her a second, Lugosi then took a pen and resigned the photos himself, adding a "Mrs." before her signature. The boy also showed him a list of all the actor's films, which he had compiled with great difficulty. Lugosi scrutinized it in the same way that he had studied the deed to Carfax Abbey, but contributed no new titles, although the list—as it turned out—was far

To my friend Arthur in appreciation Bela Lugosi

from complete. The boy told Lugosi how much he liked *White Zombie*, but Lugosi did not seem to remember the film, confused it with *Voodoo Man*, and then said that there were so many title changes that he could not keep up with them. This lack of memory about one of his few masterpieces was somewhat of a surprise to the boy.

The word that best describes Lugosi at this time was kindly. He was not aloof, not proud, not haughty, but instead treated his admirer as an adult (how young people like that!) and was obviously pleased that somewhere in an increasingly hostile and indifferent world there was still a solid bastion of Lugosiana. After about an hour or so, Lugosi autographed almost everything the boy had brought with him, led him out of the darkened theater, shook hands in the street, and went into a bar with his wife to slake a more easily satisfied thirst than the one he had suffered in the play.

As Shakespeare says, "Summer hath too short a lease," and soon Lugosi was once more unemployed, but constantly hoping that Hollywood would again draw upon his talent. Lugosi had heard that Universal was going to pit Abbott and Costello against the old Universal monsters—the wolf man, the Frankenstein monster, and Dracula—in a film tentatively titled *The Brain of Frankenstein*, and he wished to play the part of the vampire. In a number of letters to this writer in 1968, Don Marlowe, Lugosi's friend and agent, explained what happened. Apparently Marlowe had promised Lugosi that he would win the part. Later, when Lugosi was in New York and Marlowe on the Coast, the actor kept writing his agent about how much he was looking forward to portraying Dracula again. Although Chaney had usurped Lugosi's role in *Son of Dracula*, he was better known as the wolfman, and since he obviously could not appear in both roles, there was hope for Lugosi. Said Marlowe:

> He was a good friend of mine and had complete confidence in me. Not wanting to let him down I kept saying everything was all right, but it wasn't. Nobody at Universal wanted him. I was there every day—seeing everybody—head casting man at that time was Bob Palmer—I went to his home—I went to Lou Costello's home—I got nowhere. I finally phoned every Universal Exchange in the country and asked them to wire me collect the net amount they made on *Dracula*. They did. [1] . . . tried to make an appointment with the President of Universal. He wouldn't see me. Lugosi read in New York papers when the picture was about to start. He called me on a

Friday night eight days before the starting date, wanting to know when I was sending the contract. I told him I would call him the following Monday afternoon. He wanted to know whether anything was wrong. I assured him everything was all right.

I didn't sleep or eat the entire weekend. Early Monday morning I barged right past the secretary of the President into his office, with telegrams under my arm. He was alone.

Marlowe explained to the president that in 1931, when Universal was going broke, *Dracula* had saved the studio from closing down; that Lugosi had been paid only $500 a week for seven weeks; that a total of $3,500 was all he had ever received, even though the studio had made millions. Marlowe told all this to the president and showed him the telegrams to prove how much the studio had profited.

I said, "You owe this part to Lugosi." I went on to say, "It's his part—he is Dracula." He looked at me like I was some kind of nut—rang a buzzer—I thought surely he was calling somebody to throw me out as I was wild and yelling at him. It was sink or swim. I had to get Lugosi this part—by the way I never accepted one cent commission on this picture—Lugosi tried to pay me several times— anyhow he asked that his secretary be sent in and without saying another word to me asked the secretary to draw up a contract for Lugosi to play Dracula in this picture. He turned to me and said, "Mr. Marlowe—how much are you asking for Mr. Lugosi?" I said, "$1,500 a week with a ten week guarantee." He looked at the secretary and said nothing. She asked him what she should put down and he replied, "Exactly what Mr. Marlowe said." He turned to me and said, "Is there anything else I can do for you, Mr. Marlowe?" I said no and as I started to leave I asked him if I should call Mr. Lugosi in New York and ask him to come to California, and in a very calm voice he replied, "I would suggest you do that." I left and in my excitement I didn't even thank him. (I did later.) The contract was delivered to my office that afternoon and I called Lugosi in New York and gave him the news.

Neither Lugosi nor his wife knew what Marlowe had gone through to get him the part or that Ian Keith, who earlier had been signed to play Dracula, was dropped.

Lugosi packed his bags, traveled west, and for the last time entered the gates of Universal Studios, where so long ago he had won fame.

Shooting began on February 14, 1948, seventeen years to the day of the New York premiere of *Dracula*. Now age sixty-five, Lugosi showed that the years of sorrow, disappointment, frustration, and drug addiction had taken their toll. Although the handsome, lean features of the earlier Dracula had vanished, the makeup department did the best it could. A heavy foundation was put on to cover the wrinkles—perhaps too heavy, as it is all too readily visible—but Count Dracula was no less impressive as a man of considerable years. His age, in fact, seemed to add another layer of meaning to the Count's need for blood. Although Lugosi's face had changed, the voice, that splendid tone and accent, remained. He added to his characterization by using his cape to mask the lower part of his face, thereby emphasizing his eyes. All in all, he played his role to perfection, still the dominant, all-powerful figure, and managed, despite the exaggeration and humor, to maintain his dignity and mystique even with the comedy team.

Abbott and Costello are shipping clerks in Florida. Two cases are sent from Europe to Mr. McDougal, the proprietor of a local house of horrors, who bought them "dirt cheap." Meantime, Costello receives a telephone call from Lawrence Talbot in London warning him not to deliver the cases, for they contain the bodies of Count Dracula and Frankenstein's monster. Unfortunately the moon rises at this point, and Talbot's conversation disintegrates into growls.

That night Abbott and Costello deliver the crates to the house of horrors. Naturally the lights go out, and Costello is left with Dracula's coffin, which slowly starts to open, the candle on its lid sliding. There are a number of funny moments, of course, as Costello observes the moving candle. He calls in Abbott and reads him the legend about Dracula. Abbott says, "It's the bunk," and Costello agrees, pointing to the coffin. Poor Costello is then hypnotized by Dracula, and the Frankenstein monster rises from his box, but backs away from Costello in fear. Except for this minor lapse, the old Universal creatures are handled in a serious fashion. It is not they who are funny, but the fright they provoke. The monster is stiff and lumbering, but is able to speak, although the content of his conversation is only, "Yes, master," repeated a few times.

Dracula goes off to an island, where he plans to put the brain of a simple-minded person into the monster. To help him with the operation he has found a lady doctor (Lenore Aubert), and she, in turn, has pretended to be smitten with Costello. Meantime, another woman, an insurance investigator checking on the missing exhibits, also pretends to be interested in Costello, much to Abbott's amazement and annoyance.

Dracula is his own Continental self. When he sees Sandra, the woman doctor, he intones with all his old magic, "You look more charming than when I saw you last." Dracula has power over the doctor, but not yet of a hypnotic kind. Later, when she says that their task is "risky business," he replies: "Not as risky as those curious operations of yours that so intrigued the European police, yet much more profitable. Restore the monster for me and you shall have anything you wish." He then speaks to her about the brain: "I don't want to make Frankenstein's mistake and revive a vicious, unmanageable brute. This time the monster must have no will of his own, no fiendish intellect to oppose his master." She tells him that she has "exceeded his fondest wishes." The new brain she has chosen for the monster is "so simple, so pliable, it will obey you like a trained dog." Needless to say whose brain is meant!

Meantime, Talbot, who despite his monthly aberrations remains a good person, has come to Florida to stop Dracula's evil plans. He tells the boys about the sinister plot, but Abbott doesn't believe him, though Costello thinks it is possible. That night they are invited by Sandra to the mansion on the island. Costello is hardly enthusiastic: "It's a little past sunset, and if Dracula is here he's going to be wanting breakfast and I'm fatter than you and it ain't going to be me."

They go downstairs to search, and of course Costello encounters the monster and the caped Dracula, though Abbott sees nothing. Later Costello tells Sandra he has just fallen down the cellar stairs. Dracula, entering, comments: "How careless. You should be careful. A person can get *killed* that way." They then introduce each other. Lugosi stares intently at Lou and, with a wonderful sense of superiority mixed with arch humor, announces enthusiastically:

Ah, Wilbur. Why, I heard so much about you I feel as if we have already met. [To Sandra] I must say, my dear, I approve very *highly* of your choice. What we need today is young blood—and brains! [Costello rests his head on Lugosi's arm.] Ah, don't be bashful!

They talk about the masquerade ball they are planning to attend. Dracula says: "Ah, you young people, making the most of life—[long

"What we need today is young blood—and brains," says Lugosi to Costello. *Abbott and Costello Meet Frankenstein* (1948).

pause] *while it lasts.*" Sandra, however, says she has a splitting headache, goes upstairs, and there tells the Count that the plan is becoming too dangerous and that they ought to wait.

Dracula says, "And jeopardize the success of the operation? Never! I must warn you, my dear Sandra, I am accustomed to having my orders obeyed, especially by women with a price on their head.

She refuses and says, "Operate yourself, if you are in such a hurry." Dracula is not intimidated by this unwise show of independence:

> DRACULA: I have other ways of securing your cooperation.
> DOCTOR: You're wasting your time. My will is as strong as yours!
> DRACULA: Are you sure? [He then stares with those full Lugosi orbs.] Look into my eyes. Look! Deeper! Tell me what you see.

The look suffices. Dracula leans over and puts his head at her throat. She will now do his bidding.

Later, at a masquerade ball on the mainland, Talbot encounters Abbott and Costello and laments, "In half an hour the moon will rise and I'll turn into a wolf." When Costello replies, "You and twenty million other guys," Talbot loses his temper. He then asks that they lock him in his room. Abbott agrees, grumbling, "Why don't you hire yourself a keeper?"

Sandra, now under Dracula's power, sits with Costello and asks him to return with her.

> DOCTOR: I want to be the only one in your life. I want to be part of you. I want to be in your blood.
> COSTELLO: I think I know what you mean. Wouldn't you want a prettier fellow than me?
> DOCTOR: No. I want no one but you. You're full blooded, so round, so firm—
> COSTELLO: —so fully packed. I want to stay that way! [He clasps the rose he is carrying.] Ah, I stuck myself. I'm bleeding.
> DOCTOR: Let me see it. [She tries to examine his finger, in a parody of the Renfield scene in *Dracula*.]
> COSTELLO: Uh, uh. There ain't enough there for the two of us, if that's what you're thinking.

Sandra asks him to look into her eyes. A closeup shows the outline of a bat flying in each pupil. Lou turns his head and says, "I've looked deep enough. I don't want to look anymore." She says, "Don't you know what's going to happen now?" "I'll bite." "Oh, no. I will!" But she is interrupted by Abbott.

Soon after, however, Dracula takes Costello and Sandra to the island. Costello is locked in a wooden stock right next to the monster, and Sandra tells him: "Soon, instead of being short and chubby, you'll be big and tall, and as strong as an ox. And furthermore, you'll live forever and never grow old."

She explains that she is going to remove his brain and put it in the monster. Costello yells out to the monster in the same room, calling him Junior. He tells the silent creature, "I've had this brain for thirty years and it hasn't worked right yet."

The next night, Dracula puts the monster on one operating table and Costello on the other and turns on the electrical equipment to charge the monster. Talbot and Abbott arrive, but just as Talbot starts to free Costello, he changes into a wolf, and so Lou is caught between the reactivated monster and the raging wolfman. Finally, after a hilarious chase, with the monster pursuing Abbott and Costello, and the wolfman snarling after Dracula, the wolfman grabs the vampire (who has just changed into a bat), and both plunge over a parapet into the sea. The monster pursues the boys out onto a dock, which is set afire, and he presumably burns to death and sinks into the water. As Abbott and Costello sit in a rowboat, thinking they are safe, a cigarette suddenly appears, and the voice of the invisible man frightens them into jumping overboard.

Lugosi seemed to enjoy being back on the set, although there was at least one minor difficulty. As Don Marlowe said, "I think the only person Lugosi ever disliked was Lon Chaney, Jr. The reason was that Chaney antagonized Lugosi by calling him Pop." Lugosi's wife and son visited him on the set, and many candid pictures were taken of Bela, Jr., with other members of the cast. The film, completed on March 27, 1948, was released in July to reasonably good reviews. Lugosi received fourth billing.

Lugosi's portrayal of Dracula pleased him, but it did not impress other Hollywood studios. To them it was just a small part in another Abbott and Costello film. But Lugosi was not the only great to be linked with this team, since that pair later encountered other notables: Boris Karloff in *Abbott and Costello Meet Dr. Jekyll and Mr. Hyde* and Charles Laughton in *Abbott and Costello Meet Captain Kid*.

Lugosi hoped that his reappearance as the Count would remind Hollywood that there was still a possibility of doing a sequel to the original *Dracula*. In April, 1948, Don Marlowe, his agent, offered the studios a script called *Return of Dracula*, written by Howard Hill and Paul Castleton, but none showed any interest.

When no additional roles were offered in Hollywood, Lugosi returned to summer stock and toured the East Coast in *Arsenic and Old Lace*, a play that had previously kept both Karloff and Erich von Stroheim solvent. Lugosi spent June, 1948, learning the role and first appeared in the play on June 30 in New Hope, Pennsylvania.

In the second week of August, Lugosi—his name featured in advertisements and in theatrical programs—appeared in the play at Sea Cliff, New York, where this writer again met his hero. The boy was more than pleased that Lugosi remembered him from the previous year and was overjoyed when the actor asked him to go back to his quarters later. Between the acts the boy went backstage with the star and was astounded at the primitive conditions there, for the great Lugosi had to change his trousers in a kind of communal room. Count Dracula with his pants off was not part of the gothic myth.

Lugosi in his role of the sadistic murderer, Jonathan Brewster, played his part well and seemed far less mannered than he had the year before in *Dracula*. The matinee performance that the boy witnessed, although appearing to go smoothly and performed by an excellent cast, was not without incident. After the play the heroine indignantly stormed up to Lugosi and complained about the moment in the play when he stuffs a handkerchief in her mouth. Apparently the cloth was not entirely clean. Unfortunately Lugosi's hypnotic eyes did not quite quell the girl's tantrum, and she waxed for a considerable time, Lugosi patiently weathering the abuse.

After the play Lugosi signed autographs for his fans, leaning on the hood of his new Buick Roadmaster convertible with its California license plate. Then he invited his young admirer back to the cottage where he was staying, and they talked over his films and career. A case of Ballantine ale stood in the corner. Lugosi said that he could not understand how Karloff was so much better known and more popular than he. He deeply resented this, and as a Lugosi partisan, the writer shared his feeling of injustice. The boy suggested that perhaps part of Lugosi's trouble came from his name, unpronounceable to the average

Bela signing autographs, August, 1948.

American: he would be Bela Loo-goos-i, Bela Lu-gush-i, and so forth. The great man pondered this a moment and then dismissed it as another irreparable aspect of his career.

Lugosi talked on, took out some of the photo files that he had brought with him, and gave his devoted fan three pictures that had been taken quite recently. On one he wrote, "Arthur, I hope you like it." He also showed a stack of smaller photos that had been taken on the set of the Abbott and Costello picture. There were shots of his son, Bela, Jr., sitting with the Frankenstein monster, the wolfman, and of course with his famous father. It was a time for the young fan to resent the wheels of fate that had not given him the immortal Count as a parent.

The young admirer told Lugosi about a shrine he had in his cellar. A chemical laboratory stood at one end of the room, a collection of Lugosi photos hung on one wall, and large posters of the great man were plastered over another wall. In his fancy the boy had tried to transplant brains, to bring the dead back to life, and to raise a breed of giant vampire bats. In actuality the experiments never got beyond boiling alcohol in a retort and lighting the end to form a kind of alchemical-looking device of roaring flame. Lugosi was intrigued by this description of the shrine, and so he and his wife drove him the eight miles or so back to his house. Lugosi had to stop along the road to get cigars and smoked one on the way over, while his wife drove, since he himself did not know how.

At home Lugosi was ushered in by the beaming boy, who regretted only that not one of his friends happened to come by at this moment of supreme bliss. Lugosi, encountering the mother of the enthusiastic fan, came up to her rapidly and intoned, "Hello, Mother." Although adjusted to the fact that her son brought back strange things—salamanders, frogs, snakes—she never quite expected to meet Count Dracula himself. Lugosi then followed the boy as they descended the steps to the cellar. Would they encounter starved and revengeful slaves from Lugosi's past films? Would there be somnambulant women in glass cases or some maimed assistant huffing and puffing and grumbling? To the boy the cellar was hopelessly prosaic, but still, there *was* the shrine. Lugosi looked happily around the room. He saw the photos, the signs with his name lettered by a cooperative lobby card painter at one of the screen services in New York, a large poster from *Voodoo Man*, and stills from *Dracula, Chandu, The Raven*, and his more current films.

Bela, pleased, patted the boy's shoulder. Here, in a distant corner of the world, far from Hungary, far from Hollywood, there was proof that although his career might be in the doldrums, there still existed one of the devout.

The boy shyly showed Bela a photograph he had made of himself with Dracula makeup on. Wearing a dark suit and trying to look as maturely hypnotic as possible, the boy glowered in front of a gnarled tree. Lugosi smiled at the picture of his young imitator and asked whether he could have a copy, and of course the boy agreed. Lugosi studied it a moment more and then shook his head. "Too much sky," he said and folded back the top of the picture to give it better proportions.

Leading Lugosi back upstairs and outside, the boy delightedly took some snapshots of him, and then his wife photographed the boy and his hero together, after which the glorious moments slipped into memory as the two drove away for the evening performance. Needless to say, the boy was ecstatic and remained that way for a number of weeks.

Oddly enough the Sea Cliff performance of *Arsenic and Old Lace* that the boy had seen also had attracted the attention of a young producer by the name of Richard Gordon, and another friendship began, one far more useful to the aging actor. When the summer season ended, Lugosi was again out of work and still on the East Coast. Gordon was too young to be very influential at this time, but, as he told me in an interview in 1970, he began to accompany Lugosi in his quest for jobs.

Lugosi's horizon remained bleak, although he finally obtained a television role that fall. He played in a half-hour dramatic version of Poe's "Cask of Amontillado" and offered an excellent performance, restrained yet powerful. The direction was hardly inspired, however, and the budget interfered as well. There was only one set of stairs, and so in shot after shot Lugosi descended the same staircase, a repeated action that seemed ludicrous. Gordon was at the studio during the telecast and accompanied Lugosi to a Hungarian restaurant, the Tokay, on the East Side in New York. There, having just been paid, Lugosi bought drinks for everyone in the restaurant and celebrated grandly. He ordered beer, poured a little out of the glass, poured Scotch in, and drank that hideous concoction. By the end of the evening, the proceeds of the performance had been spent, and Lugosi was again broke and desperate.

Making a special face for the camera.

The boy and his hero.

Mr. and Mrs. Lugosi at the author's home.

Lugosi also appeared on one of Milton Berle's comedy hours in a sketch about an evil scientist. Two of the immortal lines in it were Berle's comment: "Ah, have a heart," and Lugosi's reply: "I think I will!" At another point, though somewhat repetitiously, Berle says, "Cut it out," and Lugosi nods in the affirmative. Lugosi seemed ill at ease in the sketch, and although Berle was playing for broad laughs, Lugosi was trying his best to be serious, and it was quite probable that he did not understand all the supposed humor in the first place. At one point he flubbed a line and instead of saying "the mummy," he said "the mumm," and while Berle kidded him about this, Lugosi could not return the banter. After the show Lugosi was angry at Berle, and justifiably so. During rehearsal Lugosi had learned the lines and had not planned on Berle's ad libs during the sketch. Slightly hard of hearing and never gifted at banter anyhow, Lugosi felt he was being made a fool of and probably placed Berle next to Karloff and Chaney, in his list of private dislikes.

In late October, 1948, a little newspaper advertisement appeared: "Manhasset Theatre, Friday, October 29—Bela 'Dracula' Lugosi, assisted by the Laugh Star, Sonny Parks. Free Halloween refreshments to the house!" Naturally the boy attended. The theater was a small one and its audience even smaller. Lugosi did a little sketch with his wife playing the maid in *Dracula* as he hypnotized her, and then he did a routine with the comedy star involving that hoary joke about a cemetery so wonderful that "people were dying to get in."

If the theater manager had paid more than $50 for Lugosi's presentation, he lost money, for the patrons were few. The stage act ended with a slight flurry of applause, and then the houselights were turned on so that the few dozen people could leave. The manager prevented the boy from going backstage, so he hurried outside and waited by the stage door. Not long after, Bela came out into the chill air. There was no swagger to the man stepping through the door. He seemed almost to sneak out. The boy greeted him, and Lugosi, his face lighting up, said, "Hello, Arthur," even remembering the name. There was conversation for a few minutes, but Lugosi was ill at ease. That he had appeared in a shabby act in a third-rate show to an almost empty house remained unsaid. "So it has come to this," his melancholy eyes and body seemed to say. Perhaps in his mind there was a flashback to the plush National Theater of Hungary, and Bela was once again bowing to salvos of applause and looking forward to a cast party at a charming restaurant in Budapest. But now there was silence, one bespectacled boy with devotion in his eyes, a brick wall, and a row of dim streetlights. There was still another moment, a long one. They looked at each other, but there was nothing to say, and they parted. It was the last time the boy would meet his hero.

Lugosi continued to stay in New York City. He studied his mail, hoping a new film offer would appear, but none did. Nor did a play materialize. Desperate, he reluctantly consented to make personal appearances in a horror act that played in theaters around New York City during 1949. As he said in an interview shortly before his death, "Without movie parts I was reduced to 'freak' status. I just couldn't stand it." William K. Everson, who knew Bela well during this period, has described the situation very well:

> First the theatre would run one of his movies—alas, one of the poorer ones, one that could be booked for minimum rental: usually one of the abortions like *The Ape Man* . . . and then Lugosi, on stage, would do a horror act. This sketch hardly seemed to be written at all and merely consisted of Lugosi playing around in a laboratory

with a giant gorilla and a manacled girl. The poor quality of the film had done nothing to give Lugosi an audience build-up. And in this era before the horror film had "Come back," the kids in the audience knew nothing of the serious work that Lugosi had done so the reception to the act was noisy and seldom respectful. Lugosi knew it was a wretched act and hated doing it, but at the same time it was his only income. In his performance, he gave the act far more than it deserved—but no matter whether it was well or badly received, he was always embarrassed when he left the theatre.[3]

Lugosi hoped for some way of getting out of this demeaning rut. According to a report in the New York *Herald Tribune* of June 8, 1950, Lugosi was considering a summer-theater tryout for *The Devil Also Dreams*, a play by Fritz Rotter. Francis L. Sullivan was being sought for the lead, and Angela Lansbury and Alexis Smith were being mentioned for the female roles. But nothing came of the scheme.

Lugosi was compelled to return to the wretched horror act. The December 6, 1950, issue of *Variety* said that to bolster the pre-Christmas sag in business, Lugosi's act was being booked along the Atlantic seaboard. Instead of starting at midnight, as did other similar "horror" shows, his began at 8:30. The RKO and Warner circuits booked the act in the New York–New Jersey area, where Lugosi had to endure the wise remarks and heckling of unimpressed, atomic-age teenagers. The show claimed to have the backing of Michael Todd.

William K. Everson occasionally accompanied the actor to Hungarian restaurants in New York City. "The trick," said Everson, "was to get him in a happy, receptive frame of mind." As the wine flowed, Bela's spirits soared and he spoke of the past. Without bitterness, he would "lapse into a kind of trance as he answered questions and recalled anecdotes." But Bela was still alert.

Once at the Tokay, the girl singer bounced around a little too energetically, and the whole front of her gown fell away. The view was hardly spectacular, although in 1952 it could have been considered a genuine accident and not a gimmick. Bela, however, roused from his reveries instantly, and whirled around to take in the sights much as he whirled around on Renfield when he cut his finger on the paper clip.

[3] William K. Everson, *Castle of Frankenstein*, n.d.

The period when Everson could ask him questions was brief, for after two or three more drinks Bela's mood changed and he became totally nostalgic for his days in Hungary. "Now he would get sad and wistfully poetic, frequently talking of death—not in a morbid sense, but in a sense that his life and his work were behind him, and there was nothing more to look forward to but that."

Finally Richard Gordon arranged for Lugosi to appear in England. In the first week of April, 1951, the actor sailed to Britain, where he was to start his provincial tour at the Theatre Royal in Brighton on April 30, prior to appearing in London's West End.[4]

Lugosi owned his own prop coffin—a satin-lined one with air holes—and tried to convince Gordon and others of a weird scheme: to lie in his coffin and be discovered by the customs officials. Lugosi thought it would be a great headline getter, one that would give him worldwide publicity and help his career along. But they talked him out of it by convincing him that British Customs had little sense of humor about someone trying to sneak into the country. Reluctantly Lugosi did not carry through his great plan.

Lugosi was to receive about $1,000 a week for his appearance in *Dracula* and looked forward to a great success. But the producer thought that the Lugosi name would be enough to draw people into the theater and therefore skimped on the rest of the cast. There were delays, and after many last-minute changes and worries the play opened at the Theatre Royal on June 26, almost two months late. Unfortunately some of the actors had not mastered their lines. Lugosi of course had the part committed to memory, but he was quite deaf in one ear and could not always hear when a line was missing. He waited for his cue, and when it did not come, he paused a few seconds longer and then began on his own lines. The results were not impressive, and the long tour was cut short. Despite the poor production, fans still flocked to see him. Bela signed autographs in blood-red ink and was proud of the respect and adulation that the United States no longer gave him, but his dreams of making an outstanding comeback in England never materialized.

One night Harry Ludlam, a future biographer of Bram Stoker and obviously a Lugosi admirer, went backstage to meet the actor.

[4] *Variety*, April 11, 1951.

He sat thickly in his dressing room, his cloak about his shoulders, make-up heavy on his face and red on his full lips, his deep eyes uncannily still and penetrating. It was incongruous to see one of his famous clutching hands supporting a script, as if he were still in need of one, and then the deathly voice rolled and stung—complaining of the plumbing in English hotels.

Tired and bitter, Lugosi told Ludlam:

"I look in the mirror and I say to myself, 'Can it be you once played Romeo?' " he intoned. "Always it is the same. When a film company is in the red they come to me and say, 'Okay, so we make a horror film.' And so that is what we do. It is what I always do." [5]

Meantime, Gordon, disappointed that the play did not do well, tried to get Lugosi a screen role. Finally the actor was hired to appear in a spoof called *Old Mother Riley Meets the Vampire*, one of the many films in the Mother Riley series, which had begun in the 1930's and originally was good slapstick. By 1951 the Mother Riley films had degenerated to the level of the Bowery Boys. Lugosi was told he would have a large role. He was offered only $5,000 for his appearance, but he took the money, hoping that a favorable review would help his career. Indeed many good scenes were shot of him, but Mother Riley added more scenes of his-her own (she was played by a male actor), and Lugosi's part was cut back. The film was released in April, 1952, to indifferent business in England. When American distributors were offered the property, they did not know what to do with it and reluctantly showed it in 1953 as *Vampire over London*. It did poorly. In 1964 it was released as *My Son, the Vampire*. The title was meaningless, and the box-office results were as disappointing as before.

The film opens as a young woman, just getting off a ship, is kidnapped at the pier. The scene then shifts to Scotland Yard as an official reads a report just received about a notorious person named Von Housen.

Born in Bosnick in 1894 [and therefore twelve years younger than Lugosi's real age] a descendant of Baron Von Housen, whom legend immortalized as a Vampire. For reasons of his own, Von Housen

[5] Ludlam, *Bram Stoker*, p. 175.

claims to be the earthly reproduction of his notorious ancestor, owing
his continued existence to the consumption of human blood.

Needless to say, "there is not the faintest vestige of truth to his claim,"
but the official adds that Von Housen is a "scientist of considerable
repute." Furthermore, he is "a dangerous character, not for what he
claims to be but for what he is—a fanatical scientist with a stupid gang
of men who have allowed themselves to be mesmerized by a legend."
The police conclude that the disappearance of the girl, the daughter of
an Italian scientist, is due to Von Housen and that he probably is after a
chart showing the location of large uranium deposits in South America,
deposits that Von Housen needs.

The scene then changes to the little store of Mother Riley, a comic
old reprobate who is eight weeks behind in the rent. Calling the agent
a vampire, the little old lady (played in woman's clothes by Arthur
Lucan) receives news that her Uncle Jeremiah, from Ireland, has died
and that his effects are being sent to her.

The camera now cuts to a spooky old house as a bespectacled
assistant walks upstairs into a shadow-filled room containing a coffin. A
loud snore emanates from the casket, and shortly after, the lid opens,
and Lugosi, with jet-black hair and Dracula cape, arises. When his
assistant says that he hopes Von Housen has had sufficient rest, the
scientist replies, "From now on there will be little rest for any of us."
The assistant asks him why he sleeps in his evening clothes, and Von
Housen answers, "Because I was buried in them." Moving with great
alacrity, Lugosi belies his years. His eyes, the movement of his head
and body, reveal a man of superb energy. He plays the role of Von
Housen with all of his Dracula-like authority, but is not afraid to enjoy
himself or to exaggerate and parody the mad scientist in a style
sometimes even approaching camp, but still remaining within the
confines of his role.

Von Housen descends to his laboratory and announces grandly to
his assistants, "The time has come when I have to acquaint you with
my latest achievements and my future plans." With great Lugosi
enthusiasm, he says: "At last I, Von Housen, am ready to fulfill my
destiny!" He explains to a fellow conspirator, Anton (a bearded man
from some iron curtain country), that he has created weapons that can
destroy much of the world. At the turn of a dial, "a thousand airplanes
will be destroyed! Another turn and ten battleships can be blown up at

My Son the Vampire (1952). "Because I was buried in them."

sea!" He points to some switches. "This is robot control. I intend to build fifty thousand robots." Anton is impressed and asks, "But how many have you built so far?" Lugosi's face becomes a study as his dark eyebrows majestically rise and lower before he announces rather lamely, "Er, ah—one." It is a beautiful moment.

But with the uranium, he says, nothing can stop him. He explains that his new robot, manufactured in Ireland, is being sent to him under the pseudonym of Dr. Riley. Unfortunately for Von Housen's great plans, the labels on the boxes directed to him and Mother Riley are switched. When the van arrives at Lugosi's house and the crate is brought in, he announces grandly, "My friends; this is a great moment, our victory is in sight." While the assistants open the box, he yells out: "Stop! Enough! My friends, this is the greatest moment of my life." His hands run through the straw and bring out only Uncle Jeremiah's household effects. The "greatest moment," however, proves to be a funny one as the great scientist registers surprise at the pots and pans. He asks whether he is going mad, brings his fingers up to the side of his head, and then, with a different expression on his face, says with great pomposity, "We must think! We must plan!" His eyes shoot around the room in a scheming manner. Lugosi plays this comedy to the hilt.

Meantime, the robot has been sent to Mother Riley. That night, while she is asleep, Von Housen turns on his control board and commands, "Master calling." The robot wakes up, grabs the woman, puts her in a sack, and goes outside in the street to be carried away by one of the henchmen in a truck. But when a Bobbie tells the driver not to loiter but to move on, the robot ends up with no transportation. Fortunately a classic drunk—confetti and streamers hanging from top hat and windshield—waveringly drives by and gives a lift to the robot and the mobile and muttering canvas sack containing Mother Riley. Von Housen, following the robot's progress, says admiringly with the full Lugosi authority, "Nothing can stop it now. This, my dear Anton, is *power!*" He then gives the robot further instructions and concludes proudly, "I created a robot with a living brain."

Mother Riley is installed in the house, the robot is welcomed back by Von Housen, and the arrival of the kidnapped girl is awaited. Von Housen, studying a report, is happy to know that Mother Riley's blood is of "Group three," and decides to interview his new find. She is looking at a picture of a bat over the fireplace and flapping her arms. Von Housen enters the room and tells her that the bat is his brother. Then he asks her whether she likes bats. She says that they give her the cold shivers. "A great pity," says Von Housen, shaking his head sadly. He offers her a job as a maid and promises that she will be given almost-raw liver and thick, juicy steaks full of blood. He leaves the room, saying, "Don't strain yourself, my lovely group three."

Meantime, the kidnapped girl has arrived, and Von Housen, using his hypnotic powers, tries to extract the whereabouts of the chart from her. But Mother Riley escapes from the house, tries to explain to the police that Von Housen has the kidnapped girl, is almost locked up by them, and then returns. Von Housen decides to do away with Mother Riley and programs the robot to carry out the task, musing that having a woman killed by a robot will be the "perfect crime" and that, proudly, "we make history!" Mother Riley has been busy sneaking around the house, and after many chases down dark corridors, disappearances through hidden doorways, and knock-about fights she saves the girl, and pursuing Von Housen and his henchmen in a most incongruous antique car, she arrives at the ship where the girl had left the chart in time to see Von Housen and his men apprehended by the police.

The film, a farce containing much low British humor, and filled with

My Son the Vampire. Bela and Mother Riley.

English muttering so that the sound track is not always very comprehensible to an American, is a reasonably amusing spoof. Lugosi is superb, playing the heavy moments with his old intensity and handling the humorous ones with just the right degree of levity. He seems really to be enjoying the role and shows that the mannerisms, timing, and versatility of his Hungarian theater days had not deserted him.

Then Lugosi took a ship back to New York, and in the harbor was interviewed by a television reporter. Lugosi seemed in good spirits, probably indeed had even downed a few. Smoking a cigar, he talked about the Mother Riley film and said that he had played it for comedy and hoped that it would be a success. He appeared gracious and tremendously grateful that as a man who had faded much from the scene, he was still being interviewed at all. That he thought he was on the verge of a comeback can be seen in his hopeful attitude. Perhaps he felt that his comparative success in England would be equaled in Hollywood, but he was much mistaken.

After months of waiting, Lugosi sank to a new low by appearing in a

Glen or Glenda? (1952).

minusculely budgeted sexploitation film called *Glen or Glenda?* which appeared in more explicit New York City as *I Changed My Sex.* The film, released in June, 1952, played in only a few of the low-class theaters in the country. It told the story of a transvestite and how he attempts to adjust to his problem. Finally he goes to a counselor (Lugosi). Sitting in an easychair covered with a fishnet for atmosphere, and with a skeleton in the corner of the room, Lugosi seems more like an exhausted Count Dracula than a helpful analyst. With thunder and lightning interrupting occasionally, he intones some advice. Mercifully he had little to do in the film and appears in sequences so unrelated to the others that perhaps they were an afterthought to make use of Lugosi's box-office value. The film belonged more to the hero-heroine, and he-she could have it.

Not long after, Lugosi appeared in *Bela Lugosi Meets a Brooklyn Gorilla* (known also as *The Boys from Brooklyn*), released in September, 1952. Although only four years had passed since the boy had last seen Lugosi (he had not viewed *Glen or Glenda?*), the actor was almost unrecognizable. He had aged at least ten years. Thin and haggard, he played a scientist on a lonely tropical island who tries to contend with (God preserve us!) a British imitation of Dean Martin and Jerry

Lewis. Bela put in a good performance, but the film was poor.

Depressed about his waning career and still bothered by various bodily pains, Lugosi's need for drugs grew more intense. His wife was faced each day with this growing horror. Her love for him had long gone, but she was still loyal and still concerned about him. But she was also concerned about her son and his welfare and peace of mind. With great effort and lots of psychology, she managed to wean him away from the habit by weakening his dosage each day until he was getting close to nothing.

Life had been difficult enough for her in the 1940's, when Bela was making good money and was still somewhat successful. But now all was different. His jobs, when he could get them, were demeaning. The once-proud man had been humbled. Now over seventy, he certainly wasn't as virile as he once had been, and sitting home brooding about his fate, he grew suspicious of his wife, thirty years his junior. She found his behavior unpleasant for herself and unwise for the welfare of their son.[6] On May 1, 1953, she became legally separated and sued for divorce on June 2. She complained that his "unfounded jealousy" kept her under his thumb twenty-four hours a day and that she could not even go to the dentist without his calling up to check. "I did not exaggerate," she told this writer in 1973. Despite her domestic difficulties, she was not vindictive. "I don't need alimony," she assured the court, "and I'm perfectly capable of supporting my son." She added that Bela was retired and should not be burdened with such an obligation at his age. The judge, however, felt differently and said that Bela should pay $50 a month support, if the actor's income warranted it, plus $1 a month token alimony. She said loyally, "I know if conditions change, Bela Lugosi will support his son without any order to do so." On August 4, 1953, after some deliberation, the court found that "the earning capacity of the father is insufficient to provide for child support and no order for child support is made at this time."

What were Lugosi's assets after so many years as a leading horror star? At the time of divorce he had two insurance policies, one for $5,000 and the other for $10,000. The court ordered him to keep up the premiums on these policies and not to increase the loan of $2,000 that was on them already. If he could not keep up the premiums, Mrs. Lugosi should be notified and she would try to keep them in effect.

[6] This and subsequent information comes from Lugosi's legal files in the Los Angeles County Hall of Records.

Doing a little publicity.

Besides a Buick automobile, which the wife received, his only other assets were a number of lots at Lake Elsinore, south of Los Angeles, which were to be divided between them. Thus in November everything became final and the twenty-year marriage dissolved. As Mrs. Lugosi told this writer, "Well, I lasted the longest." (In February, 1966, she married Brian Donlevy, who died in 1972. The son, Bela, Jr., became a lawyer in June, 1964. He is married, has four children, and works in Los Angeles.)

Lugosi, alone and depressed and without his son, felt his life completely empty. There was no work and little possibility for it, so inevitably he returned to drugs. From then on, his condition, both mental and physical, deteriorated further. In 1954 he appeared for a short time in a variety act in Las Vegas. Called "The Bela Lugosi Review," it was a sketch played for laughs. The Las Vegas paper said:

Dracula is burlesqued in a series of skits for big yocks as Bela Lugosi scores with patrons no matter what he does. In familiar horror make-up, he uses a big cape around his dress suit to elicit screams in a vampire skit with Joan White. He is no mean ad libber, and there is no doubt he has the affection of the audience, which is aware that the old actor still has plenty of that old spark left.[7]

The "old spark" stemmed more and more from the drugs, but he had to keep going.

In late 1954 his friend Alex Gordon (Richard's brother) collaborated with Edward Wood, Jr., on a screenplay that was shot in the first part of 1955. Planned as *The Bride of the Atom* (it also for a time had the title *The Monster of the Marshes*), it was eventually released as *Bride of the Monster*. A rose by any other name would smell as sweet, and whatever the title, this film was horrendous: the direction by the

[7] H. Ludlam, *A Biography of Dracula*, p. 175.

Bride of the Monster (1955).

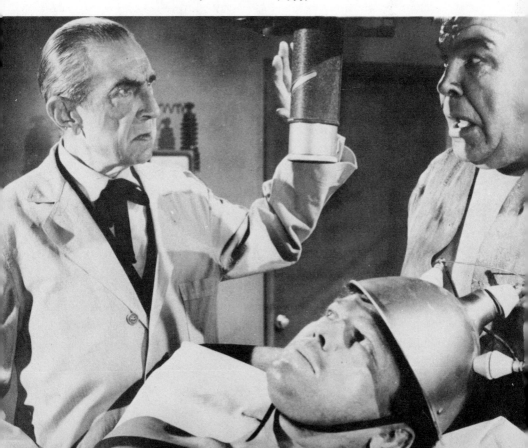

twenty-eight-year-old Wood was appropriately wooden, the acting atrocious, and the production values nil. (The atomic-ray machine is an old photo enlarger, and even the car driven by the obnoxious heroine was more than fifteen years old.)

The story seemed to be a distillation, admittedly a rather flat one, of all Lugosi's mad-scientist roles. As Dr. Eric Vornoff, he has fled Europe and isolated himself somewhere in California in a lonely house. There he conducts experiments in radiation, attempting to create beings of "superstrength and size." Some of his enlarged creations have terrified the local populace, and there is information in newspapers about the monsters. The good doctor has now switched from animals to people, and as a result, a few humans are disappearing too.

Unfortunately the film is so low-budgeted that it is comical. The giant octopus that is supposed to terrify people and kill a man before our very eyes is perhaps the most flaccid and impotent monster ever encountered. Later in the film, when Vornoff throws his adversary to the creature, the poor victim tries vainly to wrap its rubber tentacles around himself. The direction is no more gripping. Despite all these drawbacks and lines such as "Go away—now—go—go—go," Lugosi at times gives a grand performance. It may well seem hammy, but it has all the sincerity and passion of which he was capable, and occasionally he even transcends the script to become touchingly eloquent. He gives it all he has. And that is quite enough, at least for a Lugosi fan, to transform a sleazy film and amateurish conception into something else, if only for a few seconds of its sixty minutes' length. The reviewer for *Variety*, however, was not at all impressed: "Lugosi's histrionics are reduced to the ridiculous through over-direction. . . ." [8] In cold fact, the reviewer was correct. But Lugosi's role, though overdone, is somehow very personal; furthermore, it is the last time he appeared as a mad doctor.

After the film opens, with an absurd storm scene, Professor Strowski, from the "homeland," who has followed rumors about strange monsters from Europe to the United States, has finally tracked them down to Vornoff's place. Lugosi tells him, "Twenty years ago, I was banned from my homeland, parted from my wife and son, never to see them again. Why? Because I suggested to use the atomic elements for producing super beings of unthinkable strength and size. I was

[8] May 11, 1955.

classed as a madman, a charlatan, outlawed in the world of science which previously had honored me as a genius. Now here in this forsaken jungle hell I have proven that I am all right."

The similarity between Lugosi's own low state in the movie world and his fictional relation of how Vornoff was hounded out of Europe could not have escaped the actor. The world Lugosi had been experiencing in the previous few years was also a "forsaken jungle hell," and in this film, in this very scene, he was trying to prove that he too was "all right." Bela is so intense here that he makes a Freudian slip; instead of "I have proven that I was right after all," he delivers "I have proven that I am all right." Indeed he was—the dignity, charisma, and charm of the man would never diminish; only the producers were simply unwilling to make use of his aging but by no means vanishing gifts. All his unhappiness is echoed in the script as he bitterly picks up the word "home," which Professor Strowski has mentioned to him.

> Home? I have no home! Abandoned, despised, living like an animal. The jungle is my home. . . . I'll show the world that I can be its master. I will perfect my own race of people, a race of atomic supermen which will conquer the world.

Strowski agrees, saying that his government is interested in Vornoff's experiments and they want him home.

"I don't intend to return home. My plans are for myself."

"Are you mad?"

To this question Lugosi offers the old chestnut: "One is always considered mad when one discovers something that others cannot grasp."

"My government ordered me to bring you back."

"I'm afraid you will find that rather difficult."

"You see, Vornoff, I did not come alone" (Strowski pulls out a gun, apparently feeling that a gun is company).

"Neither did I, Strowski."

At this point Vornoff's helper, Lobo (Tor Johnson), attacks Strowski. Just before Vornoff feeds Strowski to the gigantic octopus, the great scientist says, "Your country offers fame and fortune, but my price is so much more great."

But Vornoff is not to enjoy his jungle hell much longer. A typically nosy female reporter shows up and is followed soon after by her police-lieutenant boyfriend. Vornoff captures both of them and then has his great moment when he is about to turn on his atomic ray, predicting, "It will hurt just for a moment but then you will emerge a woman of super strength and beauty: the bride of the atom." "You're insane," he is told, but Vornoff is not worried about such ridiculous observations. In fact, he delights in his scheme: "As soon as my experiments are completed, no one can ever touch me. I will make the law."

But his plans, as usual, turn awry. Lobo does not like seeing the girl mistreated, attacks Vornoff, and puts him in his own machine. The ray is turned on, and to the accompaniment of Lobo's happy grunts, the scientist is transformed into a being of "unthinkable strength and size." Vornoff, as the monster, now carries off the girl, but, pursued and shot at, he falls into the lake and battles the octopus. According to the script, "As the creatures struggle the fission of the atom elements that each contain has caused a culmination" in a tremendous lightning storm. "One great flash strikes the combatants," and a "great atomic mushroom of smoke comes out of the lake." The sheriff arrives in time to see the mountainside blow up and delivers the homily, "He tampered in God's domain." The film ends in a welter of explosions— an apt conclusion to such a bomb.

As the dialogue indicates, the title was originally to be *The Bride of the Atom*, but it apparently was changed to entice more viewers, even though the new title makes little sense. Actually the script seems to be a combination of the Lugosi character in *The Raven* mixed with some of his other mad-scientist roles. Derivative certainly, it captures the essence of the Lugosi screen characterization—his rise and fall, his vindication and vanquishment—even though it does it badly. It was the last time his voice would be heard on the screen. In his two remaining films he would be silent.

The little money that Lugosi received for the film was quickly spent, and the generosity of his friends had been exhausted. Without money for the drugs that he needed more and more, he could see no way out of his dilemma. Finally he summoned enough courage and on April 21, 1955, entered Los Angeles General Hospital's mental health and hygiene department and requested that he be committed for treatment. Suddenly newsmen on the scent of scandal arrived, and Lugosi made headlines, but not in the manner he had once hoped. After spending the night at General Hospital, he appeared at the Psychopathic Court

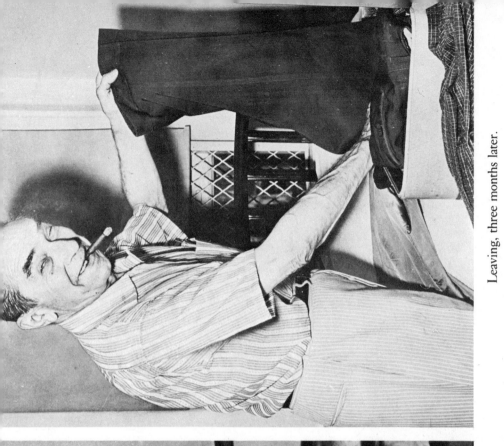

Leaving, three months later.

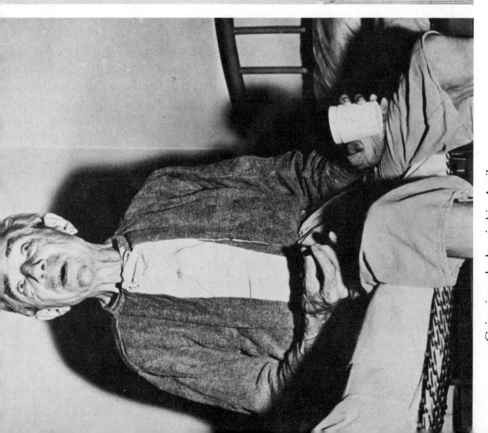

Going into the hospital in April, 1955.

the next day. He told reporters, "I don't have a dime left. I am dependent on my friends for food and a small old-age pension. I am anxious to rehabilitate myself and decided this was the only way to do it."

During the forty-five-minute hearing Lugosi told Superior Judge Wallace L. Ware, "I've been using narcotics for twenty years." The judge listened sympathetically and praised Lugosi for his voluntary action:

> The court wants to commend you for this very courageous act of yours. It is commendable that you have come forward voluntarily wanting to cure your addiction to the use of drugs.
> After all you are only seventy-two years of age. And it will be wonderful to get well and live the rest of your life as you should.[9]

The judge ruled that Lugosi be committed to Metropolitan State Hospital at Norwalk, California, for a minimum of three months or a maximum of two years. Photographs of Lugosi at this time show an incredibly haggard man, no more than 130 pounds, ample evidence that there are indeed "far worse things awaiting man than death." The doctors took him off the narcotics immediately, and he went through fantastic suffering owing to the sudden withdrawal. In an "as-told-to article" months later he said: "I cannot describe the tortures I underwent. My body grew hot, then cold. I tried to eat the bed sheets, my pyjamas. My heart beat madly. Then it seemed to stop. Every joint in my body ached." [10] In another interview he reiterated this experience:

"I used to take five or six needles a day. And when I took the cure they took it all away from me. . . . It was horrible, just horrible." [11]

A few days after Bela committed himself, the cast and crew of *Bride of the Monster* arrived at his bedside in the charity ward at General Hospital and told him that a "lavish" premiere of the just-completed movie, still known as *Bride of the Atom*, would be held (it was shown on May 11, 1955) and that the proceeds would go to a trust fund for him. He was also given the script of his next picture, *The Ghoul Goes West*, which would be postponed because of his illness.

[9] Associated Press. In New York *Daily News*, April 23, 1955.
[10] Olive Mosby, *Inquirer*, February 15, 1956.
[11] "Dracula Makes His Comeback—the Hard Way," Newark *Star Ledger*, February 15, 1956.

Bela was deeply touched by the respect and devotion of his visitors and wept unrestrainedly. "This is so heartwarming, such a miracle. I cannot believe it. To know that people have such faith in me is better than medicine. I will not let them down."

Bela said that now he had finally made up his mind "to leave the drugs alone." He said, "The drugs had me on the hook. I mean to dehook myself."

The cast and crew of the picture explained why Lugosi was so popular with them: "It was his gracious charm and his willingness to help us. He was a perfect trouper all during production. We want him to know we're all behind him to the finish and we're waiting for him to rejoin us." [12]

At the State Hospital he received encouraging letters from his still-faithful fans, this writer among them. He said later, in February, 1956:

> I was able to get out in three months because of the kind letters from all over the world. I even got a telephone call from Japan. It was hell to go through what I went through. I didn't know I had so many friends—so many people who knew about me and gave a damn about my situation. They helped cure me.

One of his correspondents who wrote frequently, a clerk in a film studio editing department, was Hope Lininger, a woman in her late thirties. Signing her letters "Hope," she was apparently of great encouragement during his incarceration. On August 2, 1955, he passed a staff health examination, and on August 5 he was released, after spending 105 days at the hospital. He announced to newsmen that he planned to start work on *The Ghoul Goes West*. "It's very cute," he said with a leer. Bela posed for a photograph with the script in one hand and his other hand dramatically raised in a fist. Lugosi appeared strong and healthy, his voice firm, a far cry from the addict who could barely walk three months before. He explained that his desire to act again plus the numerous letters of encouragement helped him over the rough spots. "I could not have done this alone," he said meaningfully. [13] To *Newsweek* he declared that his rehabilitation was "the greatest thing that ever happened to me."

[12] Los Angeles *Examiner*, April 25, 1955.
[13] Los Angeles *Times*, August 4, 1955.

As soon as Lugosi got out of the hospital, he went to see Hope, the woman who had been writing him so constantly. As he said later in an article,

> It wasn't very long before I fell very much in love with Hope. I told her that I needed her kindness, her strength, her care.
>
> "If I did not think," I said, "that you would turn me down, I would propose."
>
> "Why don't you try it?" she said.
>
> Fearfully I proposed, and Hope accepted.[14]

So the impetuous Lugosi married for the fifth and final time. The marriage ceremony took place on August 25 at a private home in Hollywood. The couple stood in front of a huge hearth, flanked by Chinese devil dogs, with the odor of burning incense. Lugosi's son, Bela, Jr., seventeen years old, was best man. Mrs. Pat Delaney, a city-jail employee, was matron of honor. The ceremony was performed by Manly P. Hall, a "writer, philosopher, ordained minister and long-time friend," according to the newspaper.[15] Hall was the same man who had hypnotized Lugosi for a scene in *Black Friday* (1940). The ceremony began with a conventional prayer and went smoothly until the Lugosi accent stumbled over some of the vows. Hall had to prompt the actor carefully through "With all my worldly goods I thee endow." His new wife said afterward, "I've been a fan of Bela's ever since I was a kid." Lugosi proposed a toast to the press and thanked the newsmen "for giving an old man a chance for a comeback." A picture of the happy couple—Lugosi with pipe and looking well—made the first page of the New York *Daily News*. They moved to an apartment in Hollywood.

In early 1956 another horror film, called *The Black Sleep*, began shooting. It told the story of a scientist during the 1870's who used a drug to induce a sleep resembling death so that he could practice his brain-surgery technique sufficiently to operate on his own wife, who is in a coma. The surgeon's previous experiments have not been

[14] "How I Beat the Curse of Dope Addiction," by Bela Lugosi as told to Lloyd Shearer.
[15] Los Angeles *Times*, August 25, 1955.

His fifth and final wife.

successful, and a number of maimed people—some dumb, some blind, some hideously scarred—remain. At the end these people escape, and with the chant of "Kill, kill" they destroy the surgeon. Lugosi was engaged for the film—not as the surgeon, but as one of the doctor's victims, Casimir, a deaf mute. That magnificent voice was stilled. Lugosi was quoted on the set as saying, "There is Basil playing my part. I used to be the big cheese. Now I'm playing just a dumb part." He added, "I have no dialogue because I was a bit worried whether I could do justice to the expectations. I'm still recuperating." [16] This last comment was mostly pride. Lugosi in all likelihood was not offered a speaking part.

The Black Sleep was a routine film, but its publicity was comparatively imaginative. On February 23, 1956, a hearse pulled in front of a high-class Hollywood restaurant, the Tail o' the Cock, and the heavily

[16] Olive Mosby, *Inquirer*, February 15, 1956.

madeup maimed creatures from the film (John Carradine all hair, one fellow all scars, other repugnant creatures, and of course Bela) sat down for lunch as photographers busily caught this peculiar scene. This entourage could hardly have been a boon to the appetite.

There were also a number of personal-appearance tours to various cities in an attempt to create some publicity for the film. Lugosi went on these, but in Portland, Oregon, in June he collapsed as he left the stage.

Just a few days before this occurrence, on June 8 and 9, Lugosi appeared in a three-performance stage presentation called *Devil's Paradise*, which was put on in Los Angeles. According to its cheaply printed brochure, it was "a dramatic play written for teenagers and adult audiences" that dealt with the methods of vast international dope rings in recruiting teenagers as prospective victims. This amateur show offered a cast of thirty-five and made this promise: "After the performance meet Mr. Bela Lugosi, the man who won a 25 year battle with dope." Already a five-year addition was made to Bela's initial exaggeration.

Obviously Lugosi's dreams for a comeback were coming to naught. He was old now and felt it. His hearing was failing even more, and as

The cast of *The Black Sleep* (1956), having lunch.

he sat by himself in growing silence, he must have brooded over what had become of his life. He was not only the horror man; he was now the drug man too. Hollywood, which could have capitalized on his fame and given him back his dignity and pride with one more meaty role, continued to ignore him.

Still wishing to act, no matter how degrading the circumstances, he received another offer and started to work again under the untalented direction and minuscule budget of Edward D. Wood, Jr., who had made the unmemorable *Glen or Glenda?* and *Bride of the Monster.* Lugosi played the "Ghoul Man," and Vampira of television fame played the "Ghoul Woman." The film is so wretched that it is almost incomprehensible.

As the film opens, Lugosi is standing by an open grave with some friends lamenting the death of his screen wife. This scene of Lugosi in a pseudo-Dracula outfit has great poignancy, for a few days later Lugosi died in the midst of shooting. Whether he was to be given any dialogue or would have had an appreciably larger part is not very clear, because the script had to be reworked after his death. In any case, Lugosi is in the film for only a couple of minutes, and some of these minutes are repeat shots, in which the same footage was printed again and again. Obviously the script was to have the Lugosi character die so that he and his wife, Vampira, could roam around and scare people. They come back to life because a space ship has landed, and the alien creatures inhabit the bodies of the recently dead. A double had to take Lugosi's part, and he marched around with the lower portion of his face covered with his cape in an unconvincing attempt to impersonate him. The film, after moldering three years, was finally released in July, 1959, and called *Plan Nine from Outer Space.* One shivers to think what the first eight plans could have been like.

During August, 1956, in the midst of shooting, Lugosi was resting at his apartment. His wife went out to buy gorceries and came back around seven o'clock. Shortly after, she was reported to have said:

> He didn't answer when I spoke so I went to him. I could feel no pulse! Apparently he must have died a very short time before I arrived. He was just terrified of death. Towards the end he was very weary, but he was still afraid of death. Three nights before he died he was sitting on the edge of the bed. I asked him if he were still afraid to die. He told me that he was. I did my best to comfort him. . . .[17]

---

[17] Barry Brown, "Drug Addiction," n.d.

Burial scene in *Plan 9 from Outer Space* (1956).

The last time he donned his Dracula cape in life.

So, on August 16, 1956, Lugosi, who had feigned death so many times during his career, would feign no more.

His wife, Hope, respecting his last wishes, lent further stature to the Lugosi legend by interring him in his Dracula cape. At his funeral there were prayers by a priest of the Blessed Sacrament Church and a violin dirge by a fellow countryman. Only sixty or so mourners attended, among them directors Zoltan Korda and Edward Wood, Jr., Bela's former wife Lillian, and of course Bela, Jr. "It was strange," Carol Borland told this writer, "for I have seen Bela lying in his coffin so often that it was a familiar sight."

The coffin was taken to Holy Cross Cemetery in Los Angeles and interred in the beautiful grotto section. When Bela was buried with his cape, fiction and fantasy finally merged with reality but alas could not vanquish it. The powers of the vampire, which he had so long imitated, would not come to his aid now. The grave remains quiet. There would be no more sequels.

During the course of his career, Lugosi had earned far in excess of half a million dollars. And yet he died completely broke, except for a building lot valued at $1,000 and $1,900 in the bank. His only legacy was his reputation. When Bela made out his last will on January 12, 1954, he left everything to his son. But under probate law, the son had to share the property with Hope, the last wife.

In 1966 Bela, Jr., and Hope brought suit against Universal Pictures. They charged breach of contract, unjust enrichment, and asked for an accounting. They felt that Universal was profiting from toys, dolls, games, paint kits, and other products featuring his likeness as Dracula.[18] The suit dragged on for six years before a court decided that Lugosi's heirs were entitled to share in the money Universal had made from his image.[19] In January, 1974, after two more years of haggling, the Los Angeles County Supreme Court awarded $53,023—final vindication but obviously no consolation to the dead Lugosi.[20]

The simple stone above his grave reads: "Bela Lugosi, 1882–1956, Beloved Father." But it is not as father to a child that he will generally be remembered; rather as father to a great myth and legend, the embodiment of Dracula. The passionate intensity that he gave his roles—that which made him dynamic, impulsive, and darkly romantic

[18] *Variety*, June 6, 1966.
[19] *Time*, February 14, 1972.
[20] Los Angeles *Times*, January 26, 1974.

and which captured the imagination of millions—had stalked him as a human being. As is true of a figure out of tragedy, that which raised him above other men would also bring him down, as if the flower of his personality carried the seeds of its own destruction.

How unfortunate that this tired, weak, and unhappy man could not have lived long enough to see his life's work vindicated, to share the fame that soon would be given him by increased millions. Instead he died almost forgotten by a Hollywood that had given him the blessing and the curse of being typecast as a horror star for much of his life. The people who laughed at him and the producers who ignored him have been proved wrong in the perspective of time, for Lugosi, with all his personal and professional failings, still reigns secure and supreme as one of the few originals of the American screen.

No words could be a better epitaph than those uttered by Maria Ouspenskaya in *The Wolf Man* as she stands over the coffin of her dead son, Bela, and says in her soft, quavering voice and Slavic accent:

> The way you walked was thorny,
> Through no fault of your own—
> But as the rain enters the soil,
> The river enters the sea,
> So tears run to their predestined end.
>
> Your suffering is over, Bela, my son.
> Now you will find peace.

Filmography

The following list of Lugosi's feature films will not agree with existing reference works. For example, Hungarian sources incorrectly include him in *Casanova*, and German credits are also far from perfect. His American period is less confused, except for his numerous roles as an unbilled bit player.

The cast listings include only the more important players and do not always follow the order of their appearance on the screen. Certain minor actors who appear frequently or who were once of importance (such as Dwight Frye) have been added.

To keep Lugosi's screen work in some kind of order, the month of the date of release has been provided. Because the studio, the copyright office, the trade press, and movie reviews often disagree, these dates must be seen as somewhat of a compromise. Significant differences between the production and release of films are mentioned either here or in the text.

A LEOPÁRD (The Leopard)   1917
Star Film Company (Hungary)
  Director: Alfréd Deésy. *Screenplay:* Alphonse Daudet.
  Cast: Arisztid Olt [Lugosi's screen name for Star Film Company], Annie Góth, Klára Peterdy, Gusztáv Turán, Ila Lóth, Peter Konrády.

AZ EZREDES (The Colonel)   1917
Phoenix Film Company (Hungary)
  Director: Mihály Kertész (Michael Curtiz). Based on a story by Ferenc Herzeg. *Screenplay:* Richard Falk.
  Cast: BL, Sándor Góth, László Z. Molnár, Károly Huszár, Géza Boross, Arpad Latabar, Claire Lotto, Zoltan Szeremy, Gero Maly, Janka Csatai.

ÁLARCOSBÁL (The Masked Ball)   March, 1918
Star Film Company (Hungary)
  Director: Alfréd Deésy. Based on an opera by Giuseppe Verdi.
  Cast: Arisztid Olt [BL], Annie Góth, Norbert Dán, Robert Fiáth, Richáru Kornai, Viktor Kurd.

NÁSZDAL (Song of Marriage) April, 1918
Star Film Company (Hungary)
  Director: Alfréd Deésy. *Screenplay:* Ingác Balla and Nándor Ujhelyi.
  Cast: Arisztid Olt [BL], Klára Peterdy, Irén Barta, Richárd Kornai, Károly Lajthay.

KÜZDELEM A LÉTÉRT (A Struggle for Life) 1918
Star Film Company (Hungary)
  Director: Alfréd Deésy. *Screenplay:* Alphonse Daudet.
  Cast: Arisztid Olt [BL], Annie Góth, Klára Peterdy, Ila Lóth, Ferenc Viragh.

99 (99) 1918
Phoenix Film Company (Hungary)
  Director: Mihály Kertész (Michael Curtiz). *Screenplay:* Ivan Siklosi.
  Cast: BL, Lajos Rethey, Jeno Balassa, Zoltan Szeremy, Claire Lotto, Mihaly Varkonyi [Victor Varconi], Gyula Gal, László Z. Molnar.

TAVASZI VIHAR (The Wild Wind of Spring) 1918
Star Film Company (Hungary)
  Director: Alfréd Deésy. *Screenplay:* László Békeffy.
  Cast: Arisztid Olt [BL], Myra Corthy, Norbert Dán, Viktor Kurd, Alice Rónay, Aladár Fenyö.

AZ ÉLET KIRÁLYA (The King of Life) September, 1918
Star Film Company (Hungary)
  Director: Alfréd Deésy. Based on *The Picture of Dorian Gray*, by Oscar Wilde. *Screenplay:* József Pakots.
  Cast: Arisztid Olt [BL], Norbert Dán, Annie Góth, Ila Lóth, Camilla Hollay, Gustzáv Turán, Richárd Kornai, Viktor Kurd.

LILI (Lili) 1918
Phoenix Film Company (Hungary)
  Director: Cornélius Hintner. *Screenplay:* Jenö Faragó.
  Cast: Arisztid Olt [BL], Irén Barta, Klára Peterdy, Ila Lóth, Gustzáv Turán, Richárd Kornai.

DER FLUCH DER MENSCHHEIT (The Curse of Mankind)
  July, 1920
  1. Die Tochter der Arbeit (The Daughter of Work)
  2. Im Rausche der Milliarden (In the Delirium of Millions)
Eichberg-Film (Germany)

Director: Richard Eichberg. *Screenplay:* William Merkel and Arthur Teuber. *Photographer:* Joe Rive.

Cast: BL, Lee Parry, Violette Napierska, Felix Hecht, Robert Scholz, Willi Kaiser-Heyl, Reinhold Pasch, Paul Ludwig, Gustav Birkholz, Herr Dörr.

DER JANUSKOPF (The Janus-Head)   August, 1920
Eine Tragödie am Rande der Wirklichkeit
(A Tragedy at the Edge of Reality)
Known also as *Janus-Faced* and as *Dr. Jekyll and Mr. Hyde*
Decla Bioscop or Lipow (Germany)
Director: F. W. Murnau. Based on the story "Dr. Jekyll and Mr. Hyde," by Robert Louis Stevenson. *Screenplay:* Hans Janowitz. *Photographers:* Karl Freund and Carl Hoffmann.

Cast: BL (butler), Conrad Veidt (Dr. Warren and Mr. O'Connor), Margarete Schlegel (Grace), Willi Kaiser-Heyl, Margarete Kupfer, Jaro Fürth.

DIE FRAU IM DELPHIN oder 30
TAGE AUF DEM MEERESGRUND   September, 1920
(The Woman in the Dolphin or Thirty Days on the Bottom of the Sea)
Gaci-Film (Gamsa-Film u. Citograph GmbH) (Germany)
Director: Artur Kiekebusch-Brenken. *Screenplay:* Jan Gramatzki.

Cast: BL, Emilie Sanno m, Magnus Stifter, Ernst Pittschau, Max Zilzer, Jacques Wandryck.

DIE TEUFELSANBETER (The Devil Worshippers)
                                                   December, 1920
Ustad-Film Dr. Droop & Co. (Germany)
Director: Not listed. Based on a work by Karl May. *Screenplay:* Marie Luise Droop.

Cast: BL, Carl de Vogt, Meinhart Maur, Ilja Dubrowski.

LEDERSTRUMPF (Leatherstocking)   December, 1920
   1. Der Wildtöter (The Deerslayer)
   2. Der Letzte der Mohikaner (The Last of the Mohicans)
Luna-Film GmbH (Germany)
Released in U.S. as THE DEERSLAYER in 1923.
Director: Arthur Wellin. Based on the novels by James Fenimore Cooper.
Screenplay: Robert Heymann.

Cast: BL (Uncas), Emil Mamelok, Herta Hedén, Gottfried Krause, Eduard Eysenck, Margot Sokolowska.

DER TANZ AUF DEM VULKAN (The Dance on the Volcano)

February, 1921

1. Sybil Joung
2. Der Tod des Grossfürsten (The Death of the Grand Duke)

It is known also as *Ihre Hoheit die Tänzerin*. A shortened version in English is known as *Daughter of the Night*.

Central-Film-Vertrieb (Eichberg-Film) (Germany)

Director: Richard Eichberg. *Screenplay:* Arthur Teuber. *Photographer:* Joe Rive.

Cast: BL (Andre Fleurot), Lee Parry, Violette Napierska, Robert Scholz, Gustav Birkholz, Felix Hecht, Kurt Fuss.

NAT PINKERTON   1921?

Dua Films (Germany)

JOHANN HOPKINS DER DRITTE (John Hopkins the Third)

1921?

Dua Films (Germany)

THE SILENT COMMAND   September, 1923

Fox

Director: J. Gordon Edwards. Based on a story by Rufus King. *Screenplay:* Anthony Paul Kelly. *Photographer:* George W. Lane.

Cast: BL (Hisston), Edmund Lowe (Capt. Richard Decatur), Betty Jewel (Dolores), Carl Harbaugh (Menchen), Martin Faust (Cordoba), Gordon McEdward (Gridley), Byron Douglas (Admiral Nevins).

THE REJECTED WOMAN   May, 1924

Distinctive Pictures

Director: Albert Parker. *Screenplay:* John Lynch. *Photographer:* Roy Hunt.

Cast: BL (Jean Gagnon), Alma Rubens (Diane Du Prez); Conrad Nagel (John Leslie), Wyndham Standing (James Dunbar), George MacQuarrie (Samuel Du Prez), Antonio D'Algy (Craig Burnett), Aubrey Smith (Peter Leslie).

THE MIDNIGHT GIRL   February, 1925

Chadwick Pictures Corp.

Director: Wilfred Noy. Based on a story by Garrett Fort. *Screenplay:* Wilfred Noy and Jean Conover. *Photographers:* G. W. Bitzer and Frank Zukor.

Cast: BL (Nicholas Harmon), Dolores Cassinelli (Nina), Lila Lee (Anna), Ruby Blaine (Natalie Schuyler), Charlotte Walker (Mrs. Schuyler).

DAUGHTERS WHO PAY   May, 1925
Banner Productions

Cast: BL (Serge Oumansky), John Bowers (Dick Foster), Marguerite de la Motte (Sonia; Margaret).

HOW TO HANDLE WOMEN   June, 1928
Universal

Director: William J. Craft. *Screenplay:* Carl Krusada. *Photographer:* Arthur Todd.

Cast: BL (a bit part), Mario Carillo (Count Olaff), Glenn Tryon (Mr. Higgins), Bull Montana (Turk), Marion Nixon (Beatrice Fairbanks), Raymond Keane (Prince Hendryx), Cesare Gravina (peanut expert).

THE VEILED WOMAN   December, 1928
Fox

Director: Emmett Flynn. Based on a story by Julio DeMoraes. *Screenplay:* Douglas J. Doty. *Photographer:* Charles Clarke.

Cast: BL (bit part), Paul Vicenti (Pierre), Lia Tora (Nanon), Kenneth Thomson (Dr. Ross), Maude George (Countess De Bracchi).

PRISONERS   June, 1929
First National

Director: William A. Seiter. Based on a novel by Ferenc Molnár. *Screenplay:* Forrest Halsey. *Photographer:* Lee Garmes.

Cast: BL (Brottos), Corinne Griffith (Riza Riga), James Ford (Kepsler), Ian Keith (Nicholas Bathy), Julanne Johnston (Lenke), Anna Skeafer (Aunt Marie).

THE THIRTEENTH CHAIR   October, 1929
MGM

Director: Tod Browning. Based on the play by Bayard Veiller. *Screenplay:* Elliot Clawson. *Photographer:* Merritt B. Gerstad.

Cast: BL (Inspector Delzante), Margaret Wycherly (Madame Rosalie La Grange), Conrad Nagel (Richard Crosby), John Davidson (Edward Wales), Leila Hyams (Helen O'Neill), Mary Forbes (Lady Crosby), Holmes Herbert (Sir Roscoe Crosby).

SUCH MEN ARE DANGEROUS   March, 1930
Fox

Director: Kenneth Hawks. Based on a novel by Elinor Glyn. *Screenplay:* Ernest Vajda. *Photographers:* L. W. O'Connell and George Eastman.

Cast: BL (Dr. Goodman), Warner Baxter (Ludwig Kranz), Catherine

Dale Owen (Elinor), Albert Conti (Paul Strohm), Hedda Hopper (Muriel Wyndham), Claude Allister (Frederick Wyndham).

WILD COMPANY   July, 1930
Fox

Director: Leo McCarey. Based on a story by John Stone and Bradley King. *Screenplay:* Bradley King. *Photographer:* L. W. O'Connell.

Cast: BL (Felix Brown), Frank Albertson (Larry Grayson), H. B. Warner (Henry Grayson), Sharon Lynn (Sally), Joyce Compton (Anita), Claire McDowell (Mrs. Grayson), George Fawcett (Judge).

VIENNESE NIGHTS   November, 1930
Warner Brothers

Director: Alan Crosland. Based on a play by Sigmund Romberg and Oscar Hammerstein II. *Screenplay:* same. *Photographer:* James Van Trees.

Cast: BL (Hungarian Ambassador), Alexander Gray (Otto), Vivienne Segal (Elsa), Jean Hersholt (Hocher), Walter Pidgeon (Franz), Louise Fazenda (Gretl).

RENEGADES   November, 1930
Fox

Director: Victor Fleming. Based on the novel by Andre Armandy. *Screenplay:* Jules Furthman. *Photographer:* William O'Connell.

Cast: BL (The Marabout), Warner Baxter (Deucalion), Myrna Loy (Eleonore), Noah Beery (Machwurth), Gregory Gaye (Vologuine), George Cooper (Biloxi), C. Henry Gordon.

OH, FOR A MAN   January, 1931
Fox

Director: Hamilton MacFadden. Based on a story by Mary T. Watkins. *Screenplay:* Philip Klein and Lynn Starling. *Photographer:* Charles Clarke.

Cast: BL (bit part), Jeanette MacDonald (Carlotta Manson), Reginald Denny (Barney McGann), Albert Conti (Manager).

DRACULA   February, 1931
Universal

Director: Tod Browning. Based on novel by Hamilton Deane and John L. Balderston. *Dialogue:* Dudley Murphy. *Screenplay:* Garrett Fort. *Photographer:* Karl Freund. *Art:* Charles D. Hall.

Cast: BL (Count Dracula), Helen Chandler (Mina Seward), David Manners (Jonathan Harker), Edward Van Sloan (Van Helsing), Dwight

Frye (Renfield), Herbert Bunston (Dr. Seward), Frances Dade (Lucy Weston), Charles Gerrard (Martin).

FIFTY MILLION FRENCHMEN   March, 1931
Warner Brothers

Director: Lloyd Bacon. Based on a play by Herbert Fields, E. Ray Goetz, and Cole Porter. *Screenplay:* Joseph Jackson, Eddie Welsh, and Al Boasberg. *Photographer:* Dev Jennings.

Cast: BL (bit part), Olsen and Johnson (Simon and Peter), William Gaxton (Jack Forbes), John Halliday (Michael Cummings), Helen Broderick (Violet), Claudia Dell (Looloo Carroll), Lester Crawford (Billy Baxter).

WOMEN OF ALL NATIONS   May, 1931
Fox

Director: Raoul Walsh. *Screenplay:* Barry Connors. *Photographer:* Lucien Andriot.

Cast: BL (Prince Hassan), Victor McLaglen (Capt. Flagg), Edmund Lowe (Sgt. Quirt), Greta Nissen (Elsa), El Brendel (Olsen), Fifi Dorsay (Fifi), Marjorie White (Pee Wee), T. Roy Barnes (Captain of Marines), Humphrey Bogart (Stone).

THE BLACK CAMEL   June, 1931
Fox

Director: Hamilton MacFadden. Based on novel by Earl Derr Biggers. Screenplay and dialogue by Barry Connors and Philip Klein. *Photographer:* Dan Clark.

Cast: BL (Tarneverro), Warner Oland (Charlie Chan), Sally Eilers (Julie O'Neil), Dorothy Revier (Shelah Fane), Victor Varconi (Robert Fyfe), Dwight Frye (Jessop).

BROAD MINDED   July, 1931
First National

Director: Mervyn Le Roy. Story, screenplay, and dialogue by Bert Kalmar and Harry Ruby. *Photographer:* Sid Hickox.

Cast: BL (Pancho), Joe E. Brown (Ossie Simpson), Ona Munson (Constance), William Collier, Jr. (Jack Hackett), Marjorie White (Penelope), Holmes Herbert (John Hackett, Sr.), Margaret Livingstone (Mabel Robinson), Thelma Todd (Pancho's ladyfriend).

MURDERS IN THE RUE MORGUE   February, 1932
Universal

Director: Robert Florey. Based on the story by Edgar Allan Poe. *Screenplay:* Tom Reed and Dale Van Every. *Photographer:* Karl Freund.

Cast: BL (Dr. Mirakle), Sidney Fox (Camille L'Espanaye), Leon Waycoff (Pierre Dupin), Arlene Francis (the street girl), Betty Ross Clark (the Mother), Bert Roach (Paul), Brandon Hurst (Prefect of Police), Noble Johnson (Janos, the Black One).

WHITE ZOMBIE   July, 1932
United Artists
   Director: Victor Halperin. *Screenplay:* Garnett Weston. *Photographer:* Arthur Martinelli.
   Cast: BL ("Murder" Legendre), Madge Bellamy (Madeline), Joseph Cawthorn (Dr. Bruner), Robert Fraser (Beaumont), John Harron (Neil), Clarence Muse (Driver), Brandon Hurst (Silver).

CHANDU, THE MAGICIAN   October, 1932
Fox
   Directors: Marcel Varnel and William Cameron Menzies. Based on the radio serial by Harry A. Earnshaw, Vera M. Oldham, and R. R. Morgan. *Screenplay:* Barry Connors. *Photographer:* James Wong Howe.
   Cast: BL (Roxor) Edmund Lowe (Chandu), Irene Ware (Princess Nadji), June Vlasek (Betty Regent), Herbert Mundin (Albert Miggles), Henry B. Walthall (Robert Regent), Virginia Hammond (Dorothy).

ISLAND OF LOST SOULS   January, 1933
Paramount
   Director: Erle C. Kenton. Based on the novel by H. G. Wells. *Screenplay:* Philip Wylie and Waldemar Young. *Photographer:* Karl Struss.
   Cast: BL (Leader of the Apemen), Charles Laughton (Dr. Moreau), Richard Arlen (Edward Parker), Leila Hyams (Ruth Walker), Kathleen Burke (Lota), Arthur Hohl (Montgomery), Stanley Fields (Captain Davies).

THE DEATH KISS   January, 1933
World-Wide Pictures
   Director: Edwin L. Marin. Based on a story by Madelon St. Dennis. *Screenplay:* Gordon Kahn and Barry Barringer. *Photographer:* Norbert Brodine.
   Cast: BL (Joseph Steiner), David Manners (Franklyn Drew), Adrienne Ames (Marcia Lane), John Wray (Detective Sheehan), Vince Barnett (Officer Gulliver), Alexander Carr (Leon Grossmith), Edward Van Sloan (Tom Avery).

INTERNATIONAL HOUSE   May, 1933
Paramount
   Director: Edward Sutherland. Based on a story by Lou Heifetz and Neil

Brant. *Screenplay:* Francis Martin and Walter DeLeon. *Photographer:* Ernest Haller. Music and lyrics by Ralph Rainger and Leo Robin.

Cast: BL (General Nicholas Petronovich), W. C. Fields (Prof. Quail), Stuart Erwin (Tommy Nash), George Burns (Dr. Burns), Gracie Allen (Nurse Allen), Franklin Pangborn (Hotel Manager); appearing as themselves: Peggy Hopkins Joyce, Rudy Vallee, Sari Maritza, Col. Stoopnagle and Budd, Baby Rose Marie, Cab Calloway and orchestra.

NIGHT OF TERROR   June, 1933
Columbia

Director: Benjamin Stoloff. Based on the novel "The Public Be Damned," by Willard Mack. *Screenplay:* Beatrice Van and William Jacobs. *Photographer:* Joseph A. Valentine.

Cast: BL (Degar), Sally Blane (Mary), Wallace Ford (Tom), George Meeker (Arthur Hornsby), Tully Marshall (Professor Rinehart), Edwin Maxwell (the maniac).

THE WHISPERING SHADOW (serial)   1933
Mascot

Directors: Albert Herman and Colbert Clark. *Screenplay:* George Mogan, Colbert Clark, Wyndham Gittens, Howard Bimberg, Barney Sarecky, and Norman Hall. *Photographers:* Ernest Miller and Edgar Lyons.

Cast: BL (Prof. Strang), Henry B. Walthall (Bradley), Karl Dane (Sparks), Viva Tattersall (Vera Strang), Malcolm McGregor (Jack Foster), Robert Warwick (Raymond), Roy D'Arcy (Steinbeck), George Lewis (Bud Foster), Ethel Clayton (The Countess).

Chapter titles: 1) The Master Magician, 2) The Collapsing Room, 3) The All-Seeing Eye, 4) The Shadow Strikes, 5) Wanted for Murder, 6) The Man Who Was the Czar, 7) The Double Room, 8) The Red Circle, 9) The Fatal Secret, 10) The Death Warrant, 11) The Trap, 12) King of the World.

THE DEVIL'S IN LOVE   July, 1933
Fox

Director: William Dieterle. Based on a story by Harry Hervey. *Screenplay:* Howard Estabrook. *Photographer:* Hal Mohr.

Cast: BL (the Prosecutor), Victor Jory (Lt. Andre Morand), Loretta Young (Margot Lesesne), Vivienne Osborne (Rena), David Manners (Capt. Jean Fabien), J. Carrol Naish (Salazar), C. Henry Gordon.

THE BLACK CAT   May, 1934
Universal

Director: Edgar G. Ulmer. Based on a story by Peter Ruric and Edgar

Ulmer; suggested by the story by Edgar Allan Poe. *Screenplay:* Peter Ruric. *Photographer:* John Mescall. *Art:* Charles D. Hall.

Cast: BL (Dr. Vitus Werdegast), Boris Karloff (Hjalmar Poelzig), David Manners (Peter Alison), Jacqueline Wells (Joan Alison), Lucille Lund (Karen).

GIFT OF GAB   September, 1934
Universal

Director: Karl Freund. Based on a story by Jerry Wald and Philip G. Epstein. *Screenplay:* Rian James. *Photographer:* Harold Wenstrom and George Robinson.

Cast: BL (man in the closet), Edmund Lowe (Phillip Gabney), Gloria Stuart (Barbara), Ruth Etting (Ruth), Phil Baker (Phil), Ethel Waters (Ethel), Boris Karloff (the Phantom).

THE RETURN OF CHANDU (serial)   October, 1934
Principal

Director: Ray Taylor. Based on the radio serial by Harry Earnshaw, Vera M. Oldham, and R. R. Morgan. *Photographer:* John Hickson.

Cast: BL (Chandu), Maria Alba (Princess Nadji), Clara Kimball Young (Dorothy Regent), Lucien Prival (Vindhyan), Phillis Ludwig (Betty Regent), Dean Benton (Bob Regent), Josef Swickard (Tyba, the White Magician), Murdock McQuarrie (Voice of Ubasti).

Chapter titles: 1) The Chosen Victim, 2) The House on the Hill, 3) On the High Seas, 4) The Evil Eye, 5) The Invisible Circle, 6) Chandu's False Step, 7) The Mysterious Island, 8) The Edge of the Pit, 9) The Invisible Terror, 10) The Crushing Rock, 11) The Uplifted Knife, 12) The Knife Descends.

THE RETURN OF CHANDU (feature)   April, 1935
CHANDU ON THE MAGIC ISLAND (feature)   August, 1935

THE BEST MAN WINS   January, 1935
Columbia

Director: Erle Kenton. Based on a story by Ben. G. Kohn. *Screenplay:* Ethel Hill and Bruce Manning. *Photographer:* John Stumar. *Underwater sequences director:* E. Roy Davidson. *Photographer:* Joseph Walker.

Cast: BL (Doc Boehm), Edmund Lowe (Toby), Jack Holt (Nick), Florence Rice (Ann), Forrester Harvey (Harry), J. Farrell MacDonald (Harbor Patrol Captain).

MYSTERIOUS MR. WONG   March, 1935
Monogram

Director: William Nigh. Based on *The Twelve Coins of Confucius* by Harry Stephen Keeler. *Screenplay:* Nina Howatt. *Photographer:* Harry Neumann.

Cast: BL (Mr. Wong). Wallace Ford (Jason Barton), Arline Judge (Peg), Fred Warren (Tsung), Lotus Long (Moonflower), Robert Emmet O'Connor (McGillicuddy), Edward Peil (Jen Yu).

MARK OF THE VAMPIRE
April, 1935
MGM

Director: Tod Browning. *Screenplay:* Guy Endore and Bernard Schubert. *Photographer:* James Wong Howe.

Cast: BL (Count Mora), Lionel Barrymore (Professor), Elizabeth Allan (Irena), Lionel Atwill (Inspector Neumann), Jean Hersholt (Baron Otto), Henry Wadsworth (Fedor), Donald Meek (Doskill), Holmes Herbert (Sir Karell).

THE RAVEN
July, 1935
Universal

Director: Louis Friedlander (later Lew Landers). Suggested by the poem by Edgar Allan Poe. *Screenplay:* David Boehm. *Photographer:* Charles Stumar.

Cast: BL (Dr. Richard Vollin), Boris Karloff (Edmond Bateman), Irene Ware (Jean Thatcher), Lester Matthews (Jerry Halden), Samuel S. Hinds (Judge Thatcher), Inez Courtney (Mary Burns), Spencer Chaters (Geoffrey), Maidel Turner (Harriet), Arthur Hoyt (Chapman).

MURDER BY TELEVISION
October, 1935
Imperial-Cameo Pictures

Director: Clifford Sanforth. *Screenplay:* Joseph Donnell. *Photographers:* James Brown, Jr., and Arthur Reed. *Music:* Cliver Wallace.

Cast: BL (Arthur Perry), George Meeker (Richard Grayson), Henry Mowbray (Chief Nelson), Charles Hills Mailes, June Collyer, Huntley Gordon, Claire McDowell.

THE PHANTOM SHIP (The Mystery of the
Marie Celeste)
November, 1935*
Hammer Productions

Director: Denison Clift. Based on a story by Denison Clift. *Screenplay:* Charles Larkworthy. *Photographers:* Geoffrey Faithful and Eric Cross. *Music:* Eric Ansell.

Cast: BL (Anton Lorenzen), Shirley Grey (Sarah Briggs), Arthur Margeston (Captain Briggs), Edmund Willard (Toby Bilson), George

* Released November, 1935, in England; not released in U.S. until February, 1937.

Mozart (Tommy Dugan), Ben Welden (Boas Hoffman), Dennis Hoey (Tom Goodschild), Gibson Gowland (Andy Gillings).

THE INVISIBLE RAY   January, 1936
Universal

   Director: Lambert Hillyer. Based on a story by Howard Higgin and Douglas Hodges. *Screenplay:* John Calton. *Photographers:* George Robinson and John P. Fulton.

   Cast: BL (Dr. Benet), Boris Karloff (Dr. Janos Rukh), Frances Drake (Diane Rukh), Frank Lawton (Ronald Drake), Walter Kingsford (Sir Francis Stevens), Beulah Bondi (Lady Arabella Stevens), Violet Kemble Cooper (Mother Rukh).

POSTAL INSPECTOR   August, 1936
Universal

   Director: Otto Brower. Based on a story by Robert Presnell and Horace McCoy. *Screenplay:* Horace McCoy. *Photographer:* George Robinson.

   Cast: BL (Benez), Ricardo Cortez (Bill Davis), Patricia Ellis (Connie Larrimore), Michael Loring (Charlie Davis), David Oliver (Butch), Wallis Clark (Pottle), Arthur Loft (Richards), Guy Usher (Evans).

SHADOW OF CHINATOWN (serial)*   1936
Victory Pictures

   Director: Robert F. Hill. Based on a story by Rock Hawkey and adapted by Isadore Bernstein and Basil Dickey. *Photographer:* Bill Hyer.

   Cast: BL (Victor Poten), Herman Brix (Martin Andrews), Joan Barclay (Joan Whiting), Luana Walters (Sonya Rokoff), Charles King (Henchman).

   Chapter Titles: 1) The Arms of God, 2) The Crushing Walls, 3) 13 Ferguson Alley, 4) Death on the Wire, 5) The Sinister Ray, 6) The Sword Thrower, 7) The Noose, 8) Midnight, 9) The Last Warning, 10) The Bomb, 11) Thundering Doom, 12) Invisible Gas, 13) The Brink of Disaster, 14) The Fatal Trap, 15) The Avenging Powers.

S.O.S. COASTGUARD (serial)   August, 1937
Republic   (Released as a feature April, 1942)

   Directors: William Witney and Alan James. Based on a story by Morgan Cox and Ronald Davidson. *Screenplay:* Barry Shipman and Franklyn Adreon. *Photographer:* William Nobles. *Music:* Raoul Kraushaar.

   Cast: BL (Boroff), Ralph Byrd (Terry Kent), Maxine Doyle (Jean Norman), Herbert Rawlinson (Commander Boyle), Richard Alexander (Thorg).

   * Also released as a feature at the same time.

Chapter titles: 1) Disaster at Sea, 2) Barrage of Death, 3) The Gas Chamber, 4) The Fatal Shaft, 5) The Mystery Ship, 6) Deadly Cargo, 7) Undersea Terror, 8) The Crash, 9) Wolves at Bay, 10) The Acid Trail, 11) The Sea Battle, 12) The Deadly Circle.

SON OF FRANKENSTEIN   January, 1939
Universal
Director: Rowland V. Lee. *Screenplay:* Willis Cooper. *Photographer:* George Robinson. *Art:* Jack Otterson.
Cast: BL (Ygor), Basil Rathbone (Baron Wolf von Frankenstein), Boris Karloff (the monster), Lionel Atwill (Krogh), Josephine Hutchinson (Elsa von Frankenstein), Emma Dunn (Amelia), Donnie Dunagan (Peter von Frankenstein), Edgar Norton (Benson).

THE GORILLA   May, 1939
20th Century-Fox
Director: Allan Dwan. *Screenplay:* Rian James and Sid Silvers. *Photographer:* Edward Cronjager. *Art:* Richard Day and Lewis Creber.
Cast: BL (Peters), Jimmy Ritz (Garrity), Harry Ritz (Harrigan), Al Ritz (Mulligan), Anita Louise (Norma Denby), Patsy Kelly (Kitty), Lionel Atwill (Walter Stevens), Joseph Calleia (stranger).

THE PHANTOM CREEPS (serial)   August, 1939
Universal
Directors: Ford Beebe and Saul A. Goodkind. Based on a story by Willis Cooper. *Screenplay:* George Plympton, Basil Dickey, and Mildred Barish. *Photographer:* Jerry Ash.
Cast: BL (Dr. Alex Zorka), Robert Kent (Capt. Bob West), Regis Toomey (Jim Daly), Dorothy Arnold (Jean Drew), Edward Van Sloan (Jarvis), Edward Norris (Marsden).
Chapter titles: 1) The Menacing Power, 2) Death Stalks the Highways, 3) Crashing Towers, 4) Invisible Terror, 5) Thundering Rails, 6) The Iron Monster, 7) The Menacing Mist, 8) Trapped in the Flames, 9) Speeding Doom, 10) Phantom Footprints, 11) The Blast, 12) To Destroy the World.

NINOTCHKA   October, 1939
MGM
Director: Ernst Lubitsch. Based on story by Melchior Lengyel. Screenplay: Charles Brackett, Billy Wilder, and Walter Reisch. *Photographer:* William Daniels. *Music:* Werner R. Heymann.
Cast: BL (Razinin), Greta Garbo (Ninotchka), Melvyn Douglas (Leon),

Sig Rumann (Iranoff), Alexander Granach (Kopalski), Felix Bressart (Buljanoff), Ina Claire.

THE HUMAN MONSTER (Dark Eyes of London)

December, 1939*

Associated British Picture Corporation

Director: Walter Summers. Based on a novel by Edgar Wallace. *Screenplay:* Patrick Kirwin, Walter Summers, and J. F. Argyle. *Photographer:* Bryan Langley.

Cast: BL (Dr. Orloff), Hugh Williams (Inspector Holt), Greta Gynt (Diana Stuart), Edmon Ryan (Lieutenant O'Reilly), Wilfred Walter (Jake, the monster).

THE SAINT'S DOUBLE TROUBLE   February, 1940
RKO

Director: Jack Hively. Based on a novel by Leslie Charteris. *Screenplay:* Ben Holmes. *Photographer:* J. Roy Hunt.

Cast: BL (Partner), George Sanders (the Saint), Helene Whitney (Anne), Jonathan Hale (Fernack).

BLACK FRIDAY   March, 1940
Universal

Director: Arthur Lubin. *Screenplay:* Kurt Siodmak and Eric Taylor. *Photographer:* Elwood Bredell. *Music:* H. J. Salter.

Cast: BL (Eric Marnay), Boris Karloff (Dr. Ernest Sovac), Stanley Ridges (Prof. George Kingsley), Anne Nagel (Sunny), Anne Gwynne (Jean Sovac), Virginia Brissac (Mrs. Margaret Kingsley).

YOU'LL FIND OUT   November, 1940
RKO

Director: David Butler. Based on a story by David Butler and James V. Kern. *Screenplay:* James V. Kern. *Photographer:* Frank Redmond.

Cast: BL (Prince Saliano), Kay Kyser (himself), Peter Lorre (Professor Fenninger), Boris Karloff (Judge Mainwaring), Dennis O'Keefe (Chuck Deems), Helen Parish (Janis Bellacrest).

THE DEVIL BAT   January, 1941
Producer's Releasing Corporation

Director: Jean Yarborough. Based on a story by George Bricker. *Screenplay:* John Thomas Neville. *Photographer:* Arthur Martinelli.

---

* Released in December, 1939, in England; not released in U.S. until March, 1940.

Cast: BL (Dr. Paul Carruthers), Suzanne Kaaren (Mary Heath), Dave O'Brien (Johnny Layton), Guy Usher (Henry Morton), Yolande Mallott (Maxine), Donald Kerr (One Shot Maguire).

THE BLACK CAT   April, 1941
Universal

Director: Albert S. Rogell. Suggested by the story by Edgar Allan Poe. *Screenplay:* Robert Lees, Fred Rinaldo, Eric Taylor, and Robert Neville. *Photographer:* Stanley Cortez.

Cast: BL (Eduardo), Basil Rathbone (Hartley), Hugh Herbert (Mr. Penny), Brod Crawford (Hubert Smith), Gale Sondergaard (Abigail Doone), Alan Ladd (Richard Hartley), Anne Gwynne (Elaine Winslow), Gladys Cooper (Myrna Hartley).

THE INVISIBLE GHOST   April, 1941
Monogram

Director: Joseph H. Lewis. *Screenplay:* Al and Helen Martin. *Photographer:* Marcel Le Picard.

Cast: BL (Mr. Kessler), Polly Ann Young (Virginia), John McGuire (Ralph), Clarence Muse (Evans), Terry Walker (Cecile), Betty Compson (Mrs. Kessler).

SPOOKS RUN WILD   November, 1941
Monogram

Director: Phil Rosen. *Screenplay:* Carl Foreman and Charles Marion. *Photographer:* Marcel Le Picard.

Cast: BL (Nardo, the monster), Leo Gorcey (Muggsy), Huntz Hall (Glimpy), Bobby Jordan (Danny), David Gorcey (Peewee), "Sunshine" Sammy Morrison (Scruno), Donald Haines (Skinny), Dave O'Brien (Jeff Dixon), Dorothy Short (Linda Mason).

THE WOLF MAN   December, 1941
Universal

Director: George Waggner. *Screenplay:* Curt Siodmak. *Photographer:* Joseph Valentine. *Art:* Jack Otterson.

Cast: BL (Bela), Lon Chaney (Larry Talbot), Claude Rains (Sir John Talbot), Ralph Bellamy (Col. Harry Montford), Patric Knowles (Frank Andrews), Maria Ouspenskaya (Maleva), Evelyn Ankers (Owen Conliffe), Warren William (Dr. Lloyd).

GHOST OF FRANKENSTEIN   April, 1942
Universal

Director: Erle C. Kenton. Based on a story by Eric Taylor. *Screenplay:* W. Scott Darling. *Photographers:* Milton Krasner and Woody Bredell. *Art:* Jack Otterson.

Cast: BL (Ygor), Sir Cedric Hardwicke (Dr. Ludwig Frankenstein), Lon Chaney, Jr. (the monster), Lionel Atwill (Dr. Bohmer), Ralph Bellamy (Erik Ernst), Evelyn Ankers (Elsa Frankenstein), Dwight Frye (villager).

BLACK DRAGONS   April, 1942
Monogram

Director: William Nigh. Based on a study by Harvey Gates. *Screenplay:* Harvey H. Gates. *Photographer:* Art Reed. *Art:* Dave Milton.

Cast: BL (Dr. Melcher; Colomb), Joan Barclay (Alice), George Pembroke (Saunders), Clayton Moore (Don Martin), Robert Frazer (Hanlin), Max Hoffman, Jr. (Kerney), Irving Mitchell (Van Dyke), Edward Peil, Sr. (Wallace).

THE CORPSE VANISHES   May, 1942
Monogram

Director: Wallace Fox. *Screenplay:* Harvey Gates, Sam Robins, and Gerald Schnitzer. *Photographer:* Art Reed.

Cast: BL (Dr. Lorenz), Luana Walters (Pat Hunter), Tristram Coffin (Dr. Foster), Elizabeth Russell (Countess), Minerva Urecal (Fagah), Kenneth Harlan (Keenan), Frank Moran (Angel), Angelo Rosito (Toby).

BOWERY AT MIDNIGHT   October, 1942
Monogram

Director: Wallace Fox. *Screenplay:* Gerald Schnitzer. *Photographer:* Mack Stengler.

Cast: BL (Prof. Brenner/Karl Wagner), John Archer (Dennison), Wanda McKay (Judy), Tom Neal (Frankie Mills), Vince Barnett (Charlie), J. Farrell MacDonald (Captain Mitchell).

NIGHT MONSTER   November, 1942
Universal

Director: Ford Beebe. *Screenplay:* Clarence Upson Young. *Photographer:* Charles Van Enger. *Art:* Jack Otterson.

Cast: BL (Rolf), Irene Hervey (Dr. Lynn Harper), Don Porter (Dick Baldwin), Nils Asther (Anger Singh), Leif Erickson (Laurie), Ralph Morgan (Kurt Ingston), Lionel Atwill (Dr. King).

FRANKENSTEIN MEETS THE WOLF MAN   March, 1943
Universal

Director: Roy William Neill. *Screenplay:* Curt Siodmak. *Photographer:* George Robinson. *Art:* John Goodman.

Cast: BL (the monster), Lon Chaney, Jr. (Lawrence Talbot), Patric Knowles (Dr. Mannering), Ilona Massey (Baroness Elsa Frankenstein), Dennis Hoey (Inspector Owen), Maria Ouspenskaya (Maleva), Lionel Atwill (Mayor), Dwight Frye (Rudi).

THE APE MAN   March, 1943
Monogram

Director: William Beaudine. Based on a story by Karl Brown. *Screenplay:* Barney Sarecky. *Photographer:* Mack Stengler. *Art:* David Milton.

Cast: BL (Dr. Brewster), Wallace Ford (Jeff Carter), Louise Currie (Billie Mason), Minerva Urecal (Agatha Brewster), Henry Hall (Dr. Randall), Ralph Littlefield (Zippo), J. Farrell MacDonald (Captain).

GHOSTS ON THE LOOSE   June, 1943
Monogram

Director: William Beaudine. *Screenplay:* Kenneth Higgins. *Photographer:* Mack Stengler.

Cast: BL (Emil), Leo Gorcey (Mugs), Huntz Hall (Glimpy), Bobby Jordan (Danny), Ava Gardner (Betty), Ric Vallin (Jack), Minerva Urecal (Hilda).

THE RETURN OF THE VAMPIRE   February, 1944
Columbia

Director: Lew Landers. *Screenplay:* Griffin Jay. *Photographers:* John Stumar and L. W. O'Connell.

Cast: BL (Armand Tesla), Frieda Inescort (Lady Jane Ainsley), Nina Foch (Nicki Saunders), Roland Varno (John Ainsley), Miles Mander (Sir Frederick Fleet), Matt Willis (Andreas Obry).

VOODOO MAN   February, 1944
Monogram

Director: William Beaudine. *Screenplay:* Robert Charles. *Photographer:* Marcel Le Picard.

Cast: BL (Dr. Marlowe), John Carradine (Job), George Zucco (Nicholas), Wanda McKay (Betty), Michael Ames (Ralph), Louise Currie (Sally), Ellen Hall (Mrs. Marlowe).

RETURN OF THE APE MAN   July, 1944
Monogram

Director: Phil Rosen. *Screenplay:* Robert Charles. *Photographer:* Marcel Le Picard.

Cast: BL (Prof. Dexter), John Carradine (Prof. Gilmore), Frank Moran (ape monster), Judith Gibson (Anne), Michael Ames (Steve).

ONE BODY TOO MANY   October, 1944
Paramount

Director: Frank McDonald. *Screenplay:* Winston Miller and Maxwell Shane. *Photographer:* Fred Jackman, Jr.

Cast: BL (Larchmont), Jack Haley (Albert Tuttle), Jean Parker (Coral Dunlap), Bernard Nedell (Attorney Gellman), Blanche Yurka (Matthews), Douglas Fowley (Henry Rutherford).

THE BODY SNATCHER   February, 1945
RKO

Director: Robert Wise. Based on a story by Robert Louis Stevenson. *Screenplay:* Philip McDonald and Carlos Keith. *Photographer:* Robert de Grasse. *Producer:* Val Lewton.

Cast: BL (Joseph), Boris Karloff (Gray), Henry Daniell (Dr. MacFarlane), Edith Atwater (Meg), Russell Wade (Fettes), Rita Corday (Mrs. Marsh), Sharyn Moffett (Georgina).

ZOMBIES ON BROADWAY   April, 1945
RKO

Director: Gordon Douglas. Based on a story by Robert Faber and Charles Newman. *Screenplay:* Lawrence Kimble. *Photographer:* Jack Mackenzie.

Cast: BL (Prof. Renault), Wally Brown (Jerry Miles), Alan Carney (Mike Strager), Anne Jeffreys (Jean), Sheldon Leonard (Ace Miller).

GENIUS AT WORK   July, 1946
RKO

Director: Leslie Goodwins. *Screenplay:* Robert E. Kent and Monte Brice. *Photographer:* Robert DeGrasse and Vernon L. Walker.

Cast: BL (Stone), Alan Carney (Mike), Wally Brown (Jerry), Anne Jeffreys (Ellen), Lionel Atwill (Marsh), Marc Cramer (Rick), Ralph Dunn (Gilley).

SCARED TO DEATH   July, 1947*
Golden Gate Pictures, Inc.

Director: Christy Cabanne. Story and screenplay by W. J. Abbott. *Photographer:* (Cinecolor) Marcel Le Picard.

---

* Completed in April, 1946.

Cast: BL (Leonide), Douglas Fowley (Terry Lee), Joyce Compton (Jane), George Zucco (Dr. Van Ee), Nat Pendleton (Raymond).

ABBOTT AND COSTELLO MEET FRANKENSTEIN

July, 1948

Universal

Director: Charles T. Barton. *Screenplay:* Robert Lees, Frederic I. Rinaldo, and John Grant. *Photographer:* Charles Van Enger.

Cast: BL (Count Dracula), Bud Abbott (Chick Young), Lou Costello (Wilbur Gray), Lon Chaney, Jr. (Larry Talbot), Glenn Strange (the Frankenstein monster), Lenore Aubert (Sandra Mornay), Jane Randolph (Joan Raymond), Frank Ferguson (Mr. McDougal), Charles Bradstreet (Dr. Stevens).

OLD MOTHER RILEY MEETS THE VAMPIRE   April, 1952

(American release title, 1953: VAMPIRE OVER LONDON)

(American release title, 1964: MY SON, THE VAMPIRE)

Renown Pictures (London, England)

Director: John Gilling. *Screenplay:* Val Valentine.

Cast: BL (Von Housen, the vampire), Arthur Lucan (Mother Riley), Dora Byran (Tilly), Richard Wattis (P. C. Fields), Philip Leaver (Anton), Judith Furse (Freda).

GLEN OR GLENDA? (Appeared in New York as
I CHANGED MY SEX)   June, 1952

George Weiss Productions

Director: Edward D. Wood, Jr. *Screenplay:* Edward D. Wood, Jr.

Cast: BL, Lyle Talbot, Dolores Fuller, Daniel Davis, Timothy Farrell, Tommy Haines, Charles Crofts, and Connie Brooks.

BELA LUGOSI MEETS A BROOKLYN GORILLA

September, 1952

(American TV title: THE BOYS FROM BROOKLYN)

(British TV title: THE MONSTER MEETS THE GORILLA)

Realart Releasing Co.

Director: William Beaudine. *Screenplay:* (Yukie) Sherin Edmond and G. Seward. *Photographer:* Charles Van Enger.

Cast: BL (Dr. Zabor), Duke Mitchell (Duke Mitchell), Sammy Petrillo (Sammy Petrillo), Charlita (Nona), Muriel Landers (Salime), Al Kikume (Chief Rakos), Mickey Simpson (Chula), Milton Newberger (Bongo), Ramona the Chimp.

BRIDE OF THE MONSTER   May, 1955
Banner Films
  Director: Edward D. Wood, Jr. *Screenplay:* Edward D. Wood, Jr., and Alex
Gordon. *Photographer:* William Thompson.
  Cast: BL (Dr. Eric Vornoff), Tor Johnson (Lobo), Tony McCoy (Lt.
Dick Craig), Loretta King (Janet Lawton), Harvey Dunn (Capt. Robbins),
George Bagun (Prof. Strowski).

THE BLACK SLEEP   June, 1956
Bel-Air (released through United Artists)
  Director: Reginald Le Borg. Based on a story by Gerald Drayson Adams.
Screenplay: John C. Higgins. *Photographer:* Gordon Avil. *Music:* Les Baxter.
  Cast: BL (Casimir), Basil Rathbone (Sir Joel Cadman), Akim Tamiroff
(Odo), Lon Chaney (Mungo), John Carradine (Borg), Herbert Rudley (Dr.
Gordon Ramsay), Patricia Blake (Laurie), Phyllis Stanley (Daphne), Tor
Johnson (Curry).

PLAN 9 FROM OUTER SPACE   July, 1959
Reynolds Pictures
  Director: Edward D. Wood, Jr. *Screenplay:* Edward D. Wood, Jr.
  Cast: BL (the ghoul man), Gregory Walcott (Jeff Trent), Mona
McKinnon (Paula), Dudley Manlove (Eros), Joanna Lee (Tanna), Vampira
(the ghoul girl).

Index